AMERICAN SPIRITS

THE FAMOUS FOX SISTERS AND THE MYSTERIOUS FAD THAT HAUNTED A NATION

BARB ROSENSTOCK

CALKINS CREEK
AN IMPRINT OF ASTRA BOOKS FOR YOUNG READERS
New York

Fame is a bee.
It has a song—
It has a sting—
Ah, too, it has a wing.

—Emily Dickinson (1830–1886)

Calkins Creek
An imprint of Astra Books for Young Readers,
a division of Astra Publishing House
astrapublishinghouse.com
Printed in China

ISBN: 978-1-63592-805-1 (hc)
ISBN: 978-1-63592-806-8 (eBook)

Library of Congress Cataloging-in-Publication Data

Names: Rosenstock, Barb, author.
Title: American spirits : the famous Fox sisters and the mysterious fad that haunted a nation / Barb Rosenstock.
Description: First edition. | New York : Calkins Creek, [2025] | Includes bibliographical references. | Audience: Ages 12 and up | Audience: Grades 10-12
Identifiers: LCCN 2024024285 | ISBN 9781635928051 (hc) | ISBN 9781635928068 (eBook)
Subjects: LCSH: Spiritualism--New York (State)--Juvenile literature. | Spiritualism--United States--Juvenile literature. | Fox, Margaret, 1833-1893. | Jencken, Catherine Fox, 1836-1892. | Underhill, A. Leah (Ann Leah), 1814-1890.
Classification: LCC BF1242.U6 R67 2025 | DDC 133.909747/87--dc23/eng/20240814
LC record available at https://lccn.loc.gov/2024024285

First edition

10 9 8 7 6 5 4 3 2 1

Design by Barbara Grzeslo
The text is set in Sabon LT Std, Vendetta OT, Webster Roman WF.
Titles are set in ITC Officina Sans Std

For the truthtellers—
Barb K., who dared me,
Ann, Pam, Lesa, Candy, Deb, Betsy, Carole,
Cynthia, and Jen,
who set the bar

CONTENTS

PROLOGUE

Before the Curtain Rises

—Academy of Music, New York City, October 21, 1888

Two thousand people rustle in their seats, cough, snort, or giggle. As an audience, they're divided into believers and skeptics, cheering or hissing at each other before the show begins.

Behind the curtain stands Maggie Fox, famous since she was fourteen. She has spent a lifetime demonstrating her talent in theaters and hotels across the country.

What is she famous for?

Talking to the dead.

For this skill, Maggie has been worshipped and she's been attacked. She's comforted families and frustrated investigators. She's been linked to America's leaders in media, politics, and the arts. For forty years, gossip swirled around Maggie and her sisters, Kate and Leah. Their lives and loves splashed across newspapers from New York to London. The public still clamors for their secrets. Did three American sisters really conquer Death itself?

Maggie has promised to tell the truth, onstage, tonight.

There's only one problem.

After the life she's led, does Maggie Fox know what truth means?

*The quotes at the beginning of each chapter are from "The Medium's Statement," an interview with Maggie Fox printed in *The New York World* on October 21, 1888.

"My sister Katie and myself were very young children . . ."

Chapter 1 FOOL'S EVE

Rap. Rap. Rap.

What was that sound?

Half an hour after the light had been snuffed out, Maggie and Kate Fox snuggled under the covers. On early spring nights in rural Hydesville, New York, the chill dampness from Mud Creek seeped into a person's bones should a foot, or a finger, escape thick layers of homemade quilts. Maggie, fourteen, and Kate, who had just turned eleven, peered into the shadows near their parents' bed across the room. Sure enough, there was Mother padding about in the darkness. Father relit the candle and joined his wife in hunting for the cause of the odd noises.

Rap. Rap.

The family had moved in a few months before, in early December of 1847. The rented cottage had just four rooms—bedroom, front room, kitchen, and buttery. Mother and Father crisscrossed the floorboards, wiggled the front door latch, listened to the individual creak of each stair. They searched from the slanted loft down to the dirt cellar. Like last night, and every night of the past week, they found nothing that might make a strange rapping sound. Maggie and Kate watched their parents give up and climb back into bed. Father blew out the candle. Mother closed her eyes.

Rap. A mystery.

The Fox family's home in Hydesville, NY, from a postcard printed around 1904

The unsettling sounds continued night after night until Mother felt "almost sick." The weather that spring of 1848 wouldn't settle either. After a few warmer days, on March 29 it turned so cold that around midnight an ice wedge stopped the constant crash of New York's Niagara Falls. Religious feeling had been whipped up by waves of Christian revivals throughout the western part of the state. In Niagara's eerie silence, some of the newly faithful predicted miracles, others the world's end.

Maggie and Kate's much older brother, David, stopped by that Friday, March 31. He tried to soothe Mother's complaints about the house's strange sounds. David reminded her that soon they'd be moving out of this tiny rental to a new home on his nearby peppermint farm. The rappings were probably "the simplest things in the world." Before he returned to his wife and children, David told Mother to ignore the nighttime noises and get a good night's sleep.

The wind whistled across the marsh grasses that afternoon. Father stayed in the front room with his Bible. Maggie, Kate, and Mother went to bed before the sun set. As the bedroom darkened . . .

Rap.

Five minutes passed.

Rap. Rap.

Kate sat up and snapped her fingers.

"As fast as she made the noise with her hands or fingers, the sound was followed up in the room," Mother would later explain.

Snap. Snap. Snap.

Rap. Rap. Rap.

In the dim light, Maggie said, "Now do this just as I do. Count one, two, three, four," while clapping her hands.

Clap. Clap. Clap. Clap.

Rap. Rap. Rap. Rap.

Were the knocks responding? Mother ordered, "Count ten."

Ten raps sounded like a drumbeat.

Kate touched two of her fingers together, lightly, without making a sound. Once, twice, three times.

Rap. Rap. Rap.

"Only look, mother! It can see as well as hear!" said Kate.

It? What was It? And what could It know about her family? Mother asked the night sounds to tell her the number of children she'd born.

Rap. Rap. Rap. Rap. Rap. Rap. Rap.

Seven. Everyone knew the Fox family had six children—Leah,

Maria, Elizabeth, and David, now grown; Maggie and Kate, still at home. Mr. and Mrs. Fox were lucky parents; about half of American babies born in the mid-1800s died before their fifth birthday. There was no protection from common childhood illnesses like tuberculosis, rheumatic fever, diphtheria, or whooping cough. But the Foxes hadn't entirely escaped that all-too-common tragedy. They'd buried a stillborn baby years back. No one in Hydesville knew. Seven was the correct number.

Stunned, Mother asked the night air if the mysterious sounds were made by a human. The answer? Total silence.

Then Mother asked, "Is it a spirit?"

Rap!

Hearing his girls' voices, Father entered the bedroom. He found his wife convinced that she was speaking to an invisible presence from beyond the grave. Mother Fox later insisted she was "not a believer in haunted houses or supernatural Appearances." But a mystic strain ran through Mother's extended family. Her sister had visions of her future headstone, and her mother was known to fall into a dreamlike state and predict neighbors' funerals weeks before their deaths took place.

Maggie and Kate knew these family tales. Like most young people of their time, the sisters also grew up with popular ghost stories like author Washington Irving's "The Legend of Sleepy Hollow" and Methodist founder John Wesley's family haunt, "Old Jeffrey." Ghosts were everywhere in nineteenth-century America. Now, it seemed, the Fox family had one of their very own.

Mother intended to find out what this particularly noisy spirit wanted.

By asking simple yes-or-no questions, listening for raps or silences, Mother learned that their spirit was a man. He'd been fatally injured in the Fox family's cottage. She asked how old he was when he died. Thirty-one raps sounded, one right after the other.

The Headless Horseman Pursuing Ichabod Crane, an 1858 John Quidor painting, inspired by Washington Irving's "The Legend of Sleepy Hollow," published in 1820

Mother asked, "Will this noise continue if I call in my neighbors?"

A pause, and then . . .

Rap.

She sent her husband into the cold night to a nearby neighbor, Mrs. Redfield.

Mrs. Mary Redfield hadn't known the family long; but she'd run into the girls on the main road a few days back. *Such friendly, pretty girls!* Maggie had brown hair, dark eyes, skin like a porcelain doll. Raven-haired Kate's best feature was her unusual gray-violet eyes. They were "smart girls, bright, full of life." The girls had told Mrs. Redfield some wide-eyed tale about hearing strange sounds in the night. Mary Redfield knew the parents, Peggy and John Fox, to be sensible folk. She hadn't given Maggie and Kate's silly story a second thought.

Yet, here was John Fox at her door, after dark, insisting that Mrs. Redfield listen to these strange sounds immediately. Mary Redfield grabbed a wrap and followed her good neighbor out into the cold spring night. She expected to endure a few minutes of foolishness with the Fox girls and be in bed before nine.

Instead, she found Maggie and Kate Fox in bed, clinging together, "much frightened." Their mother, Mrs. Peggy Fox, was sitting on the bed, her face unearthly pale. To comfort the woman, Mrs. Redfield sat beside her.

"Now count five," she heard Peggy mumble.

Mary Redfield realized that Peggy Fox was talking to the night air.

The poor woman has lost her reason, Mary thought. Then, she heard a rhythm, like a beating heart.

Rap. Rap. Rap. Rap. Rap.

"Count fifteen," said Peggy.

Fifteen raps shook the bedstead. Mary both heard the sounds and felt them jar her bones. *What in this room could be making such a powerful sound?*

Peggy Fox asked the spirit to give Mary Redfield's age.

Thirty-three raps sounded one right after the other. Correct. Mary ruffled through the possibilities. *Who knew her exact age except her husband?*

Mrs. Redfield took over the questioning, "If you are an injured spirit, manifest it by three raps."

Rap. Rap. Rap.

She repeated several questions trying to prove that the raps sounded randomly. All were answered correctly, same as before. After an hour or so with the rappings, Mrs. Redfield agreed, a spirit had indeed entered the Fox family's humble cottage.

Across the bedroom, Maggie and Kate trembled. Mrs. Redfield consoled them. She told the girls they would not be harmed. As a Christian, Mary trusted that this spirit was from God. In one of the earliest accounts of that night's events, Kate replied, "we are innocent—how good it is to have a clear conscience."

Mrs. Redfield didn't ask Kate why her conscience was bothered. Then again, it's hard to think straight when talking to a dead man.

Mrs. Redfield fetched her husband. When they returned, loud raps again echoed about the Fox home. As the night went on, the Redfields brought their neighbors, who brought other neighbors. Question by question, guess after guess, the small group learned further details of the spirit's story.

The spirit had been a traveling peddler.

The peddler had been murdered.

His throat was cut with a butcher knife! He'd been robbed of $500!

How many years ago? **Rap. Rap. Rap. Rap. Rap.**

Midnight brought a new day: Saturday, April 1. At least a dozen of the Fox family's neighbors remained crammed in the house, asking questions and receiving rapped answers. Like Mary Redfield, they came anticipating a bit of nighttime fun, until the raps correctly answered personal questions about family members, living *and* dead. In the early morning hours, the rappings simply stopped. The rumors about the two girls who had first talked to the peddler's spirit were just getting started.

"All the people around . . . were called into witness . . ."

Chapter 2 LOCAL CELEBRITIES

Something was happening in western New York . . . again. In the seven decades since the American Revolution, these rolling hills had produced social revolutions by the dozens. Visionaries had founded experimental communities supporting radical ideas like equal rights for women or the abolition of slavery. New religious faiths sprung from the state's rich soil: Shakers, Mormons, and Adventists, among others. No one wanted to miss a new miracle.

Over the next days, at least three hundred people, more than six times Hydesville's population, visited the Fox home. Wagons of strangers bumped in from the countryside, lining the crossroads nearest the cottage.

Housewives in buttoned ankle boots and farmers in felt hats clomped in and milled about. *Were the strange sounds made by a spirit? Or through some kind of trick?* Once they heard the rappings answer questions, these solid, working folk were deeply shaken, some so scared they fled the house. Others stayed on in wonder, asking the invisible spirit about the past, present, and future.

Father didn't like the attention: "It has caused a great deal of trouble and anxiety . . . it is impossible for us to attend to our daily occupations." But Mother played hostess, showing off the bedroom where Maggie and Kate first talked to the spirit. She retold the story in ever more grisly detail—*the murderer had filled a bowl with the peddler's blood!*

Curiosity about the spirit and the Fox family, Maggie and Kate in particular, grew throughout the whole of Wayne County. The girls were special, either chosen by the spirit or fooling everyone. Some people insisted that Maggie and Kate were always at home when the sounds were heard. Others swore they heard rappings even when the girls were away.

Groups of curious people searched the Fox cottage and tried to recreate the sounds. They stomped the floor, knocked on the walls, dropped silverware; but nothing made that soft, rhythmic rap. Questions to the spirit continued.

Was your body buried in this house? **Rap**. *In the cellar?* **Rap**.

Four feet down? Silence. *Six feet?* Silence.

Ten feet? **Rap**.

A buried corpse would prove the truth. Led by brother David Fox, a troop of men carrying shovels and pickaxes descended the stairs to dig up the peddler's body. A series of questions, raps, and silences directed them to the cellar's center. Metal blades bit into damp dirt, easily moved as if previously disturbed. As the diggers reached three feet, a rush of frigid underground water flooded the hole, stopping the search for the peddler's bones.

In just a few weeks, the spirit had answered so many questions so accurately that residents felt responsible for finding the peddler's murderer. Excited neighbors played detective. If the peddler was killed while visiting this house, the murderer must have lived there before the

A daguerreotype of an American peddler with his trunks, around 1840–1860, much like the peddler Maggie and Kate described in their first spirit encounter

Fox family. The last names of prior renters were called. *Duesler?* Silence. *Feasler?* Silence. *Johnson?* Silence. *Weekman?* Silence. *Bell?* **Rap**.

Mr. Bell had left Hydesville about four years ago. Gossip traveled fast. Living in a nearby town, Bell knew almost immediately that he'd been accused of a murder. He asked for support against the slanderous spirit. Forty-four people signed a formal statement of Mr. Bell's good character. Though lingering rumors dogged him, Bell was never charged. The law didn't recognize the dead as reliable witnesses.

Who was this dead peddler? Guessing a name using yes or no questions could take years! Someone suggested reciting the alphabet out loud. The calling began, "A . . ." Silence. "B . . ." Silence. "C," **Rap**.

The spirit rapped initials, **C**, and the second time through the alphabet, **B**.

Communicating with the spirit wasn't easy. Sometimes the person calling the alphabet spoke too quickly or made mistakes. Answering raps often came in a flurry or with long pauses between. *Did that sound come after the M or the N? Could the spirit mean A not O?* It took time before the peddler's full name was understood—

"C h a r l e s B. R o s n a."

Who? Some would maintain that the surname was "Rosema," "Rasme," or "Rosma." No matter, none of those names were recognized by anyone in the area. On the other hand, a wandering peddler's name could easily have been forgotten if it was ever known at all.

Still, Hydesville locals tended toward belief in the spirit that had first contacted Maggie and Kate Fox. "I cannot in any way imagine how these noises can be made by any human means," said one resident. Another "examined the premises very carefully, and can find nothing . . . no cord or wire, or any thing of that kind . . ." Neighbors trusted each other, "I have no doubt but what [that] Mr. Fox and family are honest."

The spirit rumors reached the ears of area journalists. Different newspapers spun the story different ways. On April 12, 1848, the *Western Argus* covered the event in fun, "The good people . . . are in quite a fever, in consequence of the discovery of an 'under ground' *Ghost* . . ." In the May 4 *Newark Herald*, the Hydesville rappings inspired a long poem that ended with the words "APRIL FOOL." A skeptical attorney sat on the bed while Mrs. Fox asked the spirit questions. The *Syracuse Herald* published his conclusion, "I couldn't tell where the raps came from."

These local articles brought in more curiosity seekers. Maggie, Kate, and their parents were forced to abandon the cottage and stay at David's farmhouse. Within the first two weeks of April, a lawyer and writer, Mr. E. E. Lewis, arrived in Hydesville to interview those with direct knowledge of the family and its spirit.

Many good people from the hamlet of Hydesville and its wider town of Arcadia in Wayne County couldn't wait to talk. Those who'd lived in the cottage before now recounted strange happenings from years back. A hired girl remembered that she'd not only heard knocking in the bedroom; she'd fallen into the holes that she said Mr. Bell dug in the cellar. The father of another family answered nighttime knocks at the cottage; but no one was at the door. A mother remembered her eight-year-old daughter's nightly screams; icy fingers had stroked the girl's face.

Questioning the spirit grew more personal. David Fox asked how many deaths neighborhood families had suffered in the past year. The spirit rapped the exact number of dead grandparents, parents, and children. Mary Redfield asked the spirit if the baby daughter she'd buried was now in heaven.

Rap.

That simple affirmation must have given Mrs. Redfield powerful comfort. She and many of her neighbors grew convinced that they were in the presence of Something or Someone beyond their normal experience. Yet, a few locals disagreed. "They all seemed to think it was a great mystery . . . some did not think there was anything supernatural about it."

Mr. Lewis interviewed twenty-two witnesses. He questioned women who'd heard the rappings, men who'd dug up the basement, and families who'd lived in the house before. He took lengthy statements, under oath, from John, Peggy, and David Fox.

Yet Lewis did not interview Maggie or Kate. Before the twentieth century, the names of young, unmarried women rarely appeared in print. Proper women lived private lives, never public ones. Either their parents prohibited them from giving a statement or the girls refused.

The youngest Fox sisters' initial thoughts and feelings about the events in Hydesville remained unknown. Maggie and Kate were both at the center of the story—and left out of it.

In the last weeks of April, Lewis published his pamphlet, *A Report of the Mysterious Noises Heard in the House of Mr. John D. Fox*. He billed it as a truthful account of events; yet Lewis used leading language like "supernatural," and "haunt," in addition to, "murder." The *Newark Herald* warned the public that Lewis had sensationalized the facts to make money, "if the excitement should subside . . . it would . . . injure the sale . . ."

Lewis offered a reward of fifty dollars, more than a farmhand's monthly salary, to anyone who could prove that the rapping sounds had been made by a human. The reward was never collected. As the pamphlet circulated, the tale was embellished. Within weeks, truths, half-truths, and outright lies were hopelessly entangled.

Perhaps even Mother hadn't told the whole truth. In Lewis' pamphlet, Mrs. Fox said Maggie's first words to the spirit were, "Now do this just as I do." Still there was a persistent rumor that the girls had addressed the spirit by name. Though the Salem witch trials were 150 years past, in remote areas like Hydesville, belief in sorcery and evil held fast. People insisted that one of the sisters had said, "Here, Mr. Splitfoot, do as I do." Had Maggie or Kate Fox called on the devil?

"**Our eldest sister . . . was in Rochester . . . but came to Hydesville . . .**"

Chapter 3 THE DEVIL KNOCKS, A SISTER ANSWERS

Leah Fox Fish was at the piano, giving a weekly lesson to a young female student toward the end of April 1848. The girl's father, a publisher, handed Leah a newly printed pamphlet—*Mysterious Noises? The House of John D. Fox?* Leah was shocked to read more than sixty pages about her parents, her little sisters, and a peddler's rapping spirit.

Asked if the story was true, Leah responded, "If my father, mother, and brother David have certified to such a statement, it is true." *But what about the girls?*

Leah was more than twenty years older than her two youngest sisters. More like a second mother than a big sister. And it was as if Leah, along with Maria, Elizabeth, and David, had grown up in a different family altogether.

When Leah was a child, her family lived in Rochester while the Erie

Canal was first constructed. The nineteenth century's "information superhighway" connected the Atlantic to the Great Lakes. Entrepreneurs, immigrants, and entertainers had turned the rural village of Rochester into America's first boomtown city.

Worldly residents and new wealth meant expanding factories, fashionable shops, and successful banks. It also meant busy brothels, taverns, and gambling houses. Father got caught up in this loose life. Though he'd once made a decent living as a blacksmith, John Fox began gambling on cards and horses, drinking to oblivion. The more he drank, the less he worked.

Alcohol, Death, and the Devil by George Cruikshank. This 1830s drawing dramatically portrays the evils of alcohol abuse.

When Leah was less than ten, and David little more than a toddler, Mother took the children and left her drunken husband. They first stayed at Grandfather's farm near the Hudson Valley for a few years, then moved to a Rochester boardinghouse for a few more.

Mother Margaret "Peggy" Fox and father John Fox around the 1850s

In Rochester, fourteen-year-old Leah Fox met a man named Bowman Fish. It is unclear how the couple became involved or whether they legally married. Around the age of sixteen, Leah gave birth to a daughter, Elizabeth, called Lizzie. Soon, "Mr. Fish . . . became indifferent to his home and family." He traveled westward, "on business," and never returned.

Very few occupations in the nineteenth century were open to women, fewer still to abandoned mothers. Most women in Leah's circumstances had no choice but to rely on charity from male family members, marry anyone who asked, or turn to prostitution.

Leah had been different, "delighted to find myself entirely independent." She was known in Rochester as Mrs. Fish, a dark-haired, ample woman, who had managed to support herself and Lizzie for nearly twenty years. Her income as a piano teacher couldn't have been much; she probably struggled financially. Yet, she met respectable friends in Rochester, and grew from a child bride into a competent woman.

As Leah's life changed, her father's transformed even more dramatically.

> "just at this time the Power of the Lord came on the People . . . the younge man . . . fell to the floor under the Power of God . . . my wife . . . kept saying to this younge man, Jesus will Save you . . . He began to crawl on His hands and Knees . . . making his way toward the Alter . . . and this younge Brother got Saved." (excerpt from the diary of Methodist minister Michael Prindle)

Father was born again. After attending a Methodist revival meeting in the early 1830s, he stopped drinking and reunited with his wife and family. The Foxes moved to a farm near Consecon, Canada, for a fresh start. Margaretta (Maggie) was born on October 7, 1833, and Catherine (Kate/Katie/Cathy) on March 27, 1837. Though the marriage survived and the girls thrived, the farm failed. Daughter Elizabeth married, and stayed in Canada, but the rest of the Foxes returned to Rochester, which was fast becoming one of the largest cities in the United States.

In Rochester, Father set up a blacksmith shop and Mother set up housekeeping. Maggie and Kate attended school in a working-class neighborhood and made friends. They grew up around the noise of new construction and immigrants arriving from across the world. Maggie called Rochester, "My Much Loved home."

Within a few years, Father failed at city blacksmithing like he'd failed at farming. Mother and Father moved Maggie and Kate again, this time to rural Hydesville, New York. Approaching their elder years, with little money saved, Mother and Father wanted to be close to son David, a peppermint farmer. Daughter Maria had married and lived nearby also.

From the start, Maggie hated dreary Hydesville, "you Cant think of how Lonesome it is out here . . ." The girls had few friends their age. Rural school was sporadic; household chores—scrubbing shirts, sweeping ashes, carrying wood and water—were endless. Still, they had each other.

And, they had Leah's daughter, Lizzie. Though she was Maggie and Kate's niece, Lizzie was about five years older, more like a big sister. Right before the rappings started, Lizzie had finished a long visit with Maggie, Kate, and her grandparents, then returned to Rochester. Though the younger girls didn't know it, Lizzie was already on the way back to Hydesville.

Leah had packed their bags as soon as she learned about the spirit rappings. She, Lizzie, and two female friends boarded a nighttime Erie Canal packet boat. After a long night tossing on scratchy straw bedding, the group disembarked a few hundred miles away at Newark, New York. Leah hired a buggy to drive them the two miles to Hydesville.

Leah and company found the Fox cottage, which she called "the haunted house," abandoned. Guessing that her family may have gone to David's, Leah ordered the driver to continue on. They creaked through rolling hills dotted with apple orchards stripped bare, past fields of

brown earth awaiting the planting of oats and wheat.

On entering David's farmhouse, Leah received the shock of her life.

Mother's hair had turned entirely white. Whatever was causing these mysterious sounds, the situation was serious. A Methodist minister had judged the peddler's spirit evil; the Fox family was no longer welcome at his church. Though Father tried to ignore the trouble, Mother spent her days in tears, worried about the spirit's purpose. Rapping sounds were now being heard around David's farmhouse. Mother believed the spirit was following her youngest daughters.

Leah learned that Maggie and Kate were local celebrities; but opinions varied. Some people looked for miracles, others whispered about witchcraft.

For days, Leah gathered all the facts about this noisy visitor from beyond. More than once she took Maggie and Kate aside for separate questioning. Their oldest sister pushed and pried, digging until she understood the whole story.

After two weeks of questioning, Leah took charge. She convinced their parents to separate the girls. Kate would return to Rochester with Leah and Lizzie. Maggie would remain in Hydesville. Leah said she intended to "put a stop to the disturbance." Or maybe she imagined an opportunity.

Passengers on an Erie Canal packet boat. Teams of horses or mules hauled each boat from stop to stop.

"We were then taken . . . to Rochester."

Chapter 4 SPIRITS ABOUT THE HOUSE

With Kate in tow, Leah and her group boarded the return boat and settled on the benches stretched along the deck. The ropes strained and the mule teams pulled them back toward Rochester at two miles an hour. To pass the time, people told stories and often sang long into the night, anything to avoid the stuffy cabins underneath their feet. They hadn't gone more than a few miles when Leah heard . . .

Rap.

Again.

Rap.

No other passengers seemed to notice. Later, at the dinner table onboard, Leah felt some raps too, "one end of the table would jump and nearly spill the water out of our glasses."

She, Lizzie, and Kate arrived in Rochester at her small, rented house, 11 Mechanics Square, early that evening. The girls went into the yard. Inside the house Leah heard, "a dreadful sound . . . as if a heavy piece of artillery had been discharged . . ." Leah rushed outside and found the girls sitting quietly. "Why, what is the matter with you, Leah?" Kate asked.

That night, Leah, Lizzie, and Kate bedded down in the same room. The light was put out. Lizzie shrieked! Leah relit the lamp. Lizzie announced that a cold hand had skittered down her back. Kate appeared equally spooked. To settle the girls, Leah read a Bible chapter aloud. She placed the holy book under her pillow perhaps for protection. But "the instant we extinguished our light the Bible flew from under my pillow . . . the box of matches was shaken in our faces, and such a variety of performances ensued that we gave up in despair to our fate . . ."

Near dawn, the spirit quieted. Leah, Lizzie, and Kate slept for a few hours, and woke to birds singing from the chestnut trees in the square. Still, all was not entirely normal. Leah thought she heard soft raps accompanying her piano that afternoon. When the sun went down, Leah, Lizzie, and Kate went to bed, and slept well. Until just after midnight, "we were awakened by the most frightful manifestations. Tables and everything in the room below us were being moved about. Doors were opened and shut . . . There seemed to be many actors engaged in this performance . . . one Spirit was heard to dance as if with clogs . . . loud clapping of hands followed . . . after this . . . we heard . . . a large crowd walking away down stairs, through the rooms, closing the doors heavily after them."

Overnight, a single rapping spirit had increased to a crowd of performing ghosts. Leah suddenly labeled the house that she'd lived in for years "haunted." She made plans to move immediately, renting a larger home on Prospect Street sometime in May of 1848. Oddly, for someone trying to escape ghosts, the new house backed up to one of the oldest cemeteries in Rochester. Leah could see the tops of tombstones from her kitchen pantry. Right after the move, she sent for Maggie and Mother Fox.

Mount Hope Cemetery, Rochester. C. I. Hayden monument around 1860–1890. Founded in 1838, Mount Hope was one of the earliest "garden cemeteries" to feature elaborate headstones, gazebos and benches used for public recreation as well as for burials.

For the first time in their lives, the Fox women enjoyed the luxury of space. The newly built house had three floors, at least seven rooms, and a balcony that overlooked a fine parlor. They soon found that the spirits had moved in too. Leah told of beds lifted, "entirely from the floor, almost to the ceiling." She heard shuffling, giggling, and whispering, felt invisible fingers near her face. Wracked by the continued spirit disturbance, Mother insisted they needed help. "We cannot much longer stay here alone nights."

Calvin Brown, a friend of their brother David's, was in his late twenties. Mr. and Mrs. Fox had cared for the young man, who had been orphaned as a teenager. Now Calvin, a former soldier, agreed to move into Leah's and guard the women from any "evil spirits."

While Calvin slept downstairs, the spirits, evil or not, continued their antics. It was two in the morning when upstairs, Leah, Mother, and the girls awoke to the stomping sound of marching feet. Their beds were raised and slammed down repeatedly. The women dragged mattresses and blankets to the floor to try to get some rest. Mother Fox called down to Calvin for help, and someone relit a lamp.

Calvin entered the upstairs bedroom and encountered five flustered females. He wasn't about to give any spirit the satisfaction of seeing him sleep on the floor like a dog. He would "conquer or die in the attempt!" He lay down in a remaining bed, and everyone attempted to settle.

Not long after the light was put out, Calvin found himself in a vicious fight. Unseen hands grabbed a walking stick and swung it near his head. A brass candlestick flew across the room, smacked him in the face, and split his lip. Leah reported that the bed, with Calvin still in it, broke apart, "the head-board in one place, the foot-board in another . . ." How quickly these spirits had grown out of control.

The random violence continued for close to a week. One night, the entire family felt invisible slaps. After one particularly hard blow, Kate fell to the floor, unconscious. Just as her panic-stricken mother insisted on going for outside help, she moaned. Half-conscious, Kate lifted a hand to point at something invisible in the air. The family wondered if she'd been mesmerized.

Late in the eighteenth century, a German doctor, Franz Mesmer, had devised a system that cured illnesses by putting people into trances. Mesmer's treatments were introduced to the United States; even the great Benjamin Franklin had investigated the phenomenon. In addition to its medical uses, mesmerism was a popular fad, performed in theaters or at home parties. Typically, practitioners were male. The mesmerists waved their hands near clients' faces, gently stroked their arms, or looked intently into their eyes until they fell into a kind of waking sleep. It was widely assumed that young women, thought to be more sensitive, fell into trance easily.

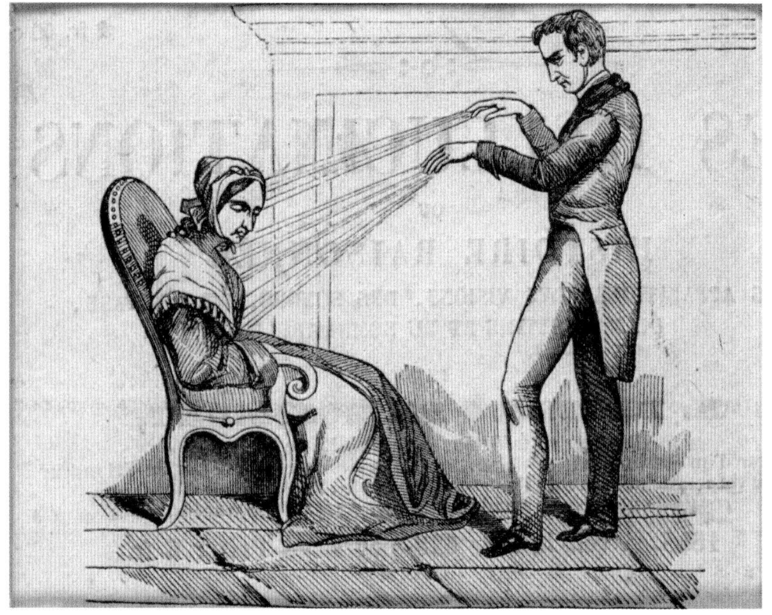

A male mesmerist entrances a female subject.

The still-woozy Kate began reciting religious poetry like an automaton, at least a hundred lines in a row. As the recitation trailed off, she awoke fully, and began sobbing. Through her tears, Kate said she'd seen the peddler, the knife, and blood, so much blood—while in her trance she'd witnessed the peddler's murder!

For weeks, Leah kept her family's astounding spirit manifestations private. Unlike in Hydesville, not a word of it appeared in Rochester's newspapers. Instead, Leah confided to a select group of friends about the strange events in her home. As these respected citizens learned of the spirits' appearances, the ghosts settled down. No more swinging, slapping, or bed-destroying; just gentle rapping, proof of an afterlife. Neighbors and acquaintances began asking for the sisters' help.

Reverend Lyman Granger told his dear friend, Reverend Lemuel Clark, that three local sisters were helping him speak to his daughter, Harriet. And Lemuel worried about Lyman's sanity. Harriet had been poisoned by her husband. She was nearly three years in her grave. So, when Lyman invited him for a visit, the concerned Lemuel was quick to accept.

On a pleasant June evening, a bit after five o'clock, Lemuel knocked at the Grangers' front door. He sat politely around a cherrywood table set for tea. Lemuel knew Lyman, his wife and daughter; but the rest of the company were strangers, including Mr. Calvin Brown, Mrs. Leah Fish, her daughter Lizzie, and Mrs. Fox with her daughter Kate. Lemuel didn't want to embarrass his host, but he did not trust this group. Someone in this room was playing a cruel trick. Lemuel Clark had every intention of protecting his friends from evildoers.

Lemuel finished saying grace. He heard soft tapping beneath the table as the party sang a hymn. Mrs. Fish had a lovely voice. Tea was poured; cakes were passed. Their gentle small talk quieted.

"Is the Spirit here?" someone asked.

Rap. Rap. Rap.

Lemuel Clark trusted his God-given senses. He listened to the raps; but never took his eyes off his fellow guests.

"Is this the Spirit of Harriet?" Silence.

When Harriet didn't respond, the group called up the Fox sisters' original spirit.

"Is it Charles?"

Rap.

"Are you the Spirit of a murdered man?"

Rap.

"Was you a peddler?"

Rap.

Lemuel heard the murdered peddler's life story told through a series of questions. All were answered either with silence, which the group took to mean **No** or with resonant raps or knocks meaning **Yes.** The powerful thuds vibrated the table.

It was probably Leah who suggested, "Shall Mr. Clark now ask questions?"

Rap.

Lemuel jumped at his chance. He asked a series of nineteen questions, beginning, "Are you a happy Spirit?"

Rap.

About halfway through, he asked, "Did God send you?"

RAP!

The rappings confounded Lemuel. The sounds could be loud or faint, hesitant or bold, slow to answer or quite rapid, like a human voice. And, as in human conversation, some questions were ignored. If the spirits stayed silent too long, the mortals regrouped with prayer and song. Most of the other guests' actions went unreported.

Lemuel followed the rappings to find their source. At first, the sounds came from under the table, but when the group sang, the raps thumped in time to the music on the table's top. Lemuel had a clear view of the hands, arms, and faces of Leah, Kate, and the rest of the company, "Not a muscle moved visibly."

"I should like to have Brother Clark see the Spirit move the table," someone said.

Now Lemuel would discover the trick! He insisted that everyone push a foot away from the table, tuck their feet into their chair rungs, and raise their hands.

"Will the Spirit please move the table to Brother Clark?" asked Lyman Granger.

The table crept across the carpet toward Lemuel. Not one teacup tipped, not a plate shifted, "I glanced around the table to see who moved a muscle . . . every countenance was mild and placid, yet bore the impress of the deepest awe . . ." Lemuel put his left hand out to resist; but the table kept coming closer as if "impelled by the strength of a man."

The table drew itself right up to Lemuel's body, then stopped. He pushed it back to its original place. Still, he remained skeptical enough to test the spirits once more. This time, Lemuel pulled the table toward himself, fully two feet from everyone else. Again, he requested that the company put hands in the air and feet on the chair rungs.

"Will the Spirit please to move the table to those on the opposite side?" he asked.

The table inched slowly away from Lemuel.

When it stopped, he searched under the table for casters or wires; he found none.

The skeptical Lemuel Clark left that evening certain he had witnessed a miracle. He wrote to his brother to share his astonishment. Though Lemuel's letters did not often specify names; Leah probably interpreted the raps and spelled all messages. Maggie was not mentioned as being at the table, but could she have been in or near the Grangers' home? Any specific actions taken by Kate, Mother, Lizzie, or Calvin can only be imagined.

Yet, their gathering—a group assembled around a table, an opening prayer or song, questions for the dead, and answering spirits—would have influence far beyond nineteenth-century Rochester. For in a few weeks between May and June of 1848, the Fox sisters—Leah, Maggie, and Kate—developed what we now call the séance.

From left: Maggie, Kate, and Leah around 1851 by famed lithographer Nathaniel Currier of the firm Currier & Ives

"I owe all my misfortune to that woman . . ."

Chapter 5 THE INFLUENCERS

The sisters called these spirit gatherings "circles." The first regular attendees were drawn from Leah's Rochester friends and acquaintances. Among the most influential were Isaac and Amy Post.

Years before, Isaac Post was the Fox family's landlord. He and his wife had remained friends with Leah after her family had moved to Hydesville. Both Isaac and Amy were prominent members of the Quaker faith and supported its then-radical ideas about equality in all forms.

In July of 1848, Amy attended the first Women's Rights Convention in Seneca Falls, New York. She was one of sixty-eight early feminists who signed the revolutionary Declaration of Sentiments, calling for equal citizenship for women in the United States.

Amy and Isaac Post were also abolitionists, passionate about ending the practice of slavery. Their spacious home served as an underground

Isaac Post and Amy Post, 1850s

railroad station assisting enslaved men, women, and children escaping from southern states into Canada. And they raised funds for their friend, speaker and writer Frederick Douglass. Douglass had escaped slavery in 1838. By 1847, he had started *The North Star*, an important antislavery newspaper. Douglass, the most famous Black man in America, exchanged frequent letters with Amy, writing, "Your family was always very dear to me . . ."

No matter how open to radical ideas he was, when Isaac Post heard rumors about rapping spirits, he "paid no more heed to it than I did of the Old Salem witch stories." However, earlier in their marriage, Amy and Isaac had buried two young sons. More recently, they suffered the death of their five-year-old daughter, Matilda. Through the Fox sisters' spirit circles, Amy and Isaac could talk to their dead children.

Leah led the circles but claimed no special powers. It was Maggie and Kate who first became known to the Posts and others in Rochester as mediums—sensitive people able to communicate between the living and the dead. Isaac Post recalled, "we do not get answers without one of the sisters [Maggie or Kate] are present, and not always then . . ." To Isaac, the two seemed "very anxious" that the family "enjoy what they did" in the circles. Isaac was so enthralled by the spirits that he didn't seem to consider the source of Maggie and Kate's noticeable anxiety.

After a few initial sessions, Isaac, Amy, their living children, and a servant, "our little Dutch girl," were regular attendees. The entire Post family "love[d] very much to ask questions." The Posts' conversations were not recorded, but it's likely their questions were those common to all mourners—*Are you there? Are you happy? Will I ever see you again?*

Isaac wrote about the answers he received through Maggie and Kate's mediumship, "They always speak of seeing Matilda, they say she is happy around us." Soon, Isaac was expressing an easy confidence in the spirits, "It [spirit communication] has been investigated by so many . . . every candid person admits that the girls do not make it." Table by table, the circle of belief widened from friends to acquaintances, from acquaintances to strangers, until it included many prominent Rochester businessmen, doctors, ministers, wives, and children . . . soon reaching the famous Frederick Douglass.

Mr. Douglass accepted at least one invitation to join a spirit circle at the Post home. Though details of this gathering did not survive, one or more of the Fox sisters would have acted as mediums. His opinion was clear; he called the rappings "*atrocious.*"

The Posts were insulted. Frederick Douglass wrote Amy Post. He didn't want to offend his friend, but wondered if there wasn't some trick. Douglass emphasized to Amy that the Fox sisters' rapping spirits had conveniently "refused to *answer*" the one personal question that would have given Frederick solid proof. Amy, on the other hand, remained a staunch believer. The emotions evoked during spirit circles

Daguerreotype of Frederick Douglass, around 1855

often brought people closer together. But the resulting conclusions—whether spirit communication was true or false—could also pull people apart.

Whether or not all people believed, the spirits were moving quickly. Before the end of summer 1848, spirit raps directed the sisters and their supporters to dig once more for proof of the peddler. Leah, Maggie, Kate, and their mother traveled with a group of roughly twenty Rochester followers back to Hydesville. The group stayed with their brother David and his family on his farm, and saw Father, who hadn't joined Mother, Kate, Maggie, and Leah in Rochester.

Early one morning, the sisters, their supporters, and David went out to the old family cottage. Wielding shovels and spades, David and the other men dug in the cellar for evidence of the peddler. Instead of the floodwaters faced that past spring, the dried, midsummer dirt floor was so hard that even with many men working, the hole deepened only a few inches each hour.

Leah, Maggie, Kate, and some female supporters crowded into the cottage, watching the men work and waiting for evidence of the peddler's body. Word that the Fox sisters were back in Hydesville spread, and soon a frenzied crowd fearing witchcraft gathered outside the cottage yelling, "crazy" and "Drag out the women! Drag them out!"

At midday, four to five feet below the cellar surface, the dirt coughed up traces of charcoal, a few teeth, strands of reddish hair, and lime, a harsh chemical used when burying bodies. These relics were set aside, and the digging resumed with the shout, "Great God! Here are the pieces of a broken bowl!"

As the pit deepened, the men hit a wood board. Using a drill, they bore through, but the drill's bit fell off and dropped into the drillhole. They used longer and longer drill bits to discover what lay under the board, but each bit fell into empty space. *A hollow space in a dirt floor? Could it be a grave?*

Those questions were never answered. Darkness came on; the diggers were exhausted. The local mob grew increasingly hostile. The sisters or their supporters asked the spirits for advice on how to proceed. Raps were heard in the cellar, as the spirits spelled a message that stopped further digging: **"Dear faithful friends, your work here is done."** "How we all reached the outside, amid the shouts . . . I cannot explain," Leah wrote. But their quest ended with the spirits' reassurance, **"God will reward you."**

The Fox sisters' supporters carried a few relics from the site. According to Leah, "Several bones were found which doctors pronounced human bones . . . from the ankle, two from the hands, and some from the skull . . ." The doctors Leah consulted were not named.

Skeptics suspected the remains were from a dead horse or calf. Leah responded, "In the name of common sense, how did they happen to be there, nearly six feet beneath the cellar bottom?" Later, when asked what the family had done with the relics, Mother Fox told a neighbor that the bones had been "sunk in the creek." Strange treatment of the precious bones from her daughters' first spirit friend.

The spirit supporters returned to Rochester, but Leah, Kate, Maggie, and Mother stayed to visit a bit longer. The sisters' presence near Hydesville encouraged daily crowds, who rode out to gawk at the original Fox cottage, then continue on to David's farm to see the Fox girls in person. In the name of curiosity, people knocked down fences, flattened peppermint beds, even climbed in David's windows.

Tired of the trouble, David opened his front door, and stood up to the crowd, "You are welcome to search the house from garret to cellar, if you do so respectfully." According to Leah, once confronted face-to-face, the local mob left without incident.

Soon, Leah, Maggie, Kate, and Mother returned to Rochester. David Fox, his family, and Father stayed on the farm. With infrequent visits, the Fox family lived separately but were united in their belief in spirits.

But at least one family member had doubts.

When the sisters returned to Rochester, Leah, and her daughter, Lizzie, sat at a spirit gathering along with Rev. Lemuel Clark, who had become a regular participant. It is likely that Maggie, Kate, and Mother Fox were present also, along with other guests. A prayer was said, a hymn sung; Leah intoned a series of questions to begin their conversation with the dead.

"Is the Spirit here?" Silence.

"Shall we have no answers?" Silence.

"Is the Spirit here?" Silence.

"I know," said Leah turning to Lizzie, "You are the cause of this silence. You have been a very wicked girl today. You have grieved the Spirit."

Rap. A loud knock burst from an empty rocking chair across the room.

Leah scolded, "I told you so . . . Spirit, has Elizabeth done wrong?"

Rap.

Tears ran down Lizzie's cheeks. Her mother used her full name, Elizabeth. Leah must be angry indeed.

"I can't help it," Lizzie said, "I just said what I thought, and if I am to blame, I can't help it."

But what had Lizzie said that was so awful? Reverend Clark couldn't imagine. Leah continued to attack, "You can help it, you must repent and ask forgiveness."

Rap.

"Must she repent, Spirit, and ask forgiveness?"

Rap.

"Will you give us answers freely if she will?"

Rap.

"I can't repent . . . I was sincere, I don't know how to repent." Lizzie sobbed.

Leah intoned, "Spirit, will we have answers if she does not repent?" Silence.

The Reverend Lemuel Clark grew more and more uncomfortable with the harsh accusations as Leah scolded, ". . . you wicked girl."

"Before this matter proceeds any further," Lemuel interrupted, "What is the girl's sin? What is she required to repent of?"

Leah related Lizzie's uncertainty toward the spirits. Lizzie worried that her mother and aunts could be accused of playing tricks. She was concerned that frequently allowing groups including men into their home made them targets of gossip. Lizzie was, "sorry the Spirit ever came . . . and . . . wished it would go away."

Lemuel understood Lizzie's concerns. Only weeks before, he too had doubted the spirits. Tonight, he was troubled. *What kind of spirit would require Lizzie's humiliation? Perhaps this was the devil's work after all!*

"Spirit, has Elizabeth done wrong in expressing such sentiments?" Leah continued.

Rap.

Leah asked seven more questions. Any action or reaction from Maggie or Kate went unnoted, but the spirit did not answer.

Lemuel Clark took over. As a minister, he felt bound to question the spirit's motives and try to protect Lizzie from evil.

"Did God send you?" Silence.

"Has she sinned against God?" Silence.

"Is it to God you require her to bow?" Silence.

It seemed Leah was correct; the spirit would not answer unless Lizzie repented.

In front of Reverend Lemuel Clark, her family, and others she knew less well, Lizzie dropped to her knees and begged forgiveness for her doubts.

Lizzie had worried for weeks about how quickly the idea of spirits had taken over her family. Recently, her mother, Leah, was claiming that she too was a medium, like Maggie and Kate. A family story quotes Lizzie scolding Leah, "Ma, how can you . . . pretend that that [rapping] is done by the spirits? . . . it's dreadfully wicked."

In early autumn of 1848, Lizzie lost everything. Leah banished her only child, shipping Lizzie eight hundred miles away to live in Illinois with the father she barely knew. The spirits were not to be doubted.

"we were frightened ourselves . . ."

Chapter 6 SPIRIT INVESTIGATORS

Like Amy Post, Eliab Capron had attended the Women's Rights Convention—one of only forty men present. It's likely he heard about the Fox sisters' rapping spirits in Seneca Falls. Capron, a newsman from Auburn, New York, was naturally curious to know more about this strange, new phenomenon. He first joined a circle at Leah's parlor table in November 1848.

Capron trusted his instincts; Maggie and Kate seemed too young to be fraudsters. Still, like any good journalist, he was determined to root out the truth. As the séance began, Capron asked the spirit if it would "rap my age." He also wrote instructions on paper, "rap four times," "rap seven." He thought of questions in his mind. All his inquiries were answered correctly.

Overwhelmed by this newfound ability to converse with spirits, Capron, like almost all early participants, was so caught up in the world of immortals, that he didn't take much note of human actions. The words communicated by the spirits were much more important than anything the people in the room were doing. As these were private gatherings, very few accounts of early séances even exist. So, what *were* Leah, Maggie or Kate actually *doing* during their spirit circles? Most participants didn't detail the sister's actions; and, unlike the dead, the sisters weren't talking.

A few days later, Capron returned to Leah's after devising what he considered a foolproof spirit test.

A small basket filled with tiny lake shells sat on Leah's table. He grabbed several shells, counted them in secret; then closed his hand, so neither Maggie, Kate, nor Leah could see. He asked the spirits for the number of shells. The raps sounded. Correct.

"I resolved to test it another way, to see if there was a possibility of my *mind* having any influence in the matter. I took a handful of shells, without knowing how many I took myself." The raps sounded. Capron then counted the shells in his hand. The number of raps precisely matched the number of shells.

The combination of correct answers and the sisters' innocent appearance convinced Eliab Capron that spirit communication was real: "the change which takes place at what is called Death is not so vast . . . as the world has generally supposed."

In the early months of 1849, Leah, Maggie, and Kate, along with a core group of followers, the Posts, Rev. Clark, Capron, and others, explored the boundaries of this new spirit world.

Before the sessions, the sisters began to ask that drapes be drawn—the spirits preferred darkness. The spirits were also known to ask participants to close their eyes during the proceedings. Was it to increase the strength of the spirit communications as Leah suggested? It certainly may have allowed the sisters a bit of freedom to act unobserved.

Yet, as proof that they remained seated, Leah, Maggie and/or Kate joined hands with the others around the table. Then the leader, typically Leah, asked the spirits to join them, "Will the Spirit come tonight?" At times, one of the sisters fell into a trancelike state. Exactly how this was accomplished went undocumented. The trances were described rather opaquely as "put her asleep," "magnetized," or "put in the clairvoyant state."

Whether the medium was in a trance or not, if a circle was successful, the group heard rappings in answer to questions. The meaning of the raps was formalized. Silence or a single rap meant **No**. Three raps meant **Yes**. Five quick raps meant **Call the alphabet**.

Working rap by rap, letter by letter, even simple messages took a long time to translate. Participants learned to be patient. After all, the messages were arriving from very far away! For a long message, the leader, assisted by the circle of sitters, guessed at words to help the communication along. The spirits typically confirmed any guesses. When the spirits were tired of talking, or frustrated by the questioning, they spelled a single word **Done**, and the spirit circle concluded.

Word of the spirit circles spread almost as fast as the cholera pandemic that swept the country. Cholera didn't discriminate, killing adults and children in the south and the north. Former US president James K. Polk suffered for two weeks, dying of cholera in Nashville at fifty-three. Arthur "Pickie" Greeley, the five-year-old son of famed New York City publisher Horace Greeley, died of cholera in less than a day.

The "black cholera" was untreatable, a mystery thought to be carried by "bad air." The contagion caused severe diarrhea, dehydrating the body so that blood thickened; sufferers' skin turned dark blue.

Cholera rampaged through big cities and small towns. To avoid panic, some state officials insisted cholera wasn't contagious. This misinformation didn't stop the pandemic; some places saw death rates as high as 10 percent. Upon learning that neighbors had cholera, people fled,

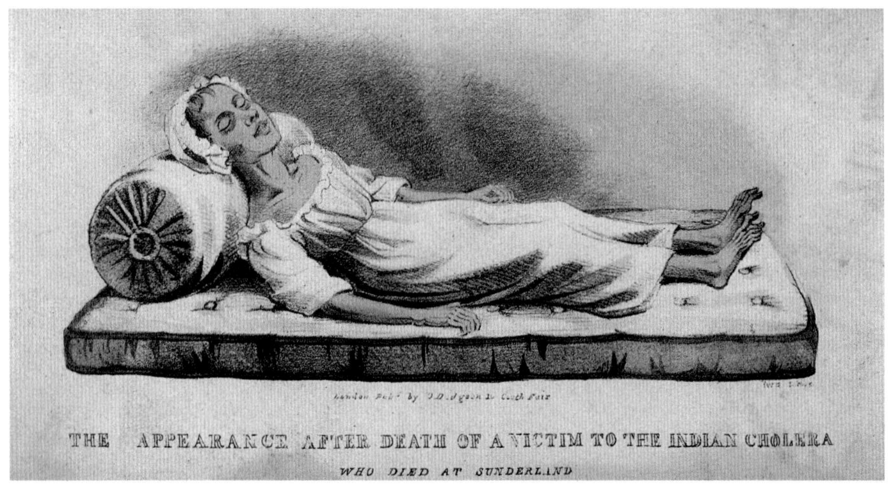

A cholera victim at death. The skin turned blue due to lack of oxygen.

which spread it further and faster. Throughout the nineteenth century, periodic waves of the disease sent more mortals than usual off to the world of spirits. Those left behind looked for answers to life's questions, both big and small. Many found them in spirit circles.

Mortals began asking the spirits for advice—who to marry, what kind of work to do, where to live. George Willets, a Post cousin from a rural New York village, attended a spirit circle. Willets was wrestling with a big decision. He wanted to know if he should join the masses of pioneers settling the "wilds of the West" in Michigan. In a sitting with Maggie and Kate, the spirit of his father told him he should move to Rochester instead. The raps directed him to apply at Rochester's railroad office, though there were no jobs available. Following the spirit's advice, Willets was hired and soon joined the sisters' core group of believers.

The spirits began to send messages not only through the sisters, but, Leah said, directed *to* them, "**Make ready for the work.**" The dead wanted Maggie, Kate, and Leah to spread the word to more of the living. But how could they do so? Decent women did not preach or perform. Leah told supporters that she and her sisters would never follow such scandalous directions, no matter what their spirit friends wished.

Despite Leah's protests, scandal haunted the Fox sisters. Neighbors complained of groups of people visiting Leah's home almost every night. She was evicted by her landlord. Leah denied that she and her sisters had begun to earn money through running spirit circles. Yet, by September of 1849, she somehow had the funds to rent a charming home on Troup Street near the expensive Third Ward, Rochester's most fashionable neighborhood.

This triangle-shaped area was bordered by water—the Erie Canal, the Genesee River and the Genesee Valley Canal. America's new canal and railroad systems had increased the flow of goods across the expanding country. Rochester's population grew 900 percent between 1810 and 1830, almost doubled again between 1840 and 1850. Business flourished—farmers became financiers, millers became millionaires.

While men made the rules for Rochester's newfound wealth, their wives created the city's blossoming society. For the first time, families in Rochester had household staff, elegant evening clothes, and places to wear them. The Fox sisters' new house snuggled near mansions full of successful neighbors with excess cash.

This improved location seemed to give the spirits courage: "**We want you to make the matter more public.**" Believers, including the Posts, Capron, and Willets, discussed the spirits' directive in depth. Some worried that going public would harm their personal reputations. Others thought it dangerous to disobey the dead.

"One morning, on awaking, we found four *coffins* drawn on the kitchen floor, of life-size, and corresponding to the different sizes of mother, myself, Margaretta [Maggie], and Katie . . ." Leah wrote.

The Fox women washed the coffins away. The drawings reappeared, "Each coffin had the drawing of its plate [metal plaque] and on them were perfectly and correctly written our respective names and ages . . ." Leah brought in supporters to witness these sinister pictures. The spirits

An infant's coffin plate. John Elgie died at only nine months old.

threatened, "**If you do not go forth and do your duty, you will soon be laid in your coffins.**"

Obeying these threatening spirits, Mr. Capron and his wife took Kate to their home in nearby Auburn to spread the spirit message. When Kate ran spirit circles for the Caprons' acquaintances, raps sounded and tables moved. The spirits' repertoire expanded to include playing guitars and touching mortal hands. Kate stayed in Auburn living with the Caprons "several weeks." Through her, the spirits converted dozens of families in the surrounding area.

Meanwhile, on an autumn evening in Rochester, the spirits asked those present, including Leah, Maggie, Isaac Post, George Willets, and others, to plan the first public presentation of spirit communication. The mortals were given an ultimatum. If they refused, the spirits would leave in twenty minutes. How spirits had clocks in the afterlife, or why dead folks would need to know the time was not questioned.

Maggie, for one, seemed to be having her own doubts about how the spirits had turned her life upside down. When the spirits threatened to leave, it is likely she who blurted, "nothing could please . . . [me] more."

Twenty minutes passed, when according to Leah, the raps spelled out, **"We will now bid you farewell."**

Despite pleas from the group, not another rap was heard that evening. Or the next. Or the one after that.

Friends called at Leah's house day after day in hopes that the spirits had returned.

"The spirits have left us," Leah repeated, sometimes through tears.

The rappings were gone, utterly gone. Believers found themselves distraught at the thought of never hearing from their loved ones again.

On day twelve of this great spirit silence, Mr. Capron and Mr. Willets knocked at the front door.

With Maggie alongside, Leah met them in the foyer, repeating the discouraging message, "The spirits have left us."

"Perhaps they will rap for us, if not for you," the men replied.

"And so they did," remembered Leah, "joyous sounds, all over the hall . . . It was like the return of long absent friends, whose value . . . we had not sufficiently appreciated."

Once the spirits had returned, the supporters would do anything to keep them happy. Though Kate remained in Auburn, the spirits in Rochester spelled out meticulous instructions for a presentation to the public. One of the more surprising must have been, **"Hire Corinthian Hall."**

Rochester's largest public hall was less than six months old. The main floor of its theater was surrounded by six tiers of seating that held well over a thousand people. The group of supporters, including Capron, Willets, and the Posts, worried that by booking such a large space, they'd be stuck with a rental bill they couldn't cover. The spirits understood money issues; they spelled reassurances that there would be **"enough to pay expenses . . ."**

In early November, the theater was booked. The spirits gave each supporter a job. Notices appeared in local papers, "Wonderful Phenomena." A bold challenge was posed to the public, "COME AND INVESTIGATE." The spirits had communicated every detail: "Doors open at 7 o'clock. Lecture to commence at 7½ [7:30]. Admittance 25 cents; 50 cents will admit a gentleman and two ladies." Latecomers could buy tickets at the door.

The spirits had become American entrepreneurs.

"that I should not give any free exhibition . . ."

Chapter 7 ALTOGETHER RIGHT, ALTOGETHER WRONG

On Wednesday, November 14, 1849, roughly four hundred people settled on wood chairs before an elegant red curtain at Corinthian Hall's third-floor theater. Part of the audience took the idea of talking to the dead seriously, others must have come to whisper about the reputations of the two Fox sisters. Behind the curtain, Leah was reportedly excited, Maggie, terrified. She had reason to be. Unlike her once-married sister, fifteen-year-old Maggie risked being labeled a loose woman, like a prostitute or an actress. What proper man would court a young woman who had appeared before an audience? The spirits had better know what they were doing.

As the curtain opened, Leah and Maggie walked toward chairs set on stage. Corinthian-style columns towered behind them, giving the hall its name. The audience applauded as important citizens, including Amy Post and Reverend Lyman Granger, seated themselves alongside Maggie

The interior of Rochester's Corinthian Hall where Maggie and Leah first appeared on stage in 1849

and Leah as the spirits had directed. The support of these well-known faces gave the idea of spirits credibility with the audience.

The spirits had also instructed that Mr. Capron give the explanatory lecture. Lectures on new ideas in science, literature, or religion were a popular form of entertainment in the nineteenth century. Capron related the entire history of the spirits in both Hydesville and Rochester. As he spoke . . .

Rap. Rap. Rap.

The audience listened with "gaping ears" to the eerie sounds.

Rap. Rap. Rap.

Capron spoke of all the respected people who had tested the spirits and found the sisters sincere.

Rap. Rap. Rap.

He explained that none of the Fox sisters knew where the sounds came from. Yet, people had asked intimate questions, and through the sisters' mediumship, received accurate answers.

Rap. Rap. Rap.

The *Daily Democrat* described the audience's initial reaction to the sounds, "the more the ghost rapped . . . the higher rose the spirit of mirth." Though many found the idea of knocking spirits ridiculous, the rapping sounds *were* mysterious—bouncing off the theater's walls, floorboards, and ceiling. The same newspaper cancelled a prewritten story labeling the rappings an obvious hoax. Its editors decided that contradicting the beliefs of prominent citizens was a risk they shouldn't take.

Capron challenged the audience to solve the mystery. The ladylike Fox sisters did not seem like swindlers. But nineteenth-century America was full of "humbug," a word used for the types of entertainment popularized by renowned promoter P. T. Barnum. Barnum's American Museum in New York exhibited objects, creatures, and people, some real, many fake, most wildly exaggerated. Americans flocked to the museum to see if the exhibits were real. The Fox sisters' claim of spirit communication fit nicely within this popular trend of investigation as entertainment.

From their ranks at Corinthian Hall, Wednesday night's audience selected a five-man committee to test Maggie and Leah and decide whether the rappings were a humbug. The crowd was invited to return to hear the results the following evening. Thursday morning, the sisters received instructions to meet the committee at a local hall. In order to prevent any preplanned trickery, the committee changed the Thursday afternoon location to the Post home. Morning or afternoon, hall or house, the spirits delivered. The five men heard a multitude of raps; and questions were answered "not altogether right and not altogether wrong."

The theater was packed Thursday night. The committee "entirely

Nineteenth-century New Yorkers explore the exhibits inside Barnum's American Museum.

failed to discover any means" by which the rappings were made by the sisters. Incredulous audience members chose a second committee.

On Friday morning, Maggie and Leah were examined by this new committee of five men: a general, a lawyer, a judge, a state chancellor, and a doctor. The doctor listened with a stethoscope to the sisters' breathing as the raps sounded. The raps were not created through ventriloquism as some had suggested. The second committee also failed to find any evidence of fraud.

Friday night's audience created a third committee, composed entirely of avid, angry Rochester skeptics. One man blustered, "If I cannot fathom the fraud, I will throw myself over Genesee Falls!" On Saturday morning, Maggie and Leah's long dresses were tied at the ankles so any movement of their feet could be seen. Raps were heard. The sisters stood on pillows. Raps were heard. They stood on a sheet of glass. Raps were heard. The knocking seemed to come from everywhere and nowhere at once.

Maggie and Leah were brought to a room at a local inn. Their supporters were ordered to remain outside. The committee's men sent in three women. Maggie and Leah were stripped. The women poured over each seam, inspecting the sister's dresses, petticoats, and stockings. They found nothing that could make rapping noises. Then, an intimate body search began. Amy Post responded to Maggie and Leah's embarrassed cries, and burst into the room to halt the examination. The committee had done enough.

Saturday night's audience was riled up, over the possibility of witchcraft, as well as questions of potential fraud. There were rumors of a vat of hot tar hidden outside Corinthian Hall ready to pour over Leah and Maggie as punishment once the trick was discovered. For the fourth night in a row, Maggie, Leah, and the others took seats onstage. When the latest committee still pronounced the sounds an utter mystery, the rowdy audience erupted.

Pop! Bang! Black smoke surfaced in patches around the theater as firecrackers exploded.

An angry mob of men rushed the stage, grabbing for Maggie and Leah. The "howling mob" would investigate these two brazen women as roughly as they wished. Police officers fought their way through the crowd and spirited Maggie and Leah out a back door. The sisters spent the night at Isaac and Amy Post's home, which had been a place of safety for so many others.

After the events at Corinthian Hall, Rochester's citizens either believed in the Fox sisters' spirits or they did not. There was little middle ground. While the city of Rochester found itself divided over spirit beliefs, local papers in nearby Buffalo were covering the growing political divisions over the issue of slavery.

The reality of keeping Black men, women, and children enslaved was unjust, a violation of human rights, and contrary to "Life, Liberty and the pursuit of Happiness," the founding ideals of the United States.

In 1799, New York had begun the gradual process of abolishing slavery. By 1804, New Jersey had been the last Northern state to pass abolition laws. Still, slavery continued unabated in the South. Public opinion on the issue was mixed; there were proslavery Northerners and antislavery Southerners. Northern abolitionists, never more than 2 percent of the population, pushed their politicians to end slavery immediately on moral grounds. But the labor of enslaved Black people was the foundation of the South's agricultural economy. Southern proslavery states rejected abolitionist interference in their business concerns, while continuing support for the racism that was entrenched in the culture. Over decades, Congress had repeatedly tried, and failed, to negotiate the "slavery question."

Newspapers, in both the North and the South, struggled to explain the tangled politics to the public. The headline for a single-column story on slavery was often long and complex: "Northern and Southern Democrats—Southern Control—The Territorial Slavery Question—Its present Position and Future Prospects—Compromise Necessary, &c."

In contrast, the Fox sisters' story was simple to headline, "A Chapter on Ghosts," and easy to summarize—Spirits Had Come to America. Even better, the tale included pretty young women, a mysterious murder, and the possibility of scandal—all elements that the reading public couldn't resist.

"we were destined for great things . . ."

Chapter 8 THE SPIRITUAL TELEGRAPH

Within days, short news items about spirits were appearing in papers as far away as Detroit, "That Rochester Ghost is still knocking at Corinthian Hall." Newspapers in Boston and Louisville ran longer accounts of the Rochester events. On November 29, 1849, the *New-York Tribune*, one of the country's most influential papers, published an unusually large, two-tiered headline—"SINGULAR REVELATIONS. COMMUNICATIONS WITH SPIRITS IN WESTERN NEW-YORK."

The *Tribune*'s editor, Horace Greeley, had been a household name for about a decade, and was associated with the slogan "Go West, young man." This famous phrase became shorthand for United States expansion from the Atlantic to the Pacific that began with the Louisiana Purchase back in 1803. Since the 1830s, Greeley had also been a liberal crusader for abolition, temperance (abstinence from alcohol), vegetarianism, and workers' and women's rights. A fan of modernism and progress in all forms, Greeley was happy to introduce his readers to the new idea of spirit communication. Written by spirit supporters Capron and Willets, the "Singular Revelations" article protected the sisters' reputations by not using their names.

Newspapers in the nineteenth century often copied stories from each other. Within weeks, versions of "Singular Revelations" circulated throughout the country's newspapers, appearing in Vermont, Kentucky, Ohio, Pennsylvania, Illinois, and North Carolina, then crossing the Atlantic to Dublin and London. The sisters' anonymity didn't last; soon Leah, Maggie, and Kate's names appeared in print for the first time.

Newspapers, later magazines and books, emphasized contrasting images for each sister. Leah was the motherly leader, "smart" and "portly." Maggie was portrayed as "gentle" yet fun-loving, "sparkling and irrepressible." Kate was seen as more somber, "dreamy," or "sensitive." All three were almost always described, most importantly, as "ladies." How much these public images corresponded with their real personalities is hard to say. Like the spirits, people saw in the Fox sisters whatever they wanted.

Stories about these three lovely American mediums appeared in hundreds of America's newspapers right alongside reports of crime, crop prices, and ads for woodstoves. So were the spirits fact or fiction? Readers couldn't tell the difference between, one way, "The matter is one well worthy of investigation," or the other, "Persons of such easy faith need *rapping* on the head." Solemn spirit messages were printed alongside obvious spirit jokes. Treated seriously or not, the story of the Fox sisters and the spirits spread farther and faster due to the invention of the telegraph.

Before telegraph wires crisscrossed the United States, news traveled only as fast as a horse could run from town to town. Samuel Morse changed the news business forever when he electronically transmitted the results of a congressional vote in Washington, DC, to a newspaper in Baltimore across a copper wire back in 1844. Editors quickly signed up to pay Morse for instant news transmissions by telegraph. Breaking news sold papers.

Much of the public didn't understand how the telegraph worked. Somehow, electrical messages flew invisibly on wires from one place to another using magnets. All people knew was what they saw: a sender, a receiver, and an operator in the middle.

The Fox sisters' new process for communicating with the dead was understood similarly. Its operators, Maggie, Kate, and Leah, worked to conquer the longest distance, that between life and death.

By the end of 1849, Kate had returned from Auburn and was once more living with Maggie, Leah, Mother, and Calvin on Rochester's Troup Street. One late winter afternoon, the three sisters were invited to the Rochester home of a family named Draper. Just as it was getting dark, the Fox sisters settled themselves at the parlor table among the other guests, joined hands, prayed, and waited for the spirits.

Rap. Rap. Rap. Rap. Rap.

The alphabet was called. Through the spirits, instructions were given to divide the party. Maggie and half the group should stay in the parlor. Kate, Leah, and the rest were sent to a room on the other side of the house. The spirit circles were resumed, and participants in both rooms heard tapping, "similar to the sounds heard in the telegraph office."

Tap. Rap. Tap. Rap. Tap.

The alphabet was called, and the group in the parlor received this message, "**Now I am ready, my friends. There will be great changes in the nineteenth century. Things that now look dark and mysterious to you, will be laid plain before your sight.**

Mysteries are going to be revealed. The world will be enlightened. I sign my name, BENJAMIN FRANKIN."

A few moments later, the other party returned to the parlor. They had received the exact same message!

This 1805 Benjamin West painting, *Benjamin Franklin Drawing Electricity from the Sky*, portrays Franklin as a scientific hero.

While alive, Benjamin Franklin had worked with invisible forces like electricity and magnetism. It made sense to many nineteenth-century Americans that their greatest inventor would be involved in this new discovery of spirit communications. Without hesitation, the Drapers' guests signed a letter published in Rochester's (fittingly named) *Daily Magnet*, faithfully attesting to Benjamin Franklin's new spiritual telegraph.

The story of Franklin's spirit appearance spread in the media. Cleveland's largest newspaper, the *Plain Dealer*, usually supportive of spirit investigation, this time suggested that Benjamin's spirit, "shut up until you have something to offer worth listening to." The long-dead Franklin didn't take that editorial advice. His popular ghost, along with that of other well-known Americans like Thomas Paine and George Washington, regularly appeared at séances for years to come.

The continued newspaper coverage created a flood of requests for spirit circles. The Fox sisters and their mother spent the first months of 1850 answering their front door. Spirit-curious people showed up to talk to the dead and the entire household was busy with spirit circles from teatime until midnight. Some nights, groups of church members, concerned about the increasing interest in the occult, gathered outside the house to protest.

In this frantic atmosphere, the number of Leah's piano students dwindled. She changed her occupation in Rochester's city directory, from "music teacher" to "mysterious knocker," and now admitted she was "forced to charge a fee" from those grateful to sit in the presence of loved ones again.

Which Fox sisters were earning their money and which sister was keeping it was discussed in the *Rochester Daily American*, "The sum thus accumulated after joint expenses of improving their attire, &c was taken . . . by Mrs. Fish. The younger sisters objected. The parties quarreled . . . and left their sister's house. The rapping ceased. A reconciliation was sought and effected. The rappings recommenced . . ."

The story also ran in Milwaukee, Nashville, New Orleans, and Pittsburgh. If true, it may have explained the real reasons behind the great spirit silence and demonstrated early tension between the sisters. Yet, these minor hints of family scandal only made the public want to know more about the Fox sisters and made their spirits more popular.

In January of 1850, Reverend Charles Hammond was attending his third spirit circle, this one at the Fox sisters' home. Though others were in the room, the spirits immediately focused their attention on Hammond. The raps directed him to join Maggie, Kate, Leah, and Mother Fox in a separate room.

There, six chairs surrounded a wood table. At its center, a flickering candle was the only source of light. Kate and Mother sat at Hammond's right, Maggie and Leah on his left. One chair remained empty. They held hands and proceeded with the séance.

Soon, "every part of the room trembled . . ." with rappings.

Hammond felt his side of the table rising off the floor. The table "passed out of the reach of us all . . ."

"Will the Spirit move the table back where it was before?" Leah asked; the spirit obeyed.

The four women sang hymns, including a new "spirit's song," probably composed by Leah, the only music teacher in the room. Hammond felt raps drumming the tabletop; then, "a transparent hand . . . presented itself before my face—I felt fingers taking hold of a lock of hair on the left side of my head . . . then a cold, death-like hand . . . over my face—three gentle raps on my left knee. . . myself and chair uplifted and moved back a few inches, and several slaps . . . on the side of my head . . . more rapid than I could count."

A spirit circle or séance, around 1853

Hammond witnessed a flurry of powerful spirit manifestations that evening. A sheet of cardboard fanned the air on its own. The window shade rolled and unrolled. A lounge chair shook as if nervous. A chest of drawers "played back and forth with inconceivable rapidity." The room itself seemed alive. "That any of the company could have performed these things, under the circumstances . . . would require a greater stretch of credulity on my part, than it would to believe it was the work of the spirits."

Soon afterward, Charles Hammond left the ministry and wrote a book about the spirits. Until his death nine years later, and presumably afterward, he remained dedicated to the power of the Fox sisters and the belief that the dead could talk.

Yet not everyone was convinced.

A prominent Rochester minister, Reverend Strong, was entertaining visitors from out of town. His guests insisted on attending a Fox séance. The reverend's teenage son, Augustus Strong, went along to what he called "the Foxy abode." Augustus remembered, "Every room, upstairs and down, was full; people were sitting on the very stairs . . ." The sisters were much too busy to see visiting guests without a prior reservation. But the spirits made time to spell out a quick message—Kate and her mother would lead a special private circle at the Strong home later that same night.

It "was a memorable evening" for Augustus who was allowed to join his father and the adult visitors. The group seated itself around a massive, mahogany table wheeled into the parlor for the occasion. Fourteen-year-old Augustus sat across from Kate Fox, who looked just about his age.

The group clasped hands and waited for the spirits to arrive. Augustus saw a slight smile on Kate's pretty face; so he winked, flirting a bit. None of the adults seemed to notice. To his shock, Kate winked back, then composed her face and began the séance.

Augustus heard raps, "under the table . . . from the floor . . . from the doors, and even from the ceiling." Questions were asked; spirit responses given. Augustus quickly realized that only "ambiguous or commonplace answers were spelled out." He amused himself watching one stately older man examine the underside of the table, find nothing, and leave that night sure "that these rappings were veritable messages from beyond the grave." Augustus Strong found Kate Fox cute and entertaining but her so-called spirits unbelievable.

It wasn't only teenagers who expressed skepticism. Another night, the middle-aged Miss Mary B. Allen joined a spirit session at the Fox sister's home. Miss Allen was principal and teacher at Allen Female Seminary, a Rochester school that Maggie and Kate had attended from time to time. Miss Allen was known as "a maiden lady, sharp and wiry, with a grain of wit which could not tolerate nonsense."

Miss Allen took a seat at the parlor table with others including Kate and Mother Fox.

This particular evening, Mother led the spirit questioning. She began, "Was there any . . . departed friends or relatives with whom Miss Allen would like to converse?"

"Yes," replied Miss Allen, "I had a grandmother whom I loved very much, and I would like to talk with her."

"Is there any particular question that Miss Allen would like to ask?" Mother continued.

"Yes, I am interested in education and I would like to know something about methods in the other world. Spelling, for example. How does my grandmother now spell the word 'scissors'?" Miss Allen asked.

As the alphabet was called seven times over, the raps spelled, "**SISSERS**."

"Oh," said Miss Allen, "that is just the way Katy Fox spelled 'scissors' when she was a scholar at my school!"

Though no response, spirit or mortal, was recorded, it's assumed that the clever Miss Allen remained a skeptic.

"I have tried to do so in every form . . ."

Chapter 9 MAKING MEDIUMS

After experiencing a Fox sisters' séance or reading about the phenomenon, people around the country began attempting spirit communication in their own homes.

Reverend Granger started to hear raps about his farm and house after attending several Fox séances. By early 1850, his teenage daughter had become the family's regular medium. Astonishingly, the Reverend continued to be awed as the spirit raps in this intimate circle answered simple questions about the family correctly.

After Kate Fox returned to Rochester, several women in Auburn suddenly discovered that they too were mediums. They fell into trances and interpreted rappings just like Kate had done. In Auburn's circles, spirits began performing all kinds of miracles, from flipping hats and playing the harp to suggesting appropriate medicines for sick relatives.

Throughout the spring of 1850, Greeley's *Weekly Tribune* published a barrage of letters about mediumship and spirit communications.

Both pro, "let us prepare ourselves for advancement in knowledge . . ." and con, "fools are not all dead . . ." He and others in the media suggested that whatever the truth was, it could only be found through further experimentation. As curious Americans ran spirit circles themselves, mediums grew more common, and spirit manifestations more varied.

Isaac Post found a new kind of mediumship, no rapping needed. Instead, guided by the spirits, Isaac's hand wrote automatically. His spirits left messages on old letters, the back of envelopes, and scrap paper, like this note from Isaac's dead mother, **"A reformation is going on in the spirit world, and these spirits seek the company of honest men like you. It will do them great good and thee no harm."**

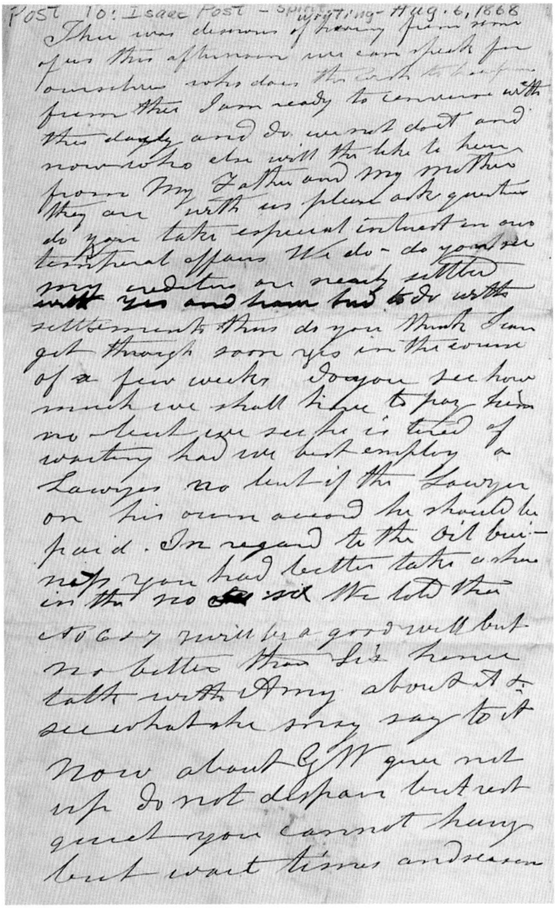
POST TO: Isaac Post - Spirit writing - Aug. 6, 1868
There was desirous of hearing from some of us this afternoon we can speak for ourselves who does the truth to hear from thee I am ready to converse with thee daily and do we not doubt and now who else will the like to hear from My Father and my mother they are with us please ask questions do you take especial interest in our temporal affairs We do - do you see my creditors are nearly settled with you and have but to do with settlements thus do you think I can get through soon yes in the course of a few weeks do you see how much we shall have to pay him no but we see he is tired of waiting had we best employ a Lawyer no but if the Lawyer on his own accord he should be paid. In regard to the oil business you had better take a share in that no sir We told thee Storey will be a good well but no better than his hence talk with Amy about it & see what she may say to it Now about G W give not up do not despair but rest quiet you cannot hurry but wait times and season

A page of Isaac Post's automatic spirit writing. Isaac took this spirit dictation in the form of a letter to himself.

Quakers, like Isaac Post, were at the forefront of American social reform not only regarding abolishing slavery but also prohibiting alcohol, treating the mentally ill, improving housing for prisoners, recognizing Native American rights, and providing public education for all. The newly discovered spirits frequently expressed messages in support for these kinds of earthly reforms. Spirits, even those who had been conservative in life, were often liberally minded after death.

After a year or two as a practicing medium, Isaac Post published a 300-page book, "without any action of his mind." It was written by the spirits of George Washington, Thomas Jefferson, William Penn, Benjamin Franklin, and Mrs. Franklin, too. Skeptical readers couldn't help wondering why spirits of people who had lived in places as different as eighteenth-century Virginia, Pennsylvania, and Massachusetts, all sounded like a nineteenth-century Quaker abolitionist from western New York.

What did Maggie, Kate, or Leah have to say about these homegrown mediums? Not much. The sisters didn't question the spirits' purposes and didn't comment on the practices of other mediums. They never specified any human actions that took place while their circles were in session. They maintained that the spirits were in charge, not the Fox sisters. Leah, Maggie, and Kate kept quiet, and let the public determine the truth. The sisters' humble attitude helped forge an honest image.

That image of innocence was spread in newspapers and magazines. One editor described Kate as "twelve years of age and evidently has no more conception of the rapping than a canary bird." Maggie was seen as "apparently 17 or 18 . . . [with] a face indicative of no superior cunning or shrewdness." Nineteenth-century news media perpetuated the belief that young women were passive, incapable of deep thought or deep deception.

It was their male followers who typically promoted the spirit cause. Eliab Capron expanded the original "Singular Revelations" article into a longer pamphlet. Capron's pamphlet gave spirit communications a religious foundation in the theology of Emanuel Swedenborg. Swedenborg, an eighteenth-century scientist and male mystic, had described the afterlife as a circular "world of spirits." Capron also wove the sisters' revelations into existing ideas set forth by yet another man, the well-known clairvoyant lecturer Andrew Jackson Davis, known as the "Poughkeepsie Seer."

Spirit communication wasn't *super*natural, Capron explained (or mansplained?). It was a scientific force that needed study, "another link in the great chain of nature's law." Mediums like the Fox sisters acted like human batteries, storing and transmitting unseen energy. Capron's publication ended with a two-page list of witnesses: doctors, judges, ministers, editors, lawyers, and prominent families throughout the country. Capron was "perfectly willing" for these witnesses to "say for themselves what their opinions are . . ." In other words, if ordinary readers didn't believe, they should ask their more distinguished neighbors. The self-published *Singular Revelations* sold enough copies for a second printing and was later expanded into a book reviewed in Greeley's *New-York Tribune*.

Another successful pamphlet about the Fox sisters' spirits came from Rochester printer D. M. Dewey. He compiled his tale into a *History of the Strange Sounds or Rappings Heard in Rochester and Western New-York and Usually Called the Mysterious Noises!* Despite the sensational title, Dewey insisted he wasn't "pro or con, in regard to the sounds being made by disembodied spirits."

But his pamphlet was hardly objective. It contained dozens of pages detailing spirit appearances, including sworn statements supporting otherworldly manifestations and instances of mediumship. A later edition included four pages of "Additional Facts," including the mysterious appearance of "a turnip covered with minute, multitudinous, and most beautifully formed mesmeric characters."

This outlandish claim of spirit writing on a vegetable didn't hurt Dewey's reputation a bit. And it didn't hurt his wallet either; his work sold an astonishing 30,000 copies. In comparison, the first runs of popular books in the 1850s, *The Scarlet Letter* or *Moby-Dick* for example, were less than 3,000 copies.

Early publications such as Capron's and Dewey's spread a generally positive message about spirits and the afterlife. Mortals had nothing to fear; death was a natural transition to another, happier world.

This idea of a happier afterworld was attractive to the public as many Americans worried that their country might not survive its galloping growth. Slavery's advocates felt the practice should be allowed to expand into the country's new western territories. Abolitionists felt the moral wrong of slavery should be stopped dead in its tracks.

Congress passed a series of laws, the Compromise of 1850, which dealt with issues of slavery in America's new territories. One of these laws allowed the voters (at the time only white males) of New Mexico, Utah, and future territories to decide whether or not slavery was permitted.

Neither those for nor against slavery liked the idea of America's citizens deciding such an essential issue. Congress worked to appease both sides. For the abolitionists, Congress prohibited slavery in the new state of California and the slave trade was banned in the capital District of Columbia. For the slaveowners, Congress passed the Fugitive Slave Act of 1850, requiring that all Black people who had escaped from slavery be returned to their owners.

One side believed slavery was a legal right. The other side knew slavery was wrong. Neither side, proslavery or antislavery, South or North, was satisfied with the Compromise of 1850. The news-reading public used spirit gossip, spirit cartoons, and spirit love stories as distractions from the realization that there seemed to be no peaceful way forward on the increasingly heated issue of slavery's expansion.

The growing popularity of spirits in the news tempted the publicity-minded Mr. Capron to expand the Fox sisters' reach. A group of prominent men had contacted him about their interest in seeing the original mediums, Maggie and Kate, demonstrate their powers in New York City.

As a believer, Mother Fox had tried to do what the spirits wanted from the first. But she had no intention of letting Mr. Capron parade her youngest, unmarried daughters in front of groups of curious men in the country's largest city.

Capron pressured Mother Fox in writing, "I this morning received a letter . . . stating that you had decided not to let Cathy [Kate] or Margaretta [Maggie] go to N.Y. at present. I regret this very much as the persons . . . there stand among the first in the nation for science and influence. It would be of great advantage to your family to have such men satisfied . . ."

Still, Mother held firm. She kept Capron and his New York City influencers waiting.

Instead, in April of 1850, just after the two-year anniversary of the peddler's spirit in Hydesville, Maggie and Leah appeared once again in Corinthian Hall. This time, Kate, who had just celebrated her thirteenth birthday, joined them onstage. She was dressed, like her sisters, in a floor-length gown. Typically, girls younger than fourteen wore short dresses, pantalets, and stockings. The long dress made Kate look more mature, and hid more of her body.

A Rochester audience once again heard the history of spirit communications, and once again, raps echoed throughout the theater. But this time, when a mob of people rushed the stage, it was in celebration.

The Fox sisters were an undeniable hit. Audience members expressed the hope that more people could be introduced to their wonderful discovery of the rapping spirits. The spirits agreed with the audience, "we were directed to **'go forth, and let the truth be known,'**" said Leah. Mother relented, allowing her daughters to spread the spirit circles into nearby smaller cities.

Nineteenth-century fashion. Until about fourteen, girls wore shorter dresses that showed their feet and ankles. Older teens and adult women wore floor-length dresses.

They left almost immediately. Maggie, Kate, Leah, Mother, and Calvin traveled by packet boat over 200 miles east to Albany, the capital city of New York State. The easternmost port of the Erie Canal, Albany had grown to about fifty thousand residents. Leah hired a business manager to book stages, rent hotel rooms, and inform reporters. The sisters' expenses ran $150/week (about $6,000/week today). The costs paid off in terms of publicity. "The people in and about Rochester have been knocked almost out of their senses lately, by a family of quite pretty young ladies . . ." gushed the *Weekly Argus*, introducing Albany's citizens to the fabulous Fox sisters.

After an evening lecture and demonstration of spirit rappings at a local theater, Albany's audience was invited to book personal conversations with the spirits. The Fox sisters set up shop at the Delavan House, the best local hotel. Their daytime schedule was entirely booked, even though talking with the dead did not come cheap. The charge for a sitting was $1 per person (about $35 today) for a group séance, and $5 for a private session (over $175 today). At the time, a New York State blacksmith like their father John Fox earned about $1.50 a day. As spirit mediums, his daughters began to regularly earn ten to twenty times that amount in a few hours.

Night after night, Albany's influential citizens threw parties in honor of the fabulous Fox sisters. The sisters and their spirits turned out to be as popular on the road as in Rochester, though they did run into at least one minor bump.

After two weeks of warm welcome in Albany, Leah, Maggie, and Kate received a shocking summons. A local minister had charged them with "blasphemy against the holy scriptures" and a warrant was issued for the sisters' arrest!

But there was no need for worry; the famous Fox sisters were given special treatment. The police didn't take them into custody, nor did the sisters appear in court. Rather, seventeen of Albany's distinguished judges and attorneys arrived at the Delavan House for a private sitting. The judges found "quiet, gracious young women," the spirits provided sound demonstrations, and the charges were dropped without further investigation.

The public could not get enough stories about mediums or spirit communication in general. The spirits sold newspapers but also created dissension. Skeptics railed against treating spirit communication as a reality. Believers railed against claims that spirit communication was fraudulent. Instead of reporting straight facts, where spirits were concerned, newspapers printed countless varying opinions.

Newspapers were in the business of keeping all their readers happy; so many editors tried to play to both sides. The *Brooklyn Eagle* wrote that contact with spirits, "rests on extremely slender foundations," but was also, "worthy of serious investigation." Cleveland's *Plain Dealer* reported, "We incline to believe them in good part the work of deception" and yet, "a great many of those involved . . . are thoroughly honest and sincere." Who knew the truth? Many Americans made up their own minds, then stopped reading anything that contradicted their beliefs.

The Fox entourage left Albany, continuing north. On May 1, 1850, the *Daily Whig* in Troy, New York crowed, "The Rochester 'Spirits' . . . are actually in town!" Troy was a small, wealthy enclave. Maggie, Kate, and Leah appeared at Apollo Hall and ran spirit circles at the luxurious Troy House hotel. After seeing the wonder and respect with which her daughters were treated by many people of the higher classes, Mother Fox agreed to let the tour continue. Next stop? New York City.

"They took a great fancy to us . . ."

Chapter 10 BIG-CITY SPIRITS

On one of the last days in May 1850, Leah, Kate, Maggie, and Mother, headed down the Hudson River. As usual, their longtime friend and protector Calvin Brown chaperoned. Eliab Capron also traveled with them to manage the big city appearance he had arranged. The Fox company had boarded the *Empire*, the largest paddle steamer in the world, for their first trip to New York City. The sisters and their party ate in the elegant, paneled dining room and visited in the plush sitting rooms, enjoying views of the passing Catskill Mountains. A day or so later, they docked at one of fifty piers lining New York Harbor, and drove "half-intoxicated" into the clamoring excitement of New York City.

By the first of June, the Fox sisters were in residence at a suite of rooms in Barnum's Hotel located at the corner of Broadway and Maiden Lane. A reporter noted the hotel's name and wrote an error-ridden news item connecting the sisters to world-famous showman

P. T. Barnum,"The daughters of Mrs. Fish, whose 'mysterious rappings' at Rochester created so much excitement awhile ago have been engaged by Mr. Barnam to 'rap at his Museum' in New York. Admission 25 cents."

The story appeared as far away as Little Rock and New Orleans, even though the original reporter didn't bother to check his facts. Barnum's Hotel was owned by a distant cousin of P. T. Barnum and *not* Barnum himself. The Fox sisters were *not* rapping at Barnum's Museum or appearing at any other public place (and certainly never for as little as a quarter!). Instead, Mr. Capron kept their demonstrations selective: "they do not mean to give any public exhibitions . . ." only, "private investigations of scientific persons and friends."

New Yorkers who attended a Fox sisters' circle were led from the Barnum Hotel's lobby, down a series of marble hallways to one of its largest parlors. The parlor contained at least one sofa, a chest of drawers, and a massive wood table that sat more than thirty. In keeping with the elegant surroundings, a deep red damask cloth draped the table, almost to the floor. Heavy curtains kept out the light.

Leah typically led the sessions, with Kate, Maggie, or both, serving as mediums. Group sessions were held six days a week, 10 a.m. 'til noon, 3 p.m. 'til 5 p.m. and 8 'til 10 p.m. Printed "Rules of Order" were posted on the doorway and the table.

Broadway, around 1850. The Fox sisters stayed down this street when first arriving in New York City. Barnum's American Museum is on the left topped by the American flag.

ATTENTION

IS SPECIALLY CALLED TO THE ENSUING

RULES OF ORDER

1. All persons present at interviews are expected to observe the order and decorum which should characterise meetings of religious solemnity and importance.

2. No controversies with reference to the truth or falsity of the communications should be entered into during their continuance.

3. All persons should follow, without delay or discussion, all directions with reference to conduct, position, &c., as compliance with directions generally ensures satisfactory manifestations, while neglect or refusal usually results in their partial or complete cessation.

4. When any individual indicated by the spirits is in communication with them, no other person should interfere, as this often occasions discontinuance of the communications.

5. The ladies in whose presence the manifestations are made will use their best exertions to satisfy all inquiries: but since the manifestations, alike in their commencement, character, and duration are *above their personal control*, they cannot promise that all persons or all inquiries will obtain answers, no manifestations being made except as the spirits will.

6. Entire truthfulness, honesty, and good faith should be observed by all who seek correct responses. Those who resort to tricks and deceptions repel all good influences, and are answered by silly or deceptive spirits, thus making the interviews unprofitable and delusive.

Admission One Dollar

One of their first visitors was *New-York Tribune* editor Horace Greeley. On June 4, 1850, just a few days after the Fox sisters' arrival, Greeley spontaneously invited a friend and turned up at Barnum's Hotel to investigate this new idea of spirit communication. Though it was off-hours, Calvin was savvy enough to usher this celebrated man and his friend in to meet the ladies.

Horace Greeley around 1844–1860 by photographic pioneer Mathew Brady, who became famous as a great documentarian of the American Civil War

Maggie and Kate curtsied politely to their important guest. First-time visitors often focused on the younger girls. Instead, Greeley shrewdly noted Leah, "seemed to be on the most familiar terms with the knocking."

Leah asked the spirits if they would converse with Mr. Greeley.

Rap. Rap. Rap.

Leah told him three sounds meant **Yes**.

Mr. Greeley was told to think of a person he knew that had passed over to the spirit world. When he had someone in mind, the questions began.

"Are you a friend?" Greeley asked. Silence.

"Are you a relative?" **Rap. Rap.**

Now Greeley was told that what he described as a "double thump on the floor," meant **Yes** also.

"How many years since you were living?" Greeley asked.

Leah directed Mr. Greeley to write a list of numbers in private, making sure only one was correct. When his list was complete, he should begin pointing to each number in turn. Greeley followed instructions; hearing nothing until he pointed to the tenth number on his list.

Rap.

He was sure that no one in the room had seen his list. Like any good newsman, Greeley double-checked his source by asking the spirit to also rap the corresponding number he'd written. Twenty-seven distinct raps echoed around the parlor. The number 27 *was* the tenth number on his list. And astonishingly, the spirit relative Greeley questioned had died exactly twenty-seven years ago.

The spirits went on to address additional questions asked by Mr. Greeley's friend. All of *his* inquiries were answered incorrectly or not at all. Despite that failure, Greeley's curiosity deepened.

Horace Greeley had worked in New York City's news business for two decades. He knew the city's politicians, performers, and police. He was as familiar with its gleaming mansions as its darkest slums. He understood its people, both honest and corrupt. He was a true New Yorker, rarely fooled. Yet Maggie, Kate, and Leah's "whole deportment exhibited . . . frankness and sincerity . . ." Greeley found himself trusting these sisters.

He wrote an article, "An Hour with the Spirits," and positioned it on page one of the next day's *New-York Tribune*. He related the events of his visit and his doubts: "We are not willing to believe that spirits have nothing better to do than make . . . thumps and raps . . ." But he also believed that mesmerism or clairvoyance had to play a role in the Fox sisters' manifestations. Greeley remained intrigued, and "hoped to have some further conversation with the 'spirits.'"

The day after Greeley's article appeared, Maggie, Kate, Leah, Mother, and a few male supporters accepted an invitation to the townhome of Rev. Dr. Rufus Griswold. The sophisticated Griswold worried that too many intelligent citizens were being duped by what he considered ghostly nonsense. Intending to expose the fraud, he asked the Fox sisters to demonstrate their 'spirits' for more than a dozen of America's most famous men.

Waiting for the Fox sisters in Griswold's parlor were best-selling novelist James Fenimore Cooper, William Cullen Bryant of the *New-York Evening Post*, George Ripley, editor of *Harper's New Monthly Magazine*, and Nathaniel Parker Willis, founder of the *Home Journal*. Rounding out the large party were three doctors, two ministers, a military general, a former secretary of the US Navy, more writers and editors, plus a businessman or two. All were chosen for their broad intelligence and utter skepticism.

At first, the sisters' group got lost in Griswold's stylish neighborhood. Griswold's guests saw them wandering outside, but didn't offer help. *After all, shouldn't the spirits be able to show them where to go?* When the Fox party finally found the correct front door, a servant ushered them in and led them to the parlor where introductions were made.

Willis, who ran a publication devoted to high fashion and current trends, described all three Fox sisters as, "considerably prettier than average." Maggie was singled out in the *New York Herald* as "a very pretty, arch-looking, black-eyed and rather modestly behaved girl."

The pretty women and the famous men arranged themselves around Griswold's parlor table, joined hands, and waited. Ten minutes passed in silence. Another ten. A half hour passed without a rap. The men grew restless.

Someone suggested the group draw closer. Chairs slid; bodies leaned forward.

Rap. Rap. Rap.

Under the floor, around the table, across the room.

"Will the Spirits converse with anyone present?" Leah asked.

Louder, faster, impossible to trace—**RAP. RAP. RAP. RAP. RAP.**

A French newspaper caricature of the Fox sisters being tested by a group of well-dressed gentlemen, most probably in New York City

One of the doctor's questions was answered correctly. One of the writers then asked questions about a dead friend. In answer, the spirits accurately communicated the deceased's city, occupation, religion, age, number of children, and the disease that killed him.

Another doctor asked questions, few raps sounded, and those that were heard were wrong.

A third doctor thought of a famous dead writer.

"Was he an American?"

"An Englishman?"

"A Scotchman?"

Rap. Rap. Rap.

"Will you tell us his name?"

Rap. Rap. Rap. Rap. Rap.

Five raps! The spirits were asking for the alphabet. As it was recited, raps spelled "**B—u—r** . . ."

"Robert Burns!" the excited group blurted. These men were so famous, they even felt comfortable interrupting the dead, who may have answered differently.

The still-very-much-alive writer, James Fenimore Cooper, was the most celebrated man at Griswold's that evening. His romantic novels such as *The Last of the Mohicans* were literary blockbusters. Cooper was sixty years old, but his thoughts went back to someone from his childhood.

"A relative?" Cooper asked the spirits.

Rap. Rap. Rap.

"A near relative?"

Rap. Rap. Rap.

"A man?"

"A woman?"

Rap. Rap. Rap.

"A daughter?" "A mother?" "A wife?" "A sister?"

Rap. Rap. Rap.

Cooper asked how many years it had been since his sister's death.

The party began counting the answering raps aloud and got mixed up. Was the number forty-five, forty-nine, or fifty-four?

The spirit was asked to rap the answer again, slowly.

Exactly fifty raps sounded. Correct.

"Did she die of consumption?" Silence.

Cooper listed several common diseases; no raps sounded.

"Did she die by accident?"

Rap. Rap. Rap.

"Was she killed by lightning?" "Was she shot?" "Was she lost at sea?" "Did she fall from a carriage?" "Was she thrown from a horse?"

Rap. Rap. Rap.

James Fenimore Cooper was thinking of Hannah, his beloved older sister, who was thrown from a horse and killed fifty years ago that month. This most famous of American writers swore that not a mortal soul in the room knew the story previously.

The next day's *Tribune* featured Ripley's article, "An Evening with the Spirits," which described the events for its readers, "with regard to their [the spirits] origin or their nature, we are as much in the dark as any of our readers. The manner and bearing of the ladies . . . create a prepossession in their favor."

Mr. Willis published an essay, "Post-Mortuum Soiree," in the next issue of his *Home Journal*, "the 'demonstration,' . . . is of sufficient extent and respectability to warrant grave attention. An electric telegraph across the Styx [in Greek mythology, the river separating life and death], before they get one across the Atlantic, would make death less of a separation from friends than a voyage to Europe . . ."

Willis, like some others in the room, tended toward spirit belief.

But another attendee from the séance at Griswold's wrote an anonymous letter to the *New-York Evening Post,* "correcting an erroneous impression . . . that the company gave countenance [approval] . . . to an absurd superstition . . . I know that several of the party are displeased . . . at the unauthorized use of their names . . ." It seemed at least some of Griswold's celebrity friends felt used by the spirits for publicity purposes.

The idea of celebrity first became prominent in the 1830s, with the advent of newspapers costing one or two cents. The new technology of steam-run printing presses could spit out cheap tabloid newspapers by the thousands. Unlike traditional papers sold by expensive subscription; newsboys hawked these "penny papers" in the streets. The penny papers combined traditional political and business news with sensational stories and scandals featuring the nation's entertainers, explorers, and artists. Penny papers, the first mass media, gained a wide readership among Americans of all classes.

Notoriety and name recognition began to have value. People bought what celebrities bought; they became interested in what celebrities found interesting. Whether Griswold's famous friends thought the Fox sisters honest or not, their interest alone helped turn Maggie, Kate, and Leah into superstars.

"wanted to establish a new religion . . ."

Chapter 11 STARDOM!

Before the end of June 1850, the Fox sisters had become New York's latest must-see sensation. From early morning until well after the gas lamps were lit, horse-drawn carriages filled with gentlemen and ladies lined the cobblestone street in front of Barnum's Hotel.

Once inside, people crowded around the parlor doors for their turn to speak with the Fox sisters' spirits. Mediumship kept Leah, Maggie, and Kate so busy that they had little time to eat. One day Mother came in from a walk with a handkerchief full of peanuts bought from a street vendor. She interrupted a séance to distribute the nuts to her hungry youngest daughters. Maggie and Kate devoured the snack while continuing their talk with the dead. Their session ended with vigorous spirits raps accompanying the singing of "Hail Columbia"—"Firm, u . . . ni . . . ted let us be, Rally-ing 'round our li . . . ber . . . ty . . ."

Singing, eating, or any spontaneous behavior concerning the dead was considered highly unusual in the nineteenth century. Death was everywhere. Mourning was inevitable. Both had strict rules of etiquette.

Doctors lacked advanced medical tools, so a corpse was watched for three days to be certain it did not awaken. Visitors came to pay their respects at this "wake," held in the parlor of the deceased's home (and yes, people considered dead were known to sit up in their coffins to the shock of those gathered to mourn them). But assuming one stayed dead, a proper burial included a fine coffin, multiple floral arrangements, and formal religious services.

Depending on one's relationship to the deceased, official mourning lasted from three months to more than two years after the funeral. Those in mourning did not attend social events and wore special dark clothing as public expressions of their grief.

Mourners at the home wake of an older woman, possibly a grandmother, around 1896

Instead of finding eating and singing with dead spirits indecent, many people attending the circles found Maggie and Kate's cheerfulness around death a sign of their closeness to the spirits. Their naïve manner supported their special connection to the happy heaven of "Summerland," an afterlife where "All is rejoicing, no mourning; all love, no fear; all Deity, no devil; all heaven, no hell."

This lighthearted, ladylike reputation created an entire market of products around the sisters and their spirits. Leah proudly recalled "Rochester Knockings" souvenirs, such as spoons, pins, cups, and sheet

The cover of "Spirit Rappings" sheet music, printed music sold often for home use, typically to be played on a piano. Note the little boy investigating the sounds, as well as the stereotyped depictions of Black people as servants.

music, being sold in the streets of New York City. A favorite Broadway actress sang "The Rochester Knockings at Barnum's Hotel," and *Mysterious Knockings*, "a new farce full of glorious fun and frolic," played at a popular theater.

Leah, Maggie, and Kate topped the exclusive guest lists of the city's elite. Dressmakers arrived at Barnum's Hotel to fit the Foxes in the latest gowns, gloves, and bonnets. Unlike most any other women of their time, their fine clothes were paid for with money earned themselves. Once they were stylishly dressed, carriages drove them in luxury to the city's finest homes.

There, butlers opened doors and ladies' maids took wraps and bonnets into elegant dressing rooms. In the dining room, ten or more courses were served by footmen: a different plate, fork, and glass for each course. Men in long frock coats and women in iridescent shot silk raised toasts. "Ladies, you are the lions of New York," editor George Ripley raved.

There were so many new people, ideas, and manners to keep track of; it was easy to feel anxious. To soothe their nerves, Maggie and Kate sipped their first glasses of chilled French champagne. The spirits had brought the Fox sisters a long way from the dirt roads of Hydesville.

Mr. Greeley suggested to Leah that she raise séance prices to five dollars a person to "keep the rabble away." She refused. That rabble was earning the family an immense amount of money. Spirit sittings brought in between $100 and $150 a day (a weekly income of $20,000 today). As manager of the household, Leah kept their earnings and ran their schedule.

Between public sittings, Leah arranged private séances, social invitations, and whatever rest time they could fit in. Maggie and Kate stretched, soaked their feet, embroidered, or read a bit to release

NOTICE.

PREVENTIVES OF

CHOLERA!

Published by order of the Sanatory Committee, under the sanction of the Medical Counsel.

BE TEMPERATE IN EATING & DRINKING!

Avoid Raw Vegetables and Unripe Fruit !.

Abstain from COLD WATER, when heated, and above all from *Ardent Spirits*, and if habit have rendered them indispensable, take much less than usual.

SLEEP AND CLOTHE WARM !

DO NOT SLEEP OR SIT IN A DRAUGHT OF AIR,

Avoid getting Wet !

Attend immediately to all disorders of the Bowels.

TAKE NO MEDICINE WITHOUT ADVICE.

Medicine and Medical Advice can be had by the poor, at all hours of the day and night, by applying at the Station House in each Ward.

CALEB S. WOODHULL, *Mayor.*

JAMES KELLY, *Chairman of Sanatory Committee.*

A public health poster during a cholera pandemic, around 1849 the strain of introducing the spirits to so many strangers. The sisters spent as many as twelve to fifteen hours a day in spirit work, with few breaks.

But Death never took a break. The cholera pandemic surged, killing 1,400 people in Chicago, 3,000 in New Orleans, 4,500 in St. Louis, thousands more in New York. At a Fourth of July celebration, US President Zachary Taylor fell ill, was diagnosed with cholera, and died five days later. Vice President Millard Fillmore was sworn into the nation's highest office. People faced a hard summer in 1850, clinging to life, and wondering more and more about what lay beyond.

Séances continued to grow in popularity. As "first in the field," the Fox sisters were prime targets for a growing number of skeptics. Each detractor had a theory: Machinery! Magnets! Vibrations! None were proven. Skeptics were incensed at believers' lack of logic. *Why did spirits need mediums or darkness? Why would immortals bother to knock at all?* A skeptical reporter from Indiana argued, "One would think that it would be as easy for ghosts to utter articulate words as to knock on chairs and tables . . ."

One early skeptic was J. Stanley Grimes, an active lecturer on mesmerism and phrenology, a nineteenth-century pseudoscience that analyzed character traits from the shape of a person's skull. Grimes had spent years in front of American audiences; he knew a bit about persuasion and performance.

In the spring of 1850, Grimes had attended a spirit circle led by a female medium in Auburn, New York. She fell into a trance; spirit raps began and people received answers to questions, but something in her manner made Grimes suspicious. When he threatened to expose her, the medium confessed. Her knockings were made by a floorboard on a lever that she pressed with her foot. She had three accomplices arranged in the circle, a neighbor and two cousins, who also knocked when necessary, and rearranged objects in the dark. The medium reported learning these tricks from "the women who practiced the same deception in Rochester."

Grimes accused the Fox sisters in a letter printed in the *New-York Tribune* on July 9, 1850. The sisters did not answer the attack themselves. Instead, respected men who believed in the sisters' spirits flooded newspapers with letters to the editor. These believers turned the tables on the medium who had confessed, accusing her of deceit. They said she'd never met the Fox sisters. Spirit supporters criticized Grimes for promoting himself using the sisters' fame. He was labeled a common huckster, his facts called obvious fictions.

New York City's papers divided into pro-Fox and anti-Fox camps. Greely's *Tribune* stayed open to the idea that spirit communication might be real and the sisters honest. Competing papers, such as the *New York Herald* and the *Evening Post,* cried fraud. In their pages, spirits were a crazy idea from upstate, like abolition or women's equality: "There are many queer people and queer things in Rochester."

The tone of the language grew harsh; the reported revelations from deceased relatives called "ludicrous," "trifling and nonsensical," "a farce." Spirit supporters were described as "dunderheads" or "fools" belonging in "lunatic asylums," their ideas dangerously "socialistic." Even the *Christian Advocate* newspaper unchristianly named everyone and everything surrounding the Fox sisters, "extreme imbecility."

Finding enough of the mainstream media hostile to their newfound beliefs, spirit supporters started their own publications, such as *Spirit Messenger*, *Spirit World*, and *Spiritual Telegraph*. These publications claimed that the spirit world was as real as the mortal one. Séance transcripts were printed as news. Folksy articles about mediums, including the famous Fox sisters, filled their pages. Readers wrote letters to the editor about the various spirit manifestations they had experienced.

However, not everything in these papers and periodicals was about the afterlife. The spiritual press appealed to their typically liberal audience with articles on the benefits of racial equality and leadership qualities in women. Other articles explained the science behind natural wonders: flowers, the human voice, or moon rays. Spiritual periodicals contained serialized fiction, book reviews, ads for upcoming lectures, wedding and birth announcements, all items common to hometown papers.

These publications helped build a spirit-believing community across the nation. The believers became known as Spiritualists and their belief system as "Modern Spiritualism." What had once been a single peddler's spirit rapping turned into a national fad and, for some, a new religion.

Unlike traditional nineteenth-century Christianity, Modern Spiritualism was a religion of inclusion. People could attend Spiritualist lectures or séances without leaving their original faith. Rejecting traditional religion's emphasis on sin and punishment, Modern Spiritualism was rooted in personal happiness on earth and in the heaven of Summerland, as well as a desire for world harmony.

While Leah embraced Modern Spiritualism as her newfound faith, Maggie and Kate never seemed to believe as deeply in the new religion they'd helped found. But they were young and female, so no one ever really cared enough to ask why.

"Katie and I were led around like lambs."

Chapter 12 SEPARATIONS

Horace Greeley's wife, Mary, was familiar with spirits long before she met the Fox sisters. During more than a decade of marriage, Mary Greeley was frequently pregnant, bore seven children, and suffered multiple miscarriages. She endured harsh nineteenth-century medical treatments like bloodletting and blistering. Perhaps under the influence of home medicines containing morphine or alcohol, Mary regularly saw visions and talked with angels.

She and Horace lived mostly separate lives. He stayed in their New York City home near the newspaper's office in lower Manhattan. Mary lived at their second residence, a farmhouse in Turtle Bay, a rural area only about three miles from the central part of the city. Horace called this farmhouse "Castle Doleful." No pictures, rugs, or curtains were allowed. Servants quit over Mary's moods. Meals were forgotten. Mary might wash the same spot on the floor for hours; leaving the rest of the house filthy. At least two of the Greeley's babies died from neglect.

Medicines, many containing opium or alcohol, were widely sold over the counter creating an addiction crisis in the nineteenth century. Women made up an estimated 60 percent of the addicts.

Other than financial support, Horace did nothing to help his wife or his children. Nineteenth-century society dictated strict roles for women and men. Men worked in the world. The house was a woman's realm. For the most part, husbands left wives, even physically or mentally ill wives, to run the home and raise the children as they saw fit.

The Greeley's third son, blond and blue-eyed Pickie, was special to both his parents. Horace doted on the sweet-natured little boy; Mary grew obsessed. Pickie was kept on a strict diet—no meats, sweets, or sauces. Mary was Pickie's sole companion. She believed her young son was a spirit medium and encouraged him to talk with angels too. If he refused, she beat him.

Mary's obsession continued even after five-year-old Pickie died of cholera. She was positive that her golden boy could return from the grave and believed in the power of the Fox sisters' mediumship to make that happen.

Near the first anniversary of Pickie's death, Horace invited the Fox entourage, which included Mother and Calvin, to spend a few late summer days in Turtle Bay. Leah, Maggie, and Kate led private circles for the Greeleys, attempting to make contact with their dead son.

At their earliest sessions, Pickie's spirit was silent, but the Fox sisters' rapping spirits mysteriously and successfully answered at least some of the Greeley's inquiries about the afterlife. As a public person, Greeley had even more reason to keep the questions he asked private. No specifics were recorded.

Emotionally, Horace wanted to believe, but he knew he had no real evidence that spirits made the rapping sounds. Trusting the American public's intelligence, he concluded, "a mere fraud could not have lived so long and spread so widely." A *New-York Tribune* editorial expressed his confidence, "these singular sounds and seeming manifestations are not produced by Mrs. Fox and her daughters, nor by any human being connected with them."

The politically and socially powerful Horace Greeley became a friend, advisor, and father figure. As the father of two baby daughters (the only Greeley children who would live to adulthood), he worried about Maggie's and Kate's futures. Spirit work had kept the girls so busy that their schooling had been neglected. A proper education would prepare Kate and Maggie to attract wealthier husbands. Horace suggested that the two sisters live with his wife, Mary, while he paid their tuitions at a nearby ladies' seminary.

The Fox family considered Greeley's offer as they ended their trip to New York City and returned home to Rochester. Greeley received a letter thanking him for his generosity, but the family felt Maggie's sporadic years of education were sufficient for a young lady of the marriageable age of seventeen. Only Kate would return to stay with Mary Greeley at the house in Turtle Bay.

In the fall of 1850, Kate attended the ladies' seminary six days a week, the most regular schooling she had ever received. Kate liked her teacher and her twice-weekly dancing lessons. After school, though, her main task was to bring Pickie back to Mary Greeley.

Mary Young Cheney Greeley, Horace Greeley's wife, around 1854

At private séances in Castle Doleful, Pickie's spirit spelled out details from his mortal life. Raps told the story of Pickie being scolded for interrupting his father's work. Mary Greeley remembered that day too! Everyday stories like these proved to Mary that her Pickie had returned from the dead. One séance led to another and another and another. Mary Greeley was too obsessed to remain satisfied. "O how I hate her!" wrote an exhausted Kate.

In a letter to Leah, Kate begged to leave Castle Doleful and return to Rochester. Leah ignored the letter and Kate remained in Turtle Bay—miserable. While Leah took care of customers in Rochester, Maggie was back on tour by November of 1850, introducing the spirits to the town of Troy, New York.

In Troy, a group of men began lurking around a house where Maggie was staying, calling out threats against witchcraft. One evening, Maggie was returning from a spirit circle accompanied by her host family. Their carriage was stopped on the road by "murderous" men; but their driver pushed the horses through and brought Maggie and her hosts home safely.

After Maggie and the family had gone to bed, an armed group of locals began hurling stones at the house. A window shattered. Maggie's host grabbed a pistol to defend his family; his wife and Maggie ran out the back door. Maggie felt a bullet whiz by. The mob stopped shooting when they realized the teenage medium wasn't alone. They wanted to kill the teenage witch, not harm a neighbor's wife.

There was no formal law enforcement in the area. A group of local Spiritualists were called in to protect Maggie Fox. The next night, "Five villanous looking fellows" returned and pushed their way into the house but were driven out by the spirit supporters.

Fearing for Maggie's life, her hosts thought it best to get her out of Troy as soon as possible. They sent a letter to Leah: "A deep plot is laid to destroy her." The hosts asked Leah to travel to Troy and escort Maggie out of town. Leah didn't answer.

The next night the anti-witch mob increased; the spirit supporters barely held them back. In Rochester, Leah received a rare Sunday telegram from Maggie's hosts, "Send your mother here or come yourself by Monday night. It is of vital importance. Answer by telegraph at once."

Leah responded asking for further details. A reply telegram insisted, "You must be here by Monday night . . ." repeating, "It is of vital importance."

Leah boarded a steam train, traveled the 200 miles to Troy, and arrived that night. A spirit supporter stepped out of the darkness carrying a loaded pistol. He escorted Leah to a waiting carriage with additional guns stacked inside. As the carriage raced into the night, Leah heard the shouts of a rowdy gang following close behind. The carriage drove through a surging mob up to the host's front door. Three strong men burst out of the house to hustle Leah inside.

Confined for her safety in a small, interior room, Maggie had been sobbing for days, "sick and nearly paralyzed with fright." Leah had no time to comfort her sister. Within minutes, the mob hurled rocks, then fired multiple shots into the house. Glass exploded around the sisters as they huddled under furniture to escape the bullets. After a long night of terror, the shooting finally stopped and the crowd scattered.

Somehow Leah smuggled Maggie out of Troy that night and brought her to a hotel in nearby Albany to recover. For weeks afterward, Maggie cried in her sleep, startled at the slightest noise, and panicked over future attacks. Maggie had felt death up close for the first time, but Leah had saved her. Her oldest sister knew how to manage their spirit angels and keep human devils at bay. Leah always knew what to do, who to meet, and where to go. From now on, as they returned home to Rochester, all Maggie had to do was follow.

"the world grew wiser and science began to investigate . . ."

Chapter 13 THE "BUFFALO GHOSTBUSTERS"

By the beginning of 1851, regular spirit circles were meeting in Boston, Cleveland, New York, Philadelphia, Providence, St. Louis, and hundreds of smaller towns. In Auburn alone, about a hundred mediums practiced among its roughly ten thousand citizens. Throughout the United States, spirits rapped messages, played instruments, remembered the past, and told of the future.

Still living at Castle Doleful, fourteen-year-old Kate was steeped in the morbid gloom surrounding Mary Greeley. Mother Fox arrived from Rochester to help her daughter manage Mrs. Greeley's spirit demands. As she continued her schooling and contacted Pickie's spirit, Kate looked for opportunities to escape Mary's oppressive home. Soon, she and Mother moved away from the Greeleys when Kate was hired as medium-in-residence for the family of wealthy match manufacturer Charles Partridge. Partridge had first experienced a séance run by

Leah, with Kate as medium. Kate had accurately chosen the names of Partridge's deceased son, brother, and cousin from a long list of other names. Partridge had heard Kate's spirits make the sounds of a ship at sea and had watched as furniture mysteriously drifted about the parlor.

A séance with a floating guitar and a writing spirit hand. Printed in *Frank Leslie's Illustrated Magazine*, April 2, 1887.

In 1851, guided by the strength of Kate's mediumship at further séances, Partridge and about twenty other men and women established one of the first organized Spiritualist groups in America. This New York Circle met consistently to investigate spirit phenomena and grew large enough to start satellite meetings in nearby towns.

With Kate and Mother busy in New York City, Leah felt it was time to take the spirits on tour once again. In February of 1851, Leah, Maggie, and Calvin left Rochester and arrived in Buffalo, New York, as miles of thick ice crept over Lake Erie. Leah and Maggie held daily sittings in front of the parlor fire at a hotel called the Phelps House. The spirits rapped, answered questions, and, as always, created more believers.

On February 16, an editor arrived with a copy of a letter to be printed in Buffalo's *Commercial Advertiser* the next day. It was written by three physicians at the University of Buffalo, Dr. Austin Flint, Dr. Charles Lee, and Dr. Charles Coventry. The editor suggested that Leah and Maggie leave town before the letter was published. Leah slammed the door in his face.

As threatened, the physicians' letter appeared in the following day's paper. The three doctors had attended a séance at the Phelps House and noticed that the rapping sounds seemed to originate closer to Maggie. Though they couldn't detect Maggie's body moving, the doctors watched her face. Each time a rap sounded her expression changed—lips pursed? eyes narrowed? The doctors gave no specific description.

The three doctors focused on the parts of the human body capable of producing rapping sounds. Observing Maggie's steady breathing, the doctors ruled out her voice. Instead, they hypothesized that she was using her joints and muscles. Such action could easily be hidden; elbows, knees, hips, and ankles were covered by long dresses. One of the doctors had a female patient whose knees knocked loudly. He explained (in language as baffling as the spirits): "the muscles inserted into the upper and inner side of the large bone of the leg (the tibia) near the knee joint, are brought into action so as to move the upper surface of the bone just named laterally upon the lower surface of the thighbone (the femur), giving rise, in fact, to a partial dislocation. . . . The return of the bone to its place is attended by another loud noise."

The doctors concluded, "*spiritual rappings* may be produced in the *knee joint*." There were no spirits at all, just some sisters with knocking knees. The "Buffalo Doctors" called the Fox sisters' spirit communication, "a waste of time, money, and credulity."

Leah knew this specific accusation had to be handled carefully. She and her sisters had thousands of followers. But Leah didn't know Buffalo or its citizens well. *Should she deny the accusations? Attack the doctors' reputations? Skip town?* It only took her a few hours to decide on a strategy.

A card, signed by Leah and Maggie, was inserted in the *Commercial Advertiser*, one day after the doctors' letter appeared. It casually addressed them as "Gents" and, in a few ladylike sentences, pushed back publicly for the first time, "we do not feel willing to rest under the imputation of being imposters, we are very willing to undergo a proper and decent examination . . . We can assure the public that there is no one more anxious than ourselves to discover the origin of these mysterious manifestations."

This clever tactic brought many to Leah and Maggie's defense. *What kind of tricksters invited accusers to examine them up close?* The Fox sisters' response to the three Buffalo doctors increased their reputation for sincerity.

The following evening, the three doctors met the two sisters for a series of examinations. Six additional witnesses were invited into the parlor of the Phelps House. Maggie and Leah sat side by side.

Did the spirits agree to participate?

Rap. Rap. Rap.

Leah and Maggie were instructed to put their heels on cushions, lower limbs extended, feet apart. The doctors knew this position kept the knee joint locked. The sisters obeyed. Questions were asked. Silence. Following the doctors' orders, the sisters were moved to a sofa. Leah was asked to place her feet on the floor; the doctors directed Maggie to sit with her legs extended. Questions were asked. Silence. Maggie put her feet on the floor. Questions were asked.

Rap. Rap. Rap.

An illustration of the Buffalo Doctors (Lee, Flint, and Coventry) examining Maggie and Leah

The doctors had to proceed carefully. In the nineteenth century, it was scandalous for unrelated men, even doctors, to touch women's bodies. Dr. Lee asked permission before he squeezed the ladies' knees through their thick dress fabric. A question was asked. Silence. He relaxed the pressure. Another question.

Rap.

The experiment was repeated. A few times, rapping sounded *while* the knees were held and Dr. Lee thought he felt a slight movement with every rap. To be certain the sounds came from the knees, the doctors wanted to immobilize the sisters' knee joints. But they hadn't come prepared with plaster or bandages to make a cast, and so, the exam ended.

The doctors printed their conclusion in the *Buffalo Medical Journal*, "The Rochester knockings emanate from the knee joint." Specifically, the knee joints of Maggie Fox. Based on their knowledge of acoustic science, the doctors theorized that the raps could be made to reverberate on nearby tables, doors, or other solid objects.

Leah responded by calling the examination "harsh" and the doctors' charges "cruel." She accused the "conceited" doctors of a lack of common sense. How could she or her sisters knock their knees for hours every day and still be able to walk? Leah said the three doctors displayed the "bigotry of modern science." She accused the doctors' intense skepticism of creating an atmosphere hostile to spirit communication. All believers knew that spirit manifestations required open minds. Leah offered two weeks of spirit demonstrations to everyone free of charge.

Crowds filled the Phelps House. The spirits began to show off a bit for the citizens of Buffalo: "a large Dinner Bell & a small tea bell sitting under the table rang . . . A violin under the table was played & moved from place to place, so far as could be discovered by 13 of us, without human agency . . ."

Believers wondered how these Buffalo doctors explained moving tables, playing instruments, and disembodied touches. The Fox sisters must have very talented knees! Dr. Lee took on the job of spokesperson, defending the doctors' conclusions in the newspapers.

The *New-York Tribune* published a letter from Dr. Lee further explaining the physiology and acoustic science behind his claim. Unfortunately, the doctor sounded as condescending as Leah had portrayed him.

His know-it-all tone helped bring defending Spiritualists out in force. Once again, believers and skeptics filled news columns with letters, helping to sell more papers. When he realized arguing with fanatic believers was futile, Dr. Lee stopped responding, "he had other business to attend to."

Later, Dr. Lee taught at a medical school. He was asked to give a scientific lecture on the rappings. His audience contained men of science, including many spirit skeptics. First, Dr. Lee lectured about acoustics, how sounds are produced, echo, and travel. Then, to demonstrate, Lee brought a local man onstage. Dr. Lee asked questions of the supposed spirits while the man cracked his ankles in response, providing, "a more striking illustration of 'spiritual knockings' than the Foxes ever dreamed of."

Dr. Lee assumed the audience would easily understand that the spirit sounds were false. Instead, after hearing the knocking correctly respond to questions, some skeptics in the audience left the lecture firm believers in spirit communication.

People *wanted* to believe. Any demonstration, even one showing how spirits might be faked, could create more spirit support instead. Dr. Lee never gave another demonstration on spirit raps. He worried, "if they [the Fox sisters] were to publicly acknowledge their imposture . . . it would not diminish the number of their followers." If facts would not convince true believers, then it was entirely possible that not even the Fox sisters could stop the spirits any longer.

"Unless it is put down soon it will do great evil."

Chapter 14 TRUTHTELLERS OR TRAITORS?

When Maggie and Leah left Buffalo at the end of March 1851, they returned to Rochester triumphant. "Money flowed to them in volume." Leah moved the family to a fine home on Troup and Sophia Street, this time right in the heart of Rochester's monied Third Ward. She hired a maid, then a cook and additional staff. Leah "had brought them all, by her own insistence and belief and assurance, to this high point of achievement." Requests for the Fox sisters to appear poured in "from all parts of the Union."

That Union's politics remained tense. Though sectionalism had been growing for decades, by 1851, almost every issue in the country was seen through opposing viewpoints: factory vs. plantation, antislavery vs. proslavery, North vs. South. Politicians' language was described as "warm." They flung insults, took offense, using language like "contempt," "abuse," and "revilement" on the floor of Congress.

In this divided time, the same Washington, DC, paper that named the Fox sisters' spirit communication one of the "Wonders of the Nineteenth Century," also ran a serialized story titled *Uncle Tom's Cabin or Life Among the Lowly*. In installments, its author, Harriet Beecher Stowe, poured forth the tragic tale of the life of Uncle Tom, a fictional, enslaved Black man.

The characters in Stowe's story, though stereotypical, humanized enslaved Black people for white nineteenth-century readers. Its emotional descriptions of slavery's injustices caught the public's attention. Stowe later claimed to have written as if in a trance, similar to the Spiritualists' automatic writing: "I did not write it . . . God wrote it . . . I merely did his dictation."

The serial was so popular, it was later published as the book *Uncle Tom's Cabin*, the greatest publishing sensation of the nineteenth century. For decades, only the Bible sold more copies.

Advertisement for the wildly successful book *Uncle Tom's Cabin*. During the Civil War, President Abraham Lincoln was said to have called the book's author, Harriet Beecher Stowe, "the little lady that started this great war."

In the North, *Uncle Tom's Cabin* was thought "admirable" and "too truthful," and abolition, once a radical idea, became more mainstream. In the South, the book was said to have been "founded on imaginary circumstances, and gross improbabilities" and frequently banned. Such differing reactions caused a "historic amount of disagreement." Americans chose a side and spewed anger at those who opposed them.

Spiritualism's critics were angry too. They believed the public was being manipulated by leaders in the media who continued to treat the spirit "delusion" as worthwhile to report as facts. C. Chauncey Burr, editor of the *Nineteenth Century Review*, and his brother, Heman, fell into this category of enraged skeptics. Calling Greeley, "the self appointed Attorney General for the hobgoblin society," the Burr brothers set out to expose spirit communication as a fraud and tell the public the truth about the Fox sisters.

The Burrs developed a lecture, "Spiritual Knockings Exposed." Audiences paid to hear Heman loudly crack his big toe inside his boot while Chauncey accused the "Rochester girls" of creating fake spirit rappings using the same method. Depending on which newspaper a person read, the brothers were either respected researchers or a complete joke. One newsman sarcastically labeled the Burrs' theory "toe-o-logy." Still, the brothers drummed up enough interest to take their toes on the road, spreading their theory in a multicity speaking tour.

Using Chauncey's notes, Heman Burr also wrote a pamphlet titled *Knocks for the Knocking*, describing the investigation of "more than fifty" mediums, specifically naming the "Rochester Rappings." After two months of research in five states, the Burrs had attended so many spirit circles, that they practically became professional sitters. After their séance studies, Heman wrote, "I can now produce 'mysterious rappings' seventeen different ways."

Like the three doctors in Buffalo, the Burrs agreed that the alleged spirit rapping could be caused by cracking joints: knees, ankles, toes, or shoulders. But the brothers also observed at least one medium snapping her fingers against a table; another who tapped a leather-booted foot against a chair leg. Mediums were caught using their feet or body weight to lift, balance, or slide parlor tables. Almost any action might go unnoticed in the dark and excitement of a séance.

Michael Faraday, one of history's most influential scientists due to his work on electromagnetism, designed this device to test the spirit phenomenon of "table-tipping." Faraday found that séance participants were unaware that they were moving the table themselves because of the ideomotor effect—the concept that thoughts can produce unconscious muscle movements.

Many of the mediums that the Burrs investigated were young women. In his pamphlet, Heman specified their ages: "nineteen," "about sixteen years," "aged about thirteen years," "A little girl ten years old." He also insulted the mediums as "feeble," "poorly educated," and "a swarm of ignorant, lying, unprincipled girls."

Those supposedly ignorant girls got the last laugh. In the séance room, the young women—brought up to be seen and not heard—were heard, but not seen. Despite Burr's criticisms, séances remained as popular as ever. When Heman's pamphlet didn't sell well, the Burr brothers looked for another way to make the public understand the spirit "fraud." What if they could get someone close to the Fox family to confess details of a hoax?

The Burrs found and interviewed Ruth Culver, a western New York woman related to David Fox's wife. A medical doctor and a local minister signed her sworn written statement.

Ruth's explanation was clear and detailed, "The Fox girls have been a great deal at my house and for about two years I was a very sincere believer in the rappings." Later, when Ruth visited the Fox sisters in Rochester, she began to "suspect that they were deceiving." Her statement told the following story:

Early in 1850, one of Ruth Culver's cousins had come to "consult the spirits." Maggie and Leah were not home, Kate would have had to run the séance alone. To "satisfy" her suspicions, Ruth asked Kate to "assist her in producing the manifestations." Kate agreed, pleased that Ruth, "should probably be able to answer all the questions he would ask." Ruth's first lesson in mediumship was at her cousin's séance. Ruth had been told to "sit next to her [Kate] and touch her arm when the right letter was called." "After I had helped her in this way a few times, she revealed to me the secret. The raps are produced by the toes."

According to Ruth, Kate and Maggie had learned the rapping trick from Leah's daughter *before* March of 1848. According to Kate, Lizzie "was the first one who produced these raps. She accidentally discovered the way of making them by playing with her toes against the foot board while in bed." All three girls, Lizzie, Maggie, and Kate, had originally practiced the trick together. But Kate confided that Lizzie turned out to be "too conscientious for mediumship."

To see if the trick was possible, Ruth practiced rapping. "At first it was very hard work to do it. Catherine [Kate] told me to warm my feet, or put them in warm water, and it would then be easier to rap." After two weeks of Kate's instruction, Ruth succeeded: "I have sometimes produced 150 raps in succession. I can rap with all the toes on both feet . . ."

Ruth's statement went on to specify the Fox sisters' séance procedures. Kate "told me how to manage to answer the questions . . ." The Fox sisters watched "the countenance and motions of the person, and in that way they could nearly always guess right." Kate taught Ruth how to alter the sounds and misdirect attention: "when I wished to make the raps sound distant on the wall, I must make them louder, and direct my own eyes earnestly to the spot where I wished them to be heard." Kate also admitted that sometimes the sisters brought in helpers. Early on in Rochester, for example, a "Dutch servant-girl rapped with her knuckles under the floor from the cellar."

Once she learned the whole truth, Ruth refused to participate further. Kate "was very much frightened." She warned Ruth that if "I meant to tell of it and expose them . . . she would swear it was a lie." People always believed the Fox sisters as "they would never suspect so young a child." Even New York City's most famous men had been fooled.

As Chauncey Burr continued a lecture tour west into Cleveland, Ohio, he readied Ruth's blockbuster confession for release. The spirits might finally be silenced.

"It is astonishing how easily it is done."

Chapter 15 SURPRISES ON TOUR

In early May of 1851, Leah received telegrams from supporters, "come immediately to Cleveland . . ." and "Burr is here, slandering you and all who believe in Spiritualism."

Chauncey Burr was lecturing at Cleveland's Melodeon Hall. His audience laughed when Burr demonstrated the many ways mediums could move objects, answer questions, or otherwise trick unsuspecting séance goers. But when Burr began insulting those who believed in the spirits of the dead, the audience hissed their disapproval.

The Burr brothers recommended believing experts like themselves, as "it is not a very safe business to trust to what men call their senses." However, their independent-minded American audience was used to making their own decisions. *Who were the Burr brothers to tell good folks who or what to believe?*

In his Cleveland lectures, Chauncey Burr called Leah, a mother and a Spiritualist, "a woman of notoriously bad character." This attack did Burr's public reputation no favors. The *Pittsburg Post* scolded, "It is not very manly or very dignified to slander a lady when she is not present." And Cleveland's *Plain Dealer* noted: "Notwithstanding the burlesques of the Burrs . . . the cause [in favor of the spirits] . . . is gaining ground on every side . . . but the greatest gain is going on among the Press."

As talk of spirits filled Cleveland's streets and the nation's newspapers, Leah had already set out for that city with a group of companions including her married sister, Maria, her nephew, Maria's two-and-a-half-year-old son, Charley, and Calvin Brown who soldiered on despite a bad cold.

The *Plain Dealer* eagerly anticipated Leah's arrival: "There are to be rapping times in Cleveland this week." Gentlemen and ladies reserved times to visit with the spirits at a busy inn called the Dunham House. Leah was leading the spirit circles for the first time without the popular mediumship of her younger sisters.

She must not have been entirely successful because the *Plain Dealer* later stated that "the strength of the spiritual battery" had increased once Maggie and Kate arrived. Even though Leah praised her sisters in the papers as "the most perfect known mediums," their arrival in Cleveland had caught Leah entirely by surprise.

Maggie and Kate had arrived in Cleveland with an older lady from Rochester named Mrs. Kedzie. Kedzie had befriended the two youngest sisters, while suggesting that they tour on their own, as a pair. Mrs. Kedzie planned to bring the girls to the western Ohio cities of Cincinnati and Columbus. Maggie and Kate agreed. They had been mediums for more than two years, working solely for Leah. Their mother and oldest sister took care of their daily needs; but it's unlikely that Maggie and Kate were allowed to keep much, if any, of the money they earned.

Maggie (left) and Kate Fox (right) around January, 1852. Daguerreotype portrait by Thomas Easterly of St. Louis.

Mrs. Kedzie planned to "Make a little Speculation of the 'Knockings'" and, it's assumed, split the proceeds with the two girls. Neither Maggie nor Kate nor Mrs. Kedzie had consulted Leah about this plan.

Leah was frustrated with the presumptuous Mrs. Kedzie and her little sisters' attempt at independence. In a letter to Amy Post she complained, "Much of my trouble is caused by the girls . . . they are always working so underhandedly." The Fox sisters already had a manager. It was Leah who would decide where and when Maggie and Kate appeared, period.

As she had back in Hydesville, Leah split her sisters up. Mrs. Kedzie could take Kate to Cincinnati with Maria and Charley. Maggie would stay with Leah and Calvin in Cleveland.

Once Kate's group got to Cincinnati, Charley fell seriously ill with a fever and Leah insisted they return to Cleveland. Little Charley's "life was despaired of . . ." and Maria, who had already lost three young sons, wanted her family together. On the other hand, the toddler's illness also threw an obstacle in Mrs. Kedzie's path to spiritual glory, riches, or both.

Mrs. Kedzie wound up with nothing to manage, as "all business was suspended" by Leah, who pleaded with the spirits to cure Charley "for several days." Letters suggest extensive conflicts between the Fox sisters around this time. Were the quarrels about money? About management? Or were any of the sisters threatening to expose whichever secrets the others held?

Whatever transpired, it didn't take long before Mrs. Kedzie hightailed it back to Rochester, calling Leah "a bad manager" and complaining of the influence their older sister held over Maggie and Kate. Whether due to spirit intervention or a strong immune system, little Charley recovered, and Maria took him back home to western New York.

With her younger sisters back in control, and sure of the support of Cleveland's news media, Leah sued Chauncey Burr for slander based on the content of his lectures. Her lawyer asked the court for $10,000 in damages (over $300,000 today). Leah's Ohio friends supposedly "arrested him," but there is no record of Burr being jailed. Instead, he posted bail and waited for his day in court. The Cleveland papers were tipped off to the lawsuit, and—as always where the Fox sisters were concerned—the story spread across the country.

In his defense, Chauncey Burr released Ruth Culver's damning statement to the press. By the end of May 1851, it was reprinted in the *New York Herald,* the most widely read daily paper in the United States.

Leah went on the attack, savaging Ruth Culver's reputation in the newspapers. "I pity her," Leah declared. She (and Kate too!) portrayed Ruth as one of their "very distant relatives" who was "shamefully slandering" the Fox family. Newspaper editors supportive of the spirits ran stories disparaging Chauncey and his brother as "itinerant, catch-penny lecturers," "dunces" and "accomplished mountebanks." In other words, liars.

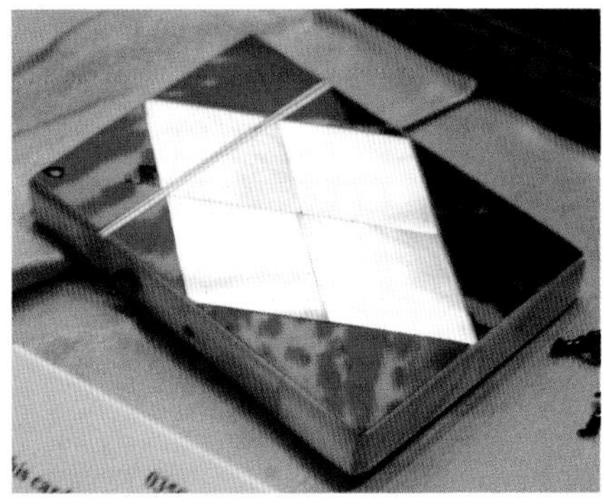

An enameled brooch and tortoiseshell calling card case belonging to Leah. In her memoirs, Leah wrote of receiving gold medals, watches, and diamonds from Ohio's spiritualists.

Regarding Leah's lawsuit against Chauncey Burr, there is no clear record of what he said, what she said, or whether they testified in court at all. Leah later told a story in which the public hated Burr so much that he was pelted with "bricks, broken eggs, sticks, and tin pans" outside the courthouse. That same courthouse, according to Leah, was cleared of rubbish as its inhabitants cheered: "Welcome to the Fox family."

Whether that self-serving story was true or not, the judge found in Leah's favor. Chauncey Burr was ordered to pay $10,000 in damages, which he likely could not afford. Within a few months Chauncey, along with his brother, Heman, fled the country. The spirit-supporting *Cincinnati Nonpareil* bragged, "The Burrs . . . left . . . under a good, stiff, spanking breeze."

It is not known whether Leah ever saw any of Chauncey Burr's money; but the lawsuit paid off in publicity. A reporter crowed, "It has become a settled fact that Burr's and the Buffalo doctors' theories are the silliest humbugs of the day." Leah boasted, "Our progress was a course of triumph."

Under Leah's direction, the Fox sisters' "Ohio Campaign" was unstoppable. The sisters received requests to appear around the state and into Kentucky throughout the summer of 1851. The demand was so great that the two youngest sisters traveled separately so they could bring the spirits to different cities at the same time.

Despite Leah's pleasure at their success, the frequent travel and public attention took its toll on her younger sisters. Kate wrote to Amy Post, "Oh so homesick. Dear Lady it is raining fast and makes me feel melancholy . . . It makes me think of other days (When I was happy)." Maggie grumbled, "We are still in Cincinnati, leave for Louisville in two weeks, and as [the popular poet] Byron says, 'I shall leave it without regret, I shall return to it without pleasure.'" Were they to live this life forever?

Mother had taken Kate to Columbus while Leah and Maggie were in Cincinnati with Calvin. As best he could, Calvin still accompanied the sisters in public though he began coughing up blood. What he thought was a bad cold turned out to be tuberculosis.

By late August of 1851, Calvin grew so gravely ill that he was near death. Propped up in a Cincinnati hotel bed, a hacking, feverish Calvin Brown made a sudden marriage proposal to his "dear sister" Leah. Before he died, he wanted to leave her something of value, his name. The loyal Calvin waited days for her response, lingering between this world and the next. Leah seemed in no hurry to answer.

Finally, she agreed, and on September 10, 1851, married Calvin, breezily admitting that the ceremony occurred on "what was supposed to be the deathbed." Positive that her new husband wouldn't last long, she expected to leave her past as an abandoned wife behind and become the respectable widow, Mrs. Calvin Brown, within days.

But Leah received another surprise in Ohio—Calvin lived.

"it was a most wonderful discovery . . ."

Chapter 16 A SCIENTIFIC FAITH

By January of 1852, there were few people in the United States who hadn't heard of the "Rochester Rappers." Yet Leah decided that it was time for the Fox sisters to leave the city that made them famous behind. Kate, Maggie, Mother, Calvin Brown, and his new wife, Leah, returned from Ohio, and moved from Rochester to New York City. An estimated 40,000 Spiritualist believers resided in that metropolis already, but with a growing population of half a million people, there was plenty of opportunity to grow the spirit cause as well.

Leah leased a "handsome" three-story brownstone at 78 West Twenty-Sixth Street, near Manhattan's Madison Square Park. Leah reduced their public hours to ease their workload, 3–5 p.m. and 8–10 p.m. only. New Yorkers knew when the Fox sisters were at home because once again carriages full of spirit seekers lined the gaslit street, this time in front of their house.

Calvin remained an invalid. He was weak, suffered sporadic fevers, and needed constant care—tuberculosis was incurable at that time. Leah didn't nurse her new husband, instead, she summoned her daughter, Lizzie, from Illinois to care for him. Though she'd been banished about four years, if Lizzie held any grudges or had any complaints, they seem to have gone (for very good reason) unspoken.

Almost five years had passed since the peddler's spirit raps had first astonished the country. The spirit actions that Kate described, "the piano was sweetly played upon by spirit fingers, the guitar was played, then taken up and carried above our heads . . ." didn't seem all that miraculous any longer. The public grew tired of the same old spirits who tipped tables, played instruments, and rapped slow messages.

Mediums began to look for ways to speed up what the press still called "the spiritual telegraph." Rapping mediums, including the Fox sisters, began pointing to an alphabet written on cards; rather than calling it aloud. Other spirits gave up raps altogether; instead, their mediums spoke aloud in spirit languages. "**Ki-e-lou-cou-ze-ta**," was an example of one such message. That single, thirteen-letter spirit word was translated by a medium's assistant into a paragraph containing forty-five words of English!

Multitudes of mediums spoke spirit messages in Greek, Latin, Spanish, and French, languages the operators of the spiritual telegraph claimed not to know. Sometimes the languages were correct, other times not. A spirit communication written in Hebrew, a language read from right to left, was found to make sense only if read from left to right. The so-called Hebrew-speaking spirit didn't understand that language's basic rules.

There were singing mediums, who warbled tunes composed by the spirits, and dancing mediums, who moved in a "very eccentric" manner. Writing mediums composed original work dictated by dead authors, among them Shakespeare, Shelley, and Poe. One skeptic suggested that authors' descendants be allowed to sue mediums for signing their relative's famous names to such dreadful new writing.

Some mediums predicted the future, other "fine, clairvoyant physician[s]" healed current illnesses. Mediums read messages through sealed envelopes or made spirit messages appear on blank slates.

An example of spirit writing on a slate. The slate was shown blank at the start of the séance, and after the spirits visited, messages to the living would appear.

Some trance mediums, like Fanny Davis and Cora Hatch, became famous public lecturers. When they delivered smart, entertaining speeches, it proved the supernatural influence of spirits. Everyone knew that women did not naturally possess the ability to speak so well in public.

There were astonishing reports of human levitation. A baby girl medium, sucking on candy, seemed to drift about the room seated in her high chair. An adult male medium was seen floating across a sixty-foot space balanced only on another man's fingertips.

The levitation of celebrity medium Daniel Dunglas Home in London, 1852

Circle participants were regularly hugged by spirit hands and kissed by spirit lips. At one séance, a skeptic asked to hold his dead wife's hand, which had been severely burned in a fire. When a hand with clawed fingers and thickened nails was put into his, he understandably left shaken to his core—and a confirmed spirit believer.

Those who wrote and thought about American life became more and more concerned about the interest in Spiritualism. To make their point, some overestimated that about one-third of the country were confirmed Spiritualists. Instead, it is more likely that of the roughly twenty-five million people living in the United States in the early 1850s, more than a million were practicing Spiritualism of some kind.

When a convention of Spiritualists was held in Cleveland in February 1852, hundreds of articles about the rapid spread of spirits were written in papers from Bangor, Maine, to New Orleans, Louisiana. The news media began to report more often on what it saw as the destructive influences of Spiritualism. The new faith was against Christianity: "the whole mass of spiritualists, so far as we know, and so far as we can judge, have cut loose from the Bible . . ." It was against logic: "an illustration of the excesses to which weak minds may be carried once they abandon the path of common sense . . ." It was against civilization: "a singular collection of dupes and fanatics, resembling more a congregation of lunatics than a company of rational creatures."

Author Ralph Waldo Emerson, one of the most popular public lecturers of the day, was among the intellectuals who came out against spirit communication. He called the spirits "a Rat-revelation, the gospel that comes by taps in the wall, and thumps in the table-drawer." Another writer, Henry David Thoreau, said that if he was made to believe such ridiculous ideas, "I would exchange my immortality for a glass of small [weak] beer." Thoreau labeled Spiritualists "idiots, inspired by the cracking of a restless board."

Skeptics particularly worried when prominent government officials—such as Ohio's US Senator Benjamin Wade, former Wisconsin governor Nathaniel Tallmadge, and New York Supreme Court Justice John Edmonds—went public about their firm belief in the ability of the dead to talk to the living.

Justice Edmonds, for example, had attended a séance at a Spiritualist's home in New York City, joining a circle of about twenty people standing around the room. Four spirit summoners were in attendance—two male mediums, plus Maggie and Kate Fox.

The séance began. Raps sounded. One of the male mediums fell into a trance and communicated a simple message from beyond. **Darken the room.** Within seconds, Edmonds and the other séance attendees started to experience the growing powers of the two original spirit mediums.

Out of the darkness, "luminous clouds" of light floated around the room. The spirits flitted about, twinkling like fairies. A wood card table opened and shut its leaf, then spun over and turned fully upside down! Shocked participants made out an empty chair crossing the room, "winding its way among the people . . . without touching them."

One of the male mediums yelled out, "Don't, I don't want to, leave me alone," before being dragged into a closet and locked in by unseen forces. Musical instruments appeared out of nowhere. They were, "played upon, separately at first, and finally all together" like a floating orchestra. When the tune ended, the instruments sailed toward the ceiling and out of reach.

Justice Edmonds's handkerchief was taken out of his pocket, tied in knots and put back. By now, the esteemed justice was frenzied, shouting in wonder to the others in the room. "I'm touched—now I am tapped on the shoulder—now they are at my feet . . ." Edmonds left that evening an unconditional believer in Spiritualism.

Modern Spiritualism called itself a scientific faith. In one aspect, that was true. It required interested parties to experiment with a variety of mediums, spirits, and phenomena. Leaders of the faith also insisted that all people should draw their own conclusions. After his séance experiment Justice Edmonds concluded that spirits were real. But real *science* requires consistent results and general agreement.

Of the twenty other people at Edmonds's séance, an unnamed man wrote about his experience as an attendee that same night. This anonymous writer was positive that the rappings sounded "always *under* or *about* the mediums" and called one of the male mediums "most peculiar and un-wholesome looking." He was suspicious of the medium's trance—"after various theatrical starts, jerks, and curious snorting and snifflings . . ." Instead of experiencing spirit lights as wonderous, the writer was, "entirely disgusted . . . of course anything done in the dark is useless . . ."

Attempting to give the séance and the mediums a fair chance, the anonymous man wrote that he "listened for about one hour and a half, to a perfect pandemonium" of "the most absurd series of noises from this closet that ever was heard" including "a chorus of 'Auld Lang Syne' . . . and scrapings of an old violincello . . ."

The same séance that turned Justice Edmonds into a true believer left this unnamed writer convinced of spirit fraud: "I left them [Justice Edmonds and the others] at last at half-past eleven, still in there, the noises going on as loud and meaningless as ever."

Despite its claims, Modern Spiritualism was not a science. A séance experiment could produce different results in different people. Manifestations were inconsistent. Spirits appeared in some situations, but not others—to some people, but not all. Sometimes, spirits answered accurately, other times stupidly—

"Does James miss his children?"

"**Yes.**" (he never had any)

"How many had he?"

"**Yes.**"

"How many boys?"

"**Yes.**"

"What did he die of?"

"**Wafer.**" (Did the spirit mishear the question? Or did some poor fool actually die after an unfortunate experience with a cookie?)

Real science knows that if a hypothesis can't be consistently proven, it's false. If everyone can't see it, it's probably not there. As more scientists, writers, and others went public with their doubts, news coverage gradually shifted to portraying spirit communication as a likely hoax. This did not stop the most prominent mediums, the Fox sisters included, from retaining their committed base of followers.

As a leader in the new religion of Modern Spiritualism, Leah's theories on spirit behavior were given great weight. With the emotional heft of dead friends and relatives behind her, she explained away any doubts or spirit inconsistencies to believers and the spiritual press.

When people asked to search the table during séances, she cautioned, "Spirits . . . are compelled to assume shapes that human eyes must not look upon." If people wondered why the well-educated dead sounded unschooled, Leah explained that spirits often took on the human characteristics of the medium. After one communication came through in poor English, Kate blurted, "You know I don't understand English grammar!" Proof of Leah's point?

Leah ultimately found one explanation that covered almost any difficult séance situation—the spirit world contained humbugs just like the mortal one—some spirits liked to play tricks; others simply lied.

With these explanations firmly believed by a mass of spirit practitioners, the Fox sisters' lives and work continued. By the middle of

1852, Lizzie had met and soon married a man named George Blauvelt. She moved out of Leah's home. Lizzie's absence left Calvin in need of care. Leah hired nurses, supervised her household servants, and continued to schedule séances for New Yorkers willing to pay for the privilege of seeing an original Fox sister.

Kate and Mother left the home of her wealthy sponsor, Charles Partridge, and moved back to Leah's. Kate seems to have still attended school, but her evenings were free to help her oldest sister with New York's spirit work. However, the Fox sisters were no longer the only celebrity mediums. Leah still received about half a dozen booking telegrams each day, but the requests for appearances seemed to slow. To keep earning the income that supported them all, they had to keep spreading the word. Once again, it fell to Maggie to take the spirits on tour.

In early October of 1852, a few days after her nineteenth birthday, Maggie Fox and her mother arrived in Philadelphia. The two women settled into the bridal parlor, a luxurious suite of rooms at Webb's Union Hotel.

Twice a day, morning and afternoon, Maggie held public hours to introduce those curious about the spirits to a séance. After five years of earning her living as a medium, Maggie knew by heart the questions that people asked of the dead: *Are you there? Are you happy? Will I ever see you again?*

Rap. Rap. Rap.

Yes. Same as always.

What could be different about Philadelphia?

"and that is where Dr. Kane met me . . ."

Chapter 17 THE DOCTOR AND THE TEENAGE MEDIUM

"It is at all times easy to create a sensation in Philadelphia," Maggie would remember about the place she called a "quiet city." In the first weeks of October 1852, Philadelphians flocked to Webb's Union Hotel to see the sensational Maggie Fox. Her public sessions were full of curious Philadelphians clamoring to hear from their dead. But after a few weeks of appearances, the spirits were proving to be a bit less popular than usual.

It was a morning in mid-October, and yet no clients were waiting. To pass the time, Maggie sat in a chair facing the sunny window and settled in to read a book of French language exercises. She heard a knock at the door but didn't get up. It was Mother who answered.

A short, well-dressed man stood in the doorway. It was unusual to see a younger man alone during morning hours. Typically, men came to see the spirits late, often in large groups, and typically after a long night of drinking.

"I beg your pardon, madam," the man said to Mother, "I have made some mistake; can you direct me to the rooms where the 'spiritual manifestations' are shown?"

"This is the place," Mother answered. "I am Mrs. Fox."

Mother didn't recognize the man, but many would have. In fact, he and the Fox sisters had shared side-by-side column space in the newspapers going back at least two years.

Images were rare in newspapers or magazines. Engravings were expensive to produce and photographic images were not easily printed. Despite consistent media attention, illustrations of the famous Fox sisters had not yet appeared in the newspapers. But a recent *Harper's Magazine* had printed *four* illustrations on the adventures of this man standing at Maggie's hotel door. Only true icons received that kind of news coverage. Thirty-two-year-old physician and explorer Elisha Kent Kane was one of them.

Dr. Kane had just returned from sixteen months away as part of the United States' Grinnell Expedition to find the lost British Arctic explorer, Sir John Franklin. When the American ships became icebound, the brave

Elisha Kent Kane in his late twenties, around 1847

crew managed to survive nine months at –40°F. They found three British graves, but not Sir Franklin's. Though Franklin's fate was still unknown, when the Grinnell Expedition returned at the end of September 1852, Kane and the crew were celebrated as national heroes.

After his Arctic journey, Kane came back to Philadelphia, his hometown. One day he "read in a penny newspaper that for one dollar the inmates of another world would rap . . . the secrets of this one . . ." On a whim, he stopped by Webb's Union Hotel during Maggie Fox's public hours and bought a ticket.

A young woman, with long, dark, shining hair sat in the window engrossed in a book. Kane was thunderstruck. Caught in the sunlight, the girl seemed to glow.

Maggie rose and came forward to meet this new client. Dr. Kane could not believe that the gorgeous young woman in this luxurious suite was the notorious medium Maggie Fox; "by Jove, I saw the 'spirit'!" he later wrote.

Dr. Kane considered himself naturally skeptical, a man of science. He assumed that spirit communication was nothing more than trickery. On the other hand, he was also grieving. Two months ago, Kane, the oldest of six brothers, had sat vigil by the sickbed of his much-loved, youngest brother, Willie, as he passed away at the age of fourteen.

The questions and answers from Maggie Fox's first séance for Dr. Kane went unrecorded. But there is no indication that Kane's questions were any different from those of other mourners. Whether or not Dr. Kane heard from his dead brother, he left Webb's Union Hotel much less impressed with the spirits than with the lovely young woman who was talking to the dead.

Kane had been on intimate terms with death before. When he was eighteen, he had almost died from rheumatic fever. Multiple recurrences of the disease kept his heart weak and his health precarious. Yet he never let fear of his own mortality keep him from adventure. After medical school, he was appointed a surgeon in the US Navy. His journeys had taken him to South America, China, India, Africa, and finally, the Arctic.

As soon as he was back home, Dr. Kane started planning a return trip to the frozen north. Like many scientists of the time, he thought there could be an ice-free ocean, an "open polar sea," above Greenland. To be the first to discover this sea or return the lost Sir Franklin to Great Britain's Queen Victoria would ensure fame and fortune forever.

Kane's influential family supported their adventurous son financially as he put together a second expedition to the Arctic. Elisha lectured in East Coast cities to raise additional funds. The handsome Dr. Kane knew how to entertain while describing the mysteries of the frigid northlands. His lively eyes, dark, curly hair, and mustache made him the face of Arctic exploration in America. By the time he met Maggie Fox, Dr. Elisha Kent Kane's name had appeared in the country's newspapers and magazines hundreds, likely thousands, of times.

As a naval officer, Dr. Kane had trained to be a leader. He was sure of his opinions and was used to being obeyed. He returned to Maggie's hotel suite the next day with some blunt advice: "This is no life for you, my child." Dr. Kane thought young Miss Maggie Fox should give up spirit rapping and finish her schooling.

For her part, Maggie had just met Dr. Kane. Yes, he was older. Yes, he was famous. Yes, he was wildly handsome. But his patronizing advice was unrealistic for a working-class teenager. *Give up the spirits? Why? How?*

Dr. Kane returned to see Maggie Fox every day. He showed up at Webb's Union Hotel once a day, often twice, sometimes more. He came alone; he brought friends. He sat through multiple séances. During one spirit circle, Kane handed Maggie a question on a slip of paper.

"Were you ever in love?"

"Ask the spirits," Maggie wrote back playfully.

Frequent invitations began to arrive for Maggie, properly addressed to her mother as a chaperone, "Dr. Kane will call at three o'clock P.M., for the purpose of accompanying Mrs. and Miss Fox upon an afternoon drive."

When Maggie and Mother had spirit business, they couldn't get away. But often enough, Dr. Kane ushered Maggie and her mother in his carriage to visit the famous sights of his hometown: Independence Hall, Fairmount Park, and the US Mint.

After these carriage rides, bouquets of "the richest and rarest" flowers arrived for Maggie, their seductive scent filling the bridal suite. Before long, Kane's notes addressed her directly, "Dr. Kane leaves for New York on Monday; might he ask Miss Fox at what hour she would be disengaged before his departure?"

Despite his growing interest in Maggie, Dr. Kane refused to believe that spirits tipped tables, rang bells, or rapped messages to communicate. He explained, "Although I am still skeptical as to our friends in the other country [the dead], I am a firm believer in my friends in this."

Whenever the two celebrity friends saw each other, Mother Fox accompanied them. Unmarried men and women were chaperoned to keep their relationships property chaste before marriage. Public displays of affection were forbidden. No hugging or hand-holding. A well-bred young woman would not dare to take the arm of a young man in public until they were engaged!

Still, Maggie and Elisha grew close enough to begin using each other's first names in conversation. In letters, though, the famous explorer's manner stayed impeccably formal:

> *My Dear Miss Fox,*
>
> *The day is so beautiful that I feel tempted to repent my indoor imprisonment. If you will do me the kind-*

ness to . . . take a quiet drive, I will call for you at your own hour.

With respect, very faithfully your servant,

E. K. Kane.

For more than a decade, Elisha Kent Kane had managed to remain one of Philadelphia's most eligible bachelors. Even though chaperoned, people noticed how much time he was spending with Maggie Fox. The thirteen-year age difference between Maggie and Elisha was normal for a courting couple of their time, but Philadelphia society gossiped due to their class difference. *Why her? A spirit rapper?* People noted that Maggie took Elisha's arm while walking. *Was he just being kind to the poor girl? Or was she an overly forward social climber?* An inappropriate relationship with the working-class Maggie Fox could ruin the son of an upper-crust family like the Kanes. But the two celebrities had more in common than most people understood. They were both explorers—one of the Earth, the other of the mind. They were both ambitious for fame and money, willing to stray from more traditional paths.

Elisha Kane often had business meetings in New York City and traveled there toward the end of 1852. Wanting to get to know Maggie's family, he made plans to take a large party of friends to an evening séance at Leah's Manhattan home and did Mrs. Fox the favor of personally carrying letters to Kate.

When Kate met Elisha, she thought him "a very pleasant gentleman." Before long, the youngest Fox sister was writing to Elisha like a brother. Elisha didn't believe that either Maggie or Kate was deceiving the public on purpose; but he considered the sisters' profession disreputable. In a letter to Kate, Elisha set forth his reasons that she (and Maggie too!) should stop working as mediums, "practice in anything hardens us . . . you do things now which you would never have dreamed of doing years ago . . . The older you grow the more difficult it will be to liberate yourself from this thing."

No matter which city he was in, Elisha sent lavish gifts for Maggie, addressed to Mother Fox, "I could not resist the temptation of sending the accompanying little trifle of ermine, for Miss Margaretta's throat."

As the new year, 1853, began, Elisha returned to Philadelphia, acting like a man head over heels in love. The gifts of books or sheet music and cozy, winter drives continued. "Tell Miss Maggie to dress warmly." Elisha's "favorite cousin" began to chaperone the couple. She, too, found Miss Maggie Fox charming.

From observing and speaking with higher-class séance clients, Maggie had learned to carry herself well. She possessed "a winning grace," "reserve" and "self-control" appropriate for "a soul far above her present calling . . ." She'd acquired the skills of an entertainer. Maggie Fox was "joyous," excellent at "repartee and mimicry." She made Elisha laugh.

She also had practice in the essential séance skill of listening with grave attention. On one outing that included his chaperoning cousin, Elisha walked Maggie through Philadelphia's Laurel Hill Cemetery. "Leading her to the family vault of the Kanes . . . he knocked on the iron door, and repeated lines from the poet Longfellow's "Psalm of Life."

Art is long, and Time is fleeting;
And our hearts, though stout and brave,
Still, like muffled drums, are beating
Funeral marches to the grave.

Hinting at their future (though pretty morbidly for a boyfriend), Elisha told Maggie, "Here, Margaret, will be *your* last resting place!" They lingered in front of Willie's grave, and Elisha confided that his

Couples walk in Laurel Hill Cemetery, Philadelphia, around 1850, the location of one of Maggie and Elisha's first dates

little brother "had suffered much in the delirium of his last illness." Elisha appreciated her quiet empathy, "Maggie, you are a godsend to me!" Elisha's cousin took Maggie aside, "Elisha loves you; I can see that!"

He knew there were barriers to a serious relationship. Elisha had been promised early on to a wealthy young woman chosen by his family. But he found such society women tiresome, "simpering behind an embroidered screen or teapot." Maggie was young and charming, but ill-educated. Elisha wrote, "if I had my way with you, I would send you to school and learn you to live your life over again." But the biggest obstacle for Elisha was that Maggie worked as a spirit medium, "an obscure and *ambiguous* profession."

As he grew to love Maggie, Elisha disparaged her work more often. He called mediumship "weary," "dreary," and full of "deceit." Maggie didn't take him too seriously at first. In fact, Elisha's moralizing about her profession made her teasingly start calling him "preacher." He found the nickname both funny and appropriate, using it to sign letters to Maggie.

The more Elisha cared for Maggie, the more he seemed to criticize her. The more he fell in love, the more he realized exactly how unsuitable his family would find the teenage spirit rapper. He set upon a course of improving Maggie's manners and morals to fit her for "a high position in society." She was to always appear "very gentle and quiet, and modest, and retiring . . ." He advised her on proper clothing, "Wear your undersleeves and spencer [articles of dress that covered the arms and chest] always when you have company." To keep his affection, he expected her to change. Elisha gave Maggie a diamond ring set in black enamel. He proposed marriage; Maggie couldn't believe he was serious and turned him down.

Their relationship hit a rougher patch. Maggie liked spending time with Elisha but didn't trust him. She knew he was keeping their budding romance a secret from his parents. Maggie was afraid of "thinking too much" of him. When she addressed him as "My dear friend—" Elisha scolded that all the "warmth and affection seem to be on my side."

He addressed her as "darling," and later, "sweet pet," and "sugar plum"; he thought her "loveable." But Elisha's letters also contained condescension disguised as compliment: "You have more *brain* than I gave you credit for," or, "I had no idea you wrote or thought so well."

Maggie Fox was used to managing difficult men of the middle and upper classes, whether drunk, rude, or simply full of themselves. She was a practiced, phenomenal flirt, "Now, Doctor—be candid!—am I not correct when I say you are an enigma past finding out? You know I am."

Elisha found her notoriety embarrassing, "It haunts me to see you perched over a two-penny song [sheet music] with 'Margaretta' in great big print underneath you." He worried about gossip, "I was unwilling to call upon you to-night for fear of *talk*." When a news story focused on *his* looks and personality, instead of his science, he found that appalling too: "How disgusting is this life, to be discussed by the papers! I need not be so proud, Maggie, for I am no better than the 'rappers.'"

Elisha Kent Kane was as attracted to Maggie Fox as he was repulsed by the talent that had made her famous. Despite having attended multiple Fox sisters' séances, he had no solid proof of spirits. Maggie may not have let him in on whatever spirit secrets she was keeping. Perhaps in response to public rumors, Kate had written Elisha bluntly, "you should know that the sounds are not made by machinery. Neither do I know how the rappings are produced." When Elisha tried, and failed, to figure out how the rappings occurred, he gave up: "I believe the only thing I ever was afraid of was, this *confounded thing being found out*. I would not know it myself for ten thousand dollars."

Though typically sure of his own intelligence, Elisha Kent Kane couldn't help but wonder—*What if Maggie Fox was deceiving the whole world? Couldn't a woman like that deceive him?* Her profession required her to sit in the dark with strangers, often men, holding hands. This behavior sat entirely outside the social rules for a young woman who might one day be worthy to become the wife of the illustrious (and honestly, quite arrogant) Dr. Kane.

After a few months of wild infatuation, Elisha expressed doubts about their future. He ended a letter to Maggie in a fit of doom about their celebrity romance, "Remember then, as sort of a dream, that Doctor Kane of the Arctic Seas loved Maggie Fox of the Spirit Rappings."

"There were several champagne bottles in the room . . ."

Chapter 18 SHOULD I STAY OR SHOULD I GO?

By the end of January of 1853, the Fox women were reunited once again in New York City. Neither Maggie nor Kate followed Elisha's advice to quit mediumship. Their cosmopolitan life of séances, parties, and champagne toasts went on as usual. Elisha would be one of the first to comment on Maggie and Kate's fondness for alcohol, warning, "Tell Katie to drink no champagne, and do you [you should] follow the same advice." But neither sister paid attention to Elisha's guidance on drinking either. Maggie and Kate drank wines, including champagne and brandy, but kept how much they drank, and how frequently, yet another secret.

As Elisha sourced a crew and supplies for his upcoming Arctic expedition, "examining recruits, inventing cooking stoves, pricing rounds of beef," he was often on the road. He was scheduled to speak in Baltimore, deliver a presentation at the Smithsonian Institution in Washington, DC, and attend meetings in Philadelphia before coming back to New York. Despite his unease with her background, he couldn't seem to forget Maggie Fox.

He returned to writing affectionately. "Maggie darling—" he fussed, "Why do you not write to me? Have you forgotten your friend? . . . how very, very, very much I love you . . ." He asked for a lock of her hair. Most of all, he wanted to see her when he returned to New York. "How can I meet you dear Maggie, away from suspicion, away from Mrs.__ [Leah Brown]." He couldn't just show up at the Fox sisters' house on West Twenty-Sixth Street.

Because Leah hated him. She had met Elisha that past autumn when he brought friends to a séance at her home. Afterward, Leah referred to Elisha as "a vain, pompous little man" and worried about his fascination with her teenage sister. Leah had seen this kind of behavior before.

As a teenager, Leah had been swept off her feet by the older Mr. Fish. She'd loved him, given birth to his child, and was abandoned before she turned twenty. After that early harsh experience, Leah's intuition regarding men (and spirits!) grew stronger.

Though it was not public knowledge, a few years earlier, Elisha almost certainly had a sexual relationship with a young woman who became pregnant. One of his friends crudely teased, "How awful 'tis that these women will now & then get themselves with child . . . What an ardent lover must you be Elisha. I have heard you generally leave a mark on anything which you touch." It looks like Elisha covered the woman's expenses until she gave birth, then went on with his life, forgetting both her and their child.

Leah felt that a man like Elisha Kent Kane might sleep with, but would never marry, a young woman like Maggie Fox. Elisha could ruin

Maggie's life and ruin the Fox sisters' business in the process. Leah had come much too far to hand Dr. Kane that power.

Leah kept Maggie busy with séances and kept her chaperoned. She insisted that Maggie limit further involvement with the spirit-skeptical Elisha. Mother Fox sided with Leah, understanding that she'd let her teenage daughter's relationship with the experienced Dr. Kane go too far.

Elisha was obsessed. Letters, gifts, or telegrams arrived almost every day. "I miss you when I look over my crowded table with its books and papers . . . I miss you when listening to the empty nonsense of my fashionable friends . . ."

Writing to Maggie, Elisha promised to come back to New York City if she would sneak out with Kate and meet him in a popular art gallery: "walk past it at exactly four o'clock on Saturday afternoon, I will be there." Maggie primly refused: "The idea seems to me so unbecoming." She suggested Elisha make the effort to ask Leah's permission. He did not do so, instead complaining to a friend about Maggie's "Devil of a sister."

Once he'd returned to New York, Elisha stopped by without warning to try to catch Maggie at home. Mother turned him away. Without asking Leah or Mother, he hired a carriage to drive Maggie to a dressmaker so he could buy her some new clothes. If the rendezvous ever took place, Elisha and Maggie kept it secret.

Whenever they were away from one another, Maggie and Elisha carried on an extensive correspondence, sometimes undercover. Elisha, or "Ly" as Maggie now called him, often asked her to address communications to him using false names, "Cousin Peter" or "F. Webster." Notes from Elisha to Maggie were passed from his friends to Kate behind Leah's back.

While Leah stayed at home in New York, in February of 1853,

Maggie, Kate, and Mother went on tour to Washington, DC. They settled in to lead séances at Mrs. Sullivan's, a high-end boardinghouse.

The nation's capital city was getting ready to inaugurate a new president the following month. Democratic "dark horse" candidate, Franklin Pierce of New Hampshire, had won election that past November. His party platform pledged to avoid conflicts on slavery. Pierce, a Northerner, believed that the Compromise of 1850 had solved the slavery issue, declaring, "We have been carried in safety through a perilous crisis . . ." He wanted Americans to concentrate on prosperity and peace.

And indeed, the next few years were "a time of relative tranquility." But just because President Pierce wanted to sweep the issue of slavery under the rug, didn't mean it went away. His refusal to address it kept the sides from talking and solidified divisions between North and South. A Southern representative called abolition "a curse to the country." A Northern senator railed, "Am I obliged, as a member of the Government of the United States, to acknowledge your title to a slave? No sir, never." No one listened; both sides dug in.

After days full of political clashes, congressmen in Washington, DC, needed simple diversion (or actual help from the spirits!). Government and military officials packed Maggie and Kate's séances at Mrs. Sullivan's boardinghouse.

"Only imagine Maggie and me and dear Mother before a crowd of drunken Senators," Kate complained in a letter to Leah. In the spirit circles, men leered at the sisters and made "low remarks." Kate wrote, "I am tired of my life." Maggie agreed, later describing a "tiresome life . . . tiresome because I have to meet with all kinds of people."

Both sisters had already seen more of the United States than most young women (or men) of their time. They had stayed in the finest rooms at the country's best hotels. They were "visited daily by many of the nation's most-respected and intelligent citizens," including celebrities, intellectuals, leaders in the media and politics. On the other hand, they were never home for long, had few (if any?) same-age friends, and worked constantly.

Fame had its obligations and took its toll. Even when Maggie and Kate were exhausted, sad, or disinterested, they still had to make the rounds of social functions, whether in Washington, DC, or any city in which they appeared. The youngest Fox sisters turned to multiple glasses of wine to cope with long evenings filled with prying strangers.

A typically elegant New York City dinner party between 1856 and 1862.

As a celebrity himself, Elisha understood Maggie's life on tour, and the many temptations put in her path. "How does Washington come on? Many beaux? Many believers? Many friends? Answer these questions you wicked little Maggie."

At times, Elisha still questioned their relationship. In answer to one of his letters accusing her of indifference, Maggie finally admitted, "*know* I have loved you and love you still."

Just weeks later, Elisha Kent Kane arrived in Washington, DC, and raised some eyebrows when his traveling cases were brought to Mrs. Sullivan's. Tongues wagged about two celebrities, Dr. Kane and Maggie Fox, staying in the same boardinghouse. Elisha put up with the gossip to sleep just one floor above the young woman he wanted, "Is it any wonder that I long to look—only to look—at that dear little deceitful mouth of yours."

As she aged, Mother Fox appeared increasingly lax about chaperoning her attractive teenage daughters. Though her exact role in spirit matters remains almost entirely unknown, while in Washington, DC, Mrs. Fox didn't control events in the séance parlor as strictly as Leah had always done.

In one session around her sixteenth birthday, Kate was bothered by "a very fine-looking man" who drunkenly yelled, "This is all a humbug, but it is worth a dollar to sit in the light of Miss Kate's eyes." Kate was being compared to women who sold themselves, and knew "if my sister, Leah, was with us, they would not dare insult us."

Maggie took long carriage rides with Elisha, past the White House, the still unfinished Capitol Building, and out to "old country inns," all apparently unchaperoned. Elisha wrote of "her warm kisses on his lips, her long hair sweeping his cheeks." He would remember America's capital as the city where Maggie "first gave me your confidence, and with it, your love." But what exactly did Maggie confide? Her spirit secrets, her longing for Elisha, or her growing preference for a different kind of life?

Elisha began interrupting Maggie while in session, sending in notes, "Come out for a moment from those coarse people . . . Surely you can rest a minute! Come dearest fluttering bird! Come!"

Distracted by desire, Maggie kept clients waiting, and at least once, left mid-séance. Elisha—his words, his eyes, his hands, his lips—held a fascination with which the dead could not compete.

Elisha's expedition to the Arctic was set to leave toward the end of May 1853. As he finalized preparations, he also made firm plans for Maggie to be tutored in the country town of Crooksville, outside Philadelphia, while he was gone. When Maggie was ready, she'd enter a formal ladies' seminary to receive a proper nineteenth-century education in languages, music, and manners.

Maggie's future schooling and living expenses were to be secretly funded by Elisha. His friend, Cornelius Grinnell, son of the Arctic expedition's major sponsor, would manage Maggie's finances while Elisha was away. If Maggie completed the education Elisha set out for her and became the "refined, educated, conscientious woman," his family background required, he promised to marry her, "for my Maggie is a lady; and by the time she has a course of . . . music and French, nobody will know her as the spirit-rapping original phenomenon."

Only a handful of people knew his plans, and Elisha asked Maggie to keep it that way. He said he loved her but felt obligated to keep his parents, and the wider public, in the dark until she was properly educated, and he had returned from the Arctic in triumph. Maggie loved and believed in Elisha, agreeing to his plan.

Leah raged at Maggie's decision and fumed at Mother too. Without Leah's knowledge, Elisha had obtained written permission from Mother to send Maggie to school. *How could Maggie let an unrelated, unmarried man pay for her education and living expenses without a public engagement? What kind of mother let her do so?*

Mother, Kate, and Maggie returned to New York from Washington, DC, to face Leah's wrath. Maggie stood her ground. "What have I ever done that I should be denied the pleasures of a quiet home, the blessings of love . . . I have given my whole time to this subject for six years. I think I have done my part." She wanted a more normal life. She intended to leave the notorious medium, Maggie Fox, behind, and become the respectable wife of a world-famous Arctic explorer, *Mrs.* Elisha Kent Kane.

When Leah realized she'd lost the battle over Maggie's future, she asked Elisha for money instead. If Maggie was to be away at school, Leah's income would suffer. The expense of Calvin's long illness had drained the family funds. Leah owned nice furniture and lovely clothes, but was somehow a month behind on the rent. *Could Dr. Kane lend her $100?*

Elisha did not give "the old wretch" exactly what she asked for. Instead, he "sent her $75 . . ." Leah took his money but never wrote a word of thanks.

On May 4, 1853, Calvin Brown finally succumbed to tuberculosis. The family attended his funeral, held in New York City. Their Spiritualist friend, Justice John Edmonds, who had been forced to retire from New York's Supreme Court due to his beliefs, delivered a eulogy, "purported to come from the spirit world." Rappings were heard throughout the service. The Foxes brought Calvin's body back to Rochester, where he was buried, "a husband, a son, and a brother—and a linch-pin in the cause of Spiritualism."

During the spring of 1853, Maggie and Elisha kept in touch by letter and telegram. While she remained in New York, he had expedition business in multiple East Coast cities. He was in final rewrites for a book about his first Arctic expedition; she was finishing prior séance commitments. She was packing for school; he was packing for the Arctic. His rheumatic fever flared; she worried about his health. He worried whether she could stay away from the spirits without his steadying influence.

"Shall I go, or stay?" he asked.

Maggie's answer was clear: Go. As a young woman of the nineteenth century, she understood that it was his job to explore the world; it was her job to wait for his return. Neither would be easy.

As part of her new life, Maggie promised Elisha "solemnly never to rap again." Yet it proved more difficult to leave the spirits than anticipated. In New York City, Maggie was surrounded by believers who clamored for her to help them talk to their dead. Since she lived in the same house, Leah and Kate expected her assistance in running evening sessions. Still, Maggie managed to keep her promise . . . until she heard from the First Lady of the United States.

First Lady Jane Pierce turned to spirit communication after a recent tragedy. Two months before her husband's inauguration, she'd witnessed the gruesome death of their eleven-year-old son, Bennie. The boy had been standing between cars when their train derailed, decapitating him. Haunted by the accident, Jane Pierce grew desperate to hear from her child: *Are you there? Are you happy? Will I ever see you again?*

To avoid involving the President, Jane Pierce made quiet arrangements to leave Washington. She asked to meet secretly with Maggie Fox in New York. "Don't rap for Mrs. Pierce," Elisha ordered. But if she could help her country's First Lady, how could Maggie refuse?

Maggie Fox held at least one séance, possibly more, for First Lady Jane Pierce. These meetings were kept entirely out of the newspapers. The exact location, topics of conversation, or any messages received from Bennie's spirit are unknown.

Elisha was disappointed in Maggie's broken promise; but even he couldn't resist asking for a bit of celebrity gossip, "Tell me how Mrs. Pierce got on!" Maggie's response, if any, did not survive.

Jane Pierce with her son Bennie prior to 1853.

Before he left, Elisha wrote Maggie some last instructions, "One final wish . . . See little of ***[Leah], and *never sleep within her house*." Just days before Maggie left for her tutor's home, Elisha arranged for an artist to paint her portrait. Maggie posed in a high-necked illusion lace dress. Elisha packed the finished painting among the few personal items he was bringing to the Arctic. He wanted her with him always.

As they parted, he wrote

> *My own Dear Darling,*
>
> *. . . Oh my Maggie, think of me, always think of me—with respect! Cling to me, always cling to me—with love! Lean on me, hope in me, bear with me—trust me! . . . . Thus live, dear Maggie, until God brings me back to you; and then . . . we will resign ourselves to a passion sanctified by love and marriage . . . Let us live for each other.*
>
> *Farewell, E. K. Kane.*

If the expedition went as planned, they'd be apart for eighteen months. If not, no one, except maybe the spirits, knew when they'd ever be together again.

Engraving of Maggie Fox made from the painting Elisha brought to the Arctic

"Dr. Kane . . . brought me away from this life."

Chapter 19 POOR GIRLS WITH PRETTY FACES

> "On the morning of the twenty seventh of May, 1853 . . . After a tedious drive of four hours, I arrived at Crookville [Crooksville] . . . about eighteen miles from Philadelphia . . . I reached the house which was to be my abode until Dr. Kane's return to our country . . ." (excerpt from Maggie Fox's journal)

Maggie settled her belongings into a spare bedroom at the family home of her tutor, Mrs. Turner. Elisha had provided a piano so Maggie could practice playing and singing; he expected his future wife to be an accomplished musician. Mrs. Turner tutored Maggie in French, German, English literature, and history, kindly treating her like a daughter. Yet, the stillness of the countryside hadn't suited Maggie in Hydesville, and it didn't suit her in Crooksville. Maggie swallowed any restlessness and concentrated on her French grammar.

On May 30, 1853, hundreds of spectators shouted three cheers, repeated three times, as Elisha's ship, the USS *Advance,* sailed out of New York harbor, headed north. The Second Grinnell Expedition's "intrepid" crew was under the leadership of what New York's *Daily Herald* called, "the indefatigable perseverance and indomitable courage" possessed by its thirty-three-year-old naval surgeon and commander.

But Dr. Elisha Kent Kane had never commanded a ship before. Many of his crew were much more experienced sailors. Still, one reporter insisted on the superior knowledge of the fledging Commander Kane, "nothing had been left undone." Elisha had calculated the supplies they'd need: salted meats, dried fruits, hard biscuits, scientific instruments, even smaller boats. He made plans to pick up additional provisions on their journey northward. He thought he had prepared well, insisting on the expedition's readiness.

As Elisha's long-planned expedition set sail, Maggie received a letter from him, "Just standing out to sea. Maggie, my own sweet pet, be comforted . . . [Cornelius] Grinnell will watch over you . . . Do not grieve, but trust." The *Advance* sailed to Newfoundland, stopped to board a few additional sailors and more than fifty sled dogs, then continued up the western coast of Greenland. Maggie received another letter posted from the town of Upernavik, in far northwest Greenland. Presumably in answer to a letter she must have written about her loneliness in Crooksville, he answered, "Don't mope like a sickly cat . . . exercise often, laugh when you can, grow as fat as you please . . ."

In July of 1853, all communication stopped. Once the *Advance* had sailed far enough north, letters could only be sent or received sporadically, when passed from ship to ship. In the nineteenth century, people wrote anyway, in the hopes that communications to loved ones would eventually show up, even if months or years late.

Though there was little *new* news, Elisha's influential family and friends supplied the newspapers with excerpts from his letters to keep his name in the public eye. The country's roughly two thousand papers began calling the journey "Dr. Kane's Arctic Expedition." In the coming months, the media reprinted and rehashed each other's old stories, and ran speculative tales about the frozen northlands. Stuck in sleepy Crooksville, Maggie "treasured all the newspaper articles she could find."

Next to unconfirmed news of Dr. Kane, Americans read speculation of another kind. The conspiratorial idea of a southern-based "Slave Power" organization began appearing in Northern newspapers. These stories spread the false claim that Slave Power agents had derailed the President's train and killed his son, Bennie. Conspiracists claimed that the Northern-born President Pierce now lived in fear of this secret group and took orders from Southern sympathizers.

Newspapers fed the conflict; Southern loyalists were "thieves," and "serving the devil"; Northern abolitionists were "crazy men" and "Atheists." The thread of ideals and traditions that held the United States together continued to fray, until armed violence broke out in the territories.

By August 1853, it was obvious to friends and family that Maggie Fox was depressed. No amount of reading about the celebrated Dr. Kane could make up for the fact that the real man, Elisha, was gone. Kate, Mother, and other New York friends made brief visits to Crooksville. These only served to remind Maggie of what she was missing. In leaving mediumship for Elisha's sake, she had also left behind an exciting life with fellow celebrities, new ideas, and lively conversation. Maggie had never been on her own. Without Elisha's encouragement, it was hard to stay dedicated to the life of a rural schoolgirl.

Maggie asked her guardian, Cornelius Grinnell, about transferring to a school in a larger town. He turned her down, "nothing could be better than the course you are now pursuing at Mrs. Turner's." Maggie

Antislavery and proslavery settlers poured into the Kansas territory to sway the vote on the question of slavery. Kansas wound up with two territorial governments, one allowing slavery, the other prohibiting it, with both sides claiming election fraud. Armed violence between the factions in the historical period "Bleeding Kansas" continued from 1854 until the start of the Civil War in 1861.

trudged on with her studies.

By summer's end 1853, spirit believers were still plentiful, though new recruits were harder to find. The Fox sisters faded from the newspapers, and their spirit business struggled. The upkeep on the West Twenty-Sixth Street house in New York became too much for Leah, Kate, and Mother. Leah moved to one apartment in Manhattan, Kate and Mother to another. Yet Leah and Kate still attracted groups of séance goers often enough to pay the bills.

In addition to private séance work, Kate took a permanent position offered by a wealthy Spiritualist who wanted to spread his beliefs to the wider public. Seventeen-year-old Kate Fox was the main attraction in a group of mediums hired to give free sittings at set hours. For these three-hour daily séances, Kate made the annual salary of $1,200, about eight times more than a female teacher earned in nineteenth-century New York City.

Despite the money and recognition, Kate seemed aimless and faced increasing public scrutiny and scorn. A fellow medium described, "poor patient Kate Fox . . . in the midst of a captious, grumbling crowd . . . repeating hour after hour the letters of the alphabet . . ." Kate's drinking continued.

Maggie, too, felt aimless, remaining in low spirits. In the autumn of 1853, she wrote Cornelius Grinnell, "I am very lonely and should love very much to go and spend a few days with my friend Mrs. Walter."

Mrs. Ellen Walter was a well-connected widow with social ties to both the Grinnell and Kane families. Elisha had suggested Mrs. Walter as an appropriate companion for Maggie before he left. It's unclear whether Elisha also knew that Ellen Walter tended toward spirit belief.

Cornelius agreed to a brief break in Maggie's studies. She traveled to New York and stayed with Mrs. Walter. But Maggie's stay in New York City was anything but brief. It lasted until after the new year 1854 and began a pattern. Maggie would spend a few weeks at Mrs. Turner's in Crooksville then take off to spend a few months at Mrs. Walter's in New York City. While in the city, Maggie did not regularly work as a medium, but she did visit her mother and Kate. She avoided Leah entirely.

To fund these city trips and other "necessary expenses," Maggie asked for larger amounts of money from Cornelius Grinnell: "Will you also please send me $80 . . ." then, "I should prefer one hundred . . ." and even, "Will you please send me one hundred and ninety dollars . . . in bills . . ." (almost $5,000 today).

The Fox sisters' profitable spirit work had protected Maggie from reality. She had no experience with financial management. She simply assumed that Elisha had left her enough money. But Elisha's naval income was only around sixty dollars a month. Cornelius Grinnell was paying Mrs. Turner ten dollars a week, more than two-thirds of Elisha's yearly pay. Maggie quickly ran through the cash he had set aside to support her.

In February of 1854, as funds dwindled, Cornelius Grinnell asked Elisha's brother, Robert Patterson Kane, for help. Both men believed that Elisha's passion for Maggie was short term. Robert called Maggie "a poor girl with a pretty face and an already disreputable association."

The two men had planned to keep the Maggie Fox situation as quiet as possible until Elisha came to his senses. But Leah had begun spreading rumors—Maggie Fox was being educated by the famous Dr. Kane "with the intention of marrying her" upon his return from the Arctic. Within a few weeks, those rumors found their way into the newspapers.

To the public, the scandalous spirit rapper Maggie Fox had no business in the heroic story of Dr. Kane of the Arctic. Cornelius Grinnell was supposed to act as Maggie's protector, but his real allegiance was to Elisha's public image. After all, it was Cornelius Grinnell's family name on the expedition and his father's money behind it.

Cornelius Grinnell and Robert Kane began denying the marriage rumors in the spring of 1854, around the time that Elisha's book about his *first* Arctic trip was published. Supported with newspapers ads paid for by his publisher and the Kane family, Elisha's true tale, *The United States Grinnell Expedition in Search of Sir John Franklin: A Personal Narrative*, sold well. Thousands of Americans craved information on their brave hero who was once again out exploring with a "hopeful and encouraging spirit." Dr. Kane's fame snowballed. The farther away he went, the more danger he faced, the more popular he became. And the value of his celebrity needed protecting.

Robert Kane wrote Cornelius Grinnell, "Miss F [Maggie] is not his

[Elisha's] mistress and holds to him no other relation than that of the recipient of his charity . . . Do you take my drift? Burn this." (Cornelius obviously didn't follow instructions.) The two men conspired to hide Elisha's romantic relationship with Maggie Fox. Instead, they portrayed Dr. Kane as selflessly helping a young girl rise from her sordid profession by providing a proper education—polishing his image as a kind of super-generous superhero.

Cornelius schemed further, writing Robert, "it has occurred to me whether by withholding funds from [Maggie] she could not be induced to return to her parents." Maggie was put on a strict budget; but oddly enough her expensive trips to New York were allowed to continue. The two men knew she was more likely to return to mediumship in the city than in Crooksville.

But Maggie kept her promise to Elisha. As far as is known, she stayed away from the séance table even when visiting friends, family, and believers. Instead, Maggie used the time with Kate, Mother, and her New York City friends to distract her from worry. Elisha was still out searching for Sir Franklin and had not returned in the fall of 1854 as expected.

Then, the world discovered that Sir Franklin would never return. Though Elisha had no way of knowing, another explorer learned from a group of the Arctic's Inuit people that Sir Franklin had died years back. Would Dr. Kane suffer a similar fate? Not if his family or his country could help it. Another of Elisha's brothers, Dr. John Kane, joined an American rescue expedition that planned to head to the Arctic from New York Harbor in the spring.

Each news article about Sir Franklin's death caused Maggie further anxiety. Dozens of well-respected newspapers ran stories, some entirely fabricated, "the bodies of Sir John Franklin and his men have been found by Dr. Kane's party, completely frozen, and in a state of perfect preservation." Maggie received letters from friends insensitively repeating news reports, "P.S. I saw in a paper last week that the Doctor would probably be absent longer than he anticipated . . . if he is only spared . . . that is all you can ask. I pray that he may be guarded safely." Prayers were not enough for Maggie; "gloom rested on the future." Her love was out there in the killing cold.

Still, Cornelius Grinnell and Robert Kane continued setting Maggie up to fail. The more time Maggie spent in New York City among Spiritualists, the more likely it was that she'd quit her studies and fall back into mediumship. Both men knew Elisha found mediumship somewhere between distasteful and disgusting. If they could force Maggie's return to the séance table, it would probably put the nail in the coffin (so to speak) to any future relationship with Elisha Kent Kane.

But Maggie did have more *brain*, as Elisha had put it, than either man expected. She brought the socially connected Mrs. Walter into her confidence about the love affair with Elisha. Maggie encouraged Mrs. Walter to read the letters she was writing him. The older woman thought Maggie's letters "sweet and touching" and approved of the couple, "What is more to be prized than a pure, devoted heart?"

Despite Elisha's emphasis on secrecy, his parents almost certainly heard the rumors about Maggie, whether from Mrs. Walter or others. The Kanes understood that Maggie Fox had her own influential friends. They also knew that Maggie had Elisha's letters, and worried about their potentially intimate content. At any time, Maggie Fox could release details of the love affair to the newspapers. The Kane family reluctantly provided Cornelius with additional funds for Maggie's support. They could only hope to tempt Maggie back to her old life and pray that would be enough to get Elisha to reject her.

While his friends and family continued plotting to separate Elisha from the young woman he called, "my own angel," he was over 3,000 miles away, living through hell.

"Dr. Kane, the Arctic explorer . . ."

Chapter 20 ARCTIC DREAMS, ARCTIC NIGHTMARES

Dear, Dear Maggie . . . In the midst of the ice and desolation I still think of you . . . Trust in my honor, dear Maggie . . . for am I not your heart? . . . your very heart of hearts—now and always!

LY.

P.S. Your portrait is a great comfort. I often gaze on its quiet loveliness.

Elisha Kent Kane had been gone about fifteen months when he wrote those words in August 1854, not knowing how he'd ever get home.

His Arctic expedition had begun successfully, even as the *Advance* sailed some of the most treacherous waters on the planet. Dr. Kane and his twenty-man crew named Canada's Kennedy Channel, took

Elisha Kane in Arctic gear, around 1855

geographical measurements, and charted iceberg-filled waters further north through the summer of 1853.

But winter in the Arctic begins early. By September, sailing was impossible. The *Advance* was encircled by ice floes in Smith Sound north of Baffin Bay. Determined to go further north, Elisha ordered the crew to pull the ship along through the thickening slush. But, within days, air temperatures lowered further until the *Advance* was frozen into the surrounding ice.

The sun went down in November. They would not see it again for months. Working in twenty-four-hour darkness, Elisha's crew built a kennel from rocks for the sled dogs (the smart dogs preferred sleeping on the ship) and a stone observatory to study the Arctic stars. Every day, Kane and others made note of the temperature, wind direction, and barometric pressure. Commander Kane organized crew members to journey far from the ship. These excursions hunted for evidence of Sir Franklin, and cached food, tents, and other supplies for future trips in the spring. Kane was along on one such trip when their planned route was blocked by a miles-wide glacier. He gave it the name Humboldt.

Midnight in September, an engraving of the USS Advance stuck in the Arctic ice

In February of 1854, temperatures reached –67°F. The sled dogs began dying by the dozens from lockjaw (tetanus). The men of the *Advance* survived on salty dried meat and tinned vegetables. Kane and his crew suffered symptoms of scurvy (vitamin C deficiency): swollen gums, loose teeth, exhaustion, severe joint pain. Left untreated, scurvy results in raging infections, internal bleeding, and heart failure—a long, torturous death.

Temperatures rose in early March. Enthusiastic about the warming weather, Commander Kane sent seven ailing crew members out to explore and hunt for fresh meat. But the erratic Arctic temperatures plunged again to more than –50°F. Three of the crew members returned barely coherent; the other four were unable to move, stranded miles away from the ship.

Dr. Kane formed a rescue mission which set off across the ice and found the men in a makeshift tent, almost dead. Dragging the incapacitated along on sledges, the rescuers struggled back to the *Advance*, enduring snow blindness and frostbite. Dr. Kane's "amputating-knives" were put to use for the first time. The chopping off of dead, blackened toes and fingers began; one crewman lost his entire foot.

In April, a group of Inuit hunters encountered the battered *Advance* and its sickly crew. One crew member spoke an Inuit language and acted as translator. Kane and his men traded needles, barrel staves, and buttons for four sled dogs and fresh walrus meat. "Experience has taught us to follow their guidance in matters of Arctic craft," Elisha noted of the Inuit. The crew began using Inuit techniques to hunt seal, preserve seal blubber, and gather green spring lichens, which helped ease their scurvy.

It was midsummer July, and then August of 1854, and still, temperatures remained cool, the pack ice did not melt, and the *Advance* couldn't move. When strong enough, the crew continued overland explorations and mapping of the Arctic terrain. Hopes of finding Sir Franklin in the area dimmed, but on one sledge trip, they spied a distant body of water that they believed to be the long-sought open polar sea.

Even if the crew's discovery had turned out to be true (future expeditions would debunk the existence of an open polar sea) the open water was too far away; the *Advance* remained stuck fast. Elisha thought about abandoning ship and returning to Upernavik, Greenland, but worried that it was too late in the year to try to make the treacherous overland trip on sledges.

Despite his initial confidence, Commander Kane had not packed all that well for the first winter—let alone for a second. When crew members discovered that polar bears had eaten or destroyed previously cached supplies, Elisha confessed doubts to his ship log, "Bad! Bad! I must look another winter in the face . . . It is horrible—yes, that is the word—to look forward to another year of disease and darkness . . ."

The punishing conditions, the amputations, and the illnesses continued. One crew member, and then another, died of "an anomalous spasmodic disorder, allied to tetanus . . ." Unable to be buried, the bodies were placed in the observatory, where they lay frozen. On a nearby rock cliff, a crew member painted a memorial, a potential headstone for them all, *Advance*, AD 1853–1854.

About half of Kane's crew balked at their inexperienced commander's decision to stay another winter. After a few days of argument, these men took some supplies, deserted the *Advance,* and set off across the ice to try to save themselves. Kane and the rest stayed with the ship and began preparations for another grueling winter.

Again using Inuit techniques, Kane and his remaining men hurried to gather moss and turf to insulate the rooms below deck. They stripped wood trim from the ship, and piled it for firewood. When the weather allowed, they hunted. Food was scarce; even when they had fresh meat (hares, fox, ptarmigan, the very occasional reindeer or polar bear), the men were usually rationed to four ounces a day. Elisha, for one, supplemented his rations by eating ship rats. (Rats, it seems, really can survive anywhere!) They hunkered down to wait for spring.

Weeks later, and more than 200 miles away, Inuit hunters found the expedition's deserters, sick, and starving on the ice. The Inuit returned them to the *Advance*. In his ship's log, Elisha grumbled about his crew's disloyalty, but took the mutinous men back onboard.

When daily sun returned in early March of 1855, outside temperatures were still close to –40°F. The *Advance* had been crushed by the ice, stripped of seven tons of wood, and looked more like a skeleton than a ship. Most of the crew were seriously ill or injured: swollen legs, missing digits, labored breathing, feverish. As the Second Grinnell Expedition struggled toward its third year, Commander Kane finally realized they'd never survive another Arctic winter. He made the decision to abandon the *Advance*.

The crew fashioned clothes from blankets. They loaded three smaller whaling boats onto long sledges. They readied the remaining dogs; but the ailing men would have to pull also. Each man was allowed only eight pounds of provisions; anything unnecessary was left behind. As their last act, they lowered and packed the ship's tattered American flag. Commander Elisha Kent Kane and his crew left the frozen USS *Advance* on May 20, 1855. They started across ice and water toward Upernavik. It was close to six hundred miles away.

Dr. Kane and his crew crossing the ice by sledge

> "There broke upon us one of the most fearful gales I have ever experienced. It had the character and the force of a cyclone. The dogs were literally blown from their harness, and it was only by throwing ourselves on our faces that we saved ourselves from being swept away . . . The snow fields before us to the south were already saturated with wet. Around the bergs the black water came directly to the surface, and the whole area was spotted with pools . . . it was impossible to prevent accidents. One of the sledges broke through, carrying six men into the water . . ." (excerpt from Kane's *Arctic Explorations)*

Elisha had never been healthy. He'd faced death many times; but this time he was sure—he would probably not survive the Arctic: "I saw that we must move or die." Trudging and slipping as he drove his men across the ice, Elisha Kent Kane reportedly carried Maggie Fox's portrait "strapped on his back."

"He wanted me to forget it."

Chapter 21 GOSSIP AND GLORY

In early October of 1855, Maggie Fox was in New York City, waiting like the rest of the country. The unknown fate of Dr. Elisha Kent Kane was one of the biggest news stories of the year. *North American Review* dedicated thirty-five pages of a single issue to Dr. Kane's chances of survival in the Arctic. Both Northerners and Southerners could be equally proud of Dr. Kane. His heroism was one of the dwindling news stories reminding Americans of their similarities instead of their differences.

The country's newspapers, both big, like, New York's *Daily Tribune*, and small, like Iowa's *Muscatine Evening Journal*, had headlined multiple stories of a rumored celebrity engagement: "Dr. Kane to Marry One of the Fox Girls," "Dr. Kane's Prospects," "Dr. Kane on a Fox Hunt."

Dr. Kane on a Fox Hunt.

The Troy *Whig* states that Dr. Kane, of the Arctic Expedition, is soon to be married to Miss Margaretta Fox the second sister of the "Fox girls" at whose residence in Hydraville, Wayne county, in N. Y. State, the spirit rappings were first manifested. Dr. Kane became acquinted with the Fox family in New York. During his absence Miss Fox, his said to be affinanced, has been attending a young ladies' school at Philadelphia. It is to be hoped the Dr. has made a good provision of crockery. It is probable his trip to the North has made him insensible to knocks.—*Sandusky Register.*

"Maggy" will cure the Dr. of his *frigidity*, for she is a kind and *warm* hearted girl. The Dr. must be a believer in the harmonial theory.

Newspaper gossip about the Kane/Fox romance

The heroic Dr. Elisha Kent Kane, still missing in the frozen northlands, was involved with an infamous spirit rapper! As real people with real feelings, Maggie and Elisha no longer mattered. The personal lives of Dr. Kane and Miss Maggie Fox were used as a product to sell newspapers. *Could it be true? Would they really marry? Was he even alive?*

Elisha and his remaining crew had spent eighty-four days crossing over ice, until they found open waters and set sail on the smaller whaling boats. One additional crew member died on the return trip. Off the coast of Greenland, Kane and his crew were finally rescued by a passing merchant ship and later transferred to the American rescue vessel.

On October 11, the American ship carrying Dr. Kane and his crew entered New York Harbor. Hundreds of clippers, schooners, sloops, barges, ferries, and steamboats raised and lowered their flags to honor the Arctic heroes. Cannons boomed from the forts lining the shore while merchants, clerks, clergy, lawyers, and omnibus drivers from Wall Street to the Bowery celebrated. "Every tongue did its best to circulate the gladdening intelligence." The *New York Times* relayed the news to the world: "DR. KANE HOME AGAIN." "The newsboys ran along the streets. . . . shouted loud and long."

Frances Flora Bond Palmer's drawing *View of New York from Brooklyn Heights*, lithographed by Nathaniel Currier, 1849

When Maggie heard cannon fire echoing off the city buildings, she wept in relief. She pleaded to meet Elisha at the docks; but Mrs. Walter forbade it. It was not proper as the couple had no formal relationship. Maggie should control herself and wait for Dr. Kane to call. Maggie stood in the sitting room. She wanted to look her best for him. She fixed her hair. She sat. She smoothed her new dress. She stood again.

At the docks, thousands of New Yorkers cheered when Elisha

and his crew disembarked. “An army of reporters” crowded around. “Remember your newspaper friends . . .” Elisha’s brother Tom had advised, “It is they who made us, and not we ourselves.” Tom Kane understood that great deeds, talents, or discoveries do not create celebrity, media attention does. Elisha was arguably the most famous man in America. He should never forget that his future success depended on public opinion.

At midday, Maggie still had received no word from Elisha. She cried into the sofa cushions, looked in the mirror, worried, rearranged the chairs, cried again. Teatime came and went. The clatter of any passing carriage sent her flying to the window. Again and again, it wasn’t her love. She waited after the sun set and into the evening. Around midnight, Mrs. Walter insisted Maggie try to sleep.

By the next morning, Elisha still had not shown up. Mother Fox stopped by to soothe her daughter and convince Maggie to stay with her and Kate. While Maggie was at Kate and Mother’s, Mrs. Walter received a visitor.

Cornelius Grinnell stood at Mrs. Walter’s front door. He carried a message—Elisha would see Maggie as soon as possible. However, for now, Dr. Kane wanted all his love letters returned. Grinnell was there to make sure he got them. Mrs. Walter refused to rummage through Maggie’s personal things without her permission and sent Grinnell away: “If Dr. Kane wants his letters, let him ask for them himself.”

When Maggie returned to Mrs. Walter’s, she was devastated to find that Elisha still had not visited. That’s when Mrs. Walter informed her that his snub was no accident.

In his first days at home, Elisha found himself lionized in the papers as an American superhero, *and* in a serious fight with his family. The Kanes were enraged at the rash of engagement stories in the press. They had no intention of allowing a spirit rapper to join their eminent family, not now, not ever. Elisha might have been a celebrity to the rest of the world, but—his family reminded him—he was also flat broke.

Elisha's book had been popular but had not yet turned a profit. The Arctic expedition and the American rescue mission had cost a fortune. Elisha was completely dependent on his parents for support. They ordered him to deny the engagement and end any relationship with Maggie Fox. This national hero was too afraid of his parents to refuse.

At nine the next morning, Elisha showed up at Mrs. Walter's front door. He asked for Maggie. His weathered face sported a thick beard, his hair was streaked with gray. He wore the dress uniform of the US Navy, blue wool cutaway coat with two rows of gilt buttons. Upset that he had ignored her for so long, Maggie refused to come downstairs. She never wanted to see him again! Elisha waited, pleading, and pacing the parlor until Mrs. Walter convinced Maggie to see the man, if only to make him leave.

Maggie stepped reluctantly down the stairs. Elisha stepped toward her. They were soon crying in each other's arms. Maggie felt his lips on her hair, his scratchy beard against her forehead. They'd waited more than two years for this one embrace.

Elisha's feelings were "the same as when we parted." But his next words cut Maggie deeply. From now on, he said, they were to treat each other as, "sister and brother." He felt he had no choice.

The media had created Dr. Kane, a larger-than-life character with, "a daring that never quailed, endurance that knew no yielding, a devotion to duty that nothing could shake . . ." There was no room in this manufactured image for the real Elisha to love a spirit rapper. Neither the public nor his family would ever welcome Maggie Fox as his partner.

Marriage proposals were legally binding in the nineteenth century. Elisha needed written evidence that he had not promised to marry Maggie Fox. Without it, Maggie (like any nineteenth-century woman) could sue Elisha for breaking his promise. In this case, Maggie certainly had letters proving that he'd made one, so she had to officially deny the engagement. Elisha handed Maggie a letter stating that there was never any promise to marry and asked her to copy it in her own handwriting.

Without a word, Maggie took the letter, copied and signed it, handing it back to him.

Needing a witness, Elisha showed Maggie's denial to Mrs. Walter. Bewildered, Mrs. Walter couldn't help but ask, "Maggie, is this so?"

Maggie could not hold back her emotions a second longer, "No—no—it is not so! Doctor Kane knows it is not!"

The most famous man in America, the man who had preached to her about honesty, the man who Maggie adored, had denied their love. Fulfilling family expectations and his own ambition, Dr. Kane set off to court his fame. He walked out the door leaving Maggie Fox heartbroken.

"if we are ever to meet again . . ."

Chapter 22 NOBODY'S BUSINESS

The very next day, Elisha made a shocking return to Mrs. Walter's. He apologized to Maggie and returned her letter denying the engagement. She didn't know who he had shown it to in the few hours since they last parted; still, she took it, and tore it to bits.

Their confusing relationship struggled forward. Some days he visited three times a day. Other days not at all. One day he brought a pushy newspaper reporter and insisted Maggie tell the man that there was no engagement. Maggie ordered Elisha and the reporter out of the house. The next day, the couple might take a carriage ride around the city like nothing had happened.

By the end of 1855, Maggie had moved from Mrs. Walter's to live with Mother and Kate. Spiritualist friends wanted the powerful Maggie Fox to return to the séance table; and off and on, she did.

Elisha wrote, "I can't bear the idea of your sitting in the dark, squeezing other people's hands . . . I touch no hands but yours; press no lips but yours . . ." Maggie's "preacher" was at it again.

Leah probably worked as a medium throughout this period, though her day-to-day life is unknown. Leah hated Elisha so much that her detailed memoirs skipped years of her own life to make sure Kane's name was not included in her version of the Fox sisters' story.

Newspaper reporters hunted for details of the romance between Dr. Kane and Maggie Fox. Some newspaper stories insisted they were engaged, others insisted they were not. Maggie was "bright" and "beautiful," but the story of marriage to the upper-class Dr. Kane was obviously "foolish," unless it was credible. No one knew the truth; everyone found it fascinating. Maggie worried, writing Elisha, "all this talk for and against cannot fail to injure you, as well as myself."

Horace Greeley agreed. Gossip was becoming news, and the powerful editor didn't like it. He used his *Tribune*'s editorial page to rail against the direction the media was headed. "If this were a monarchy, and one or both of them were of the blood royal, there would be an excuse for reports and speculation with regard to their relations to each other." (That is, unless celebrities were fast becoming American royalty?) "Whether they have been, are, may be, are not, or will be 'engaged' can be nobody's business but their own . . ." Greeley grumbled.

Maggie's friends, like Mrs. Walter, seethed. America may have thought Elisha Kent Kane was a gentleman/hero, but he was not defending young Maggie Fox's reputation to the press. It didn't take long before Mother Fox stepped in, writing Elisha, "I from this moment forbid you ever again entering my house. I forbid my daughter from receiving you . . . It is injuring her hitherto unblemished name . . ."

Elisha called at the house anyway. Maggie would not see him. He came again and again to plead with Mother Fox. He promised he was working hard on a second book. He promised that this new book would make him financially independent. He promised he'd formalize the relationship when the time was right. Maggie's "preacher" promised and promised, never once understanding why the Fox women had grown skeptical.

Maggie wrote, "I have seen you for the last time . . . I have been deceived." She tried to return his love letters; he refused to take them back. She insisted, "I must either give you up from this moment on, or give up those who are very dear to me . . ." But Maggie also insisted he remember, "you have my love."

Visit by visit, letter by letter, Elisha persuaded and reassured Mother Fox. He said he had the utmost respect for Maggie's reputation. He said he would never harm her. Before Christmas, he asked permission to take his "friend" Maggie and her sister Kate for a sleigh ride in New York City. Perhaps softened by the holidays, Mother granted his request, which only encouraged Elisha's attentions and weakened Maggie's resolve.

By spring, he was sending Maggie gifts again, like the engraved portrait of himself created for his upcoming book. No matter what his family wanted, Elisha couldn't treat Maggie like a sister or a friend. He loved her. Whether or not the world would accept it, that was his truth.

One morning in April of 1856, Elisha attended a friend's funeral. He felt sickly, tired, aware of time passing. After the service, Elisha went directly to the Foxes'. Neither Maggie nor Kate nor Mother was at home. A flustered maid put him in the parlor.

When Maggie came in, Elisha jumped from behind the parlor door, startling her. He took her in his arms. Maggie pushed him away until she heard the words, "the betrothed wife of Dr. Kane." He took a ring

One of the first media images of Kate (left) and Maggie (right) Fox, an unflattering drawing compared to their actual photographs. Note the ring on Maggie's left hand, signifying an engagement.

from his finger, and gently placed it on the ring finger of her left hand. He kissed her hand, then her lips. Maggie loved Elisha too. That was her truth. Nothing else mattered. The couple told Kate and Mother that they were to be married. From that day on, Maggie's family and friends treated them as an engaged couple. Elisha's family wouldn't even meet her. But Maggie grew confident enough in Elisha's love to make fun of the judgmental Kanes, calling them "the Royal Family."

Though he still had not made the engagement public, Elisha "cared no longer . . . for the world's opinion or its sneers . . ." and acted like it. He traveled to New York, taking Maggie out often. They ate at fine restaurants and attended the opera.

Engravings of the Arctic from his upcoming book were previewed in the news media, increasing its soaring advance sales. Yet, the final manuscript was not finished. Elisha traveled to his publisher in Philadelphia as he put the finishing touches on the book. He hated to be without Maggie: "I really can not bear to leave." She wanted him home: "It is now five days since you left, and it seems a whole year to me. Oh, my lover and friend, hasten!"

Elisha was thirty-six and couldn't wait for independence from his family. Maggie was twenty-two and talked of wedding dresses and honeymooning in Italy. Elisha's busy work schedule meant he sometimes missed a date with Maggie. Her busy social life meant she attended parties while he was out of town (and yes, she probably still drank too much champagne). He could be insecure; she could be insensitive. She lightened him up; he brought her down to earth. Neither of them was perfect; yet Maggie and Elisha seemed destined for each other. He wished "to be shut out from the big world, gazing at your dark eyes . . ." Writing a letter in the midnight moonlight, she sent him "ten thousand kisses."

By May 1856, Kate, Mother, and Maggie had moved to a fine apartment in Manhattan. Kate supported them; she had well-paying clients who remained committed to her mediumship. Her first-floor séance parlor was luxurious: thick carpets, figured silk curtains, and rosewood armchairs. Kate presided over a mahogany séance table, dressed simply in a black silk gown with a gold cross around her neck almost like a kind of Spiritualist nun. The spirits rapped out answers or spelled out predictions using an alphabet card. Mother took on Leah's old role, confidently explaining any errors: "You must not be discouraged . . . the spirits at the start often get wrong . . ."

When Elisha was in New York, he avoided Kate's séances. Whenever Kate entertained clients, he and Maggie spent hours alone on the third floor, which contained a parlor and Maggie's bedroom. Elisha called this private upper floor "a sort of sanctuary; a retreat to which we are driven by mischief-making eyes and tongues. There, like wounded deer we escape the hunters." Maggie's notoriety had first brought them together. Elisha's celebrity had kept them apart. Both now understood that fame was a two-faced monster.

Elisha turned in his final manuscript just as the summer of 1856 ended, dramatically insisting, "The book . . . has been my coffin." He was stressed, suffering the chest pains and swollen joints of recurrent rheumatic fever. Elisha struggled through the remaining dates of a lecture tour, bedridden between appearances. Maggie was troubled, "I . . . twice dreamt that you were very, *very* ill; and I waked each time weeping bitterly."

They each had a trip planned. Maggie, along with Kate and Mother, went to visit family in Canada. As soon as his second book was published, Elisha would be sailing to England to present one of the first copies to Sir Franklin's widow in London. After he returned, Maggie and Elisha intended to spend the rest of their lives together enjoying "the simple pleasure of sitting by your side . . ."

In September, Maggie, her sister and mother returned from Canada just in time for the publication of Elisha's book. Reviewers called Kane's work "magnificent," "stirring," and recommended it "be in the hands of parents and school children" everywhere. Booksellers who had ordered a thousand copies found they could sell five thousand. Kane's *Arctic Explorations* sold 150,000 copies in its first six months. Best-seller status meant Elisha only had a few months before he would be free of his family's financial control.

He and Maggie spent two weeks together before he left for England.

One evening he clasped a diamond Tiffany bracelet on her wrist, "They will all know now, Maggie . . ." (though, by that point, an invitation to meet his family might have been more appreciated).

A few evenings later, Elisha was lying on a sofa in Maggie's third-floor parlor. It was getting dark; as usual, he didn't want to leave her. He hadn't felt well and was anxious about sailing to England. "If I send for you, my own Maggie, will you come to me?" he asked.

"Certainly, I will," she answered.

"I fear you would hesitate, and yet you know you are my own—my wife!" he cried, then called for everyone in the house to come up the stairs.

Elisha and Maggie stood. He held her hand, his left arm around her waist.

In front of Kate, Mother, a maid, and a female visitor, he reportedly said, "Maggie is my wife, and I am her husband. Wherever we are, she is mine, and I am hers. Do you understand and consent to this, Maggie?"

Maggie agreed.

This simple self-marriage ceremony was perfectly legal in places across nineteenth-century America. Elisha promised Maggie that he would announce the marriage as soon as he came back from England.

A few days later, she watched his carriage drive toward the docks. A few feet up the cobblestones, it stopped, Elisha leapt out, and ran back to Maggie.

"Tell me, shall I go, or stay?" he asked.

Yes, Maggie loved him; yes, she would miss him; but of course, he should go. Maggie wouldn't keep Elisha from his busy life. Their long-sought happy ending was in sight.

Elisha left for England on October 11, 1856.

He never returned.

(BEFORE MARRIAGE)

* * * And now dear Maggie, my own dear Maggie, live a life of purity and goodness. Consecrate it to me, wear no garb upon which even the breath of an angel could leave a stain. Thus live, dear Maggie, until God brings me back to you — and then meeting my eye with the proud consciousness of virtue — we will resign ourselves to a passion sanctified by love and marriage. Golden fields shall spread before us their summer harvests. Silver lakes mirror your very breath. Let us live for each other — Farewell!

E. K. Kane.

(AFTER MARRIAGE)

Dear Wife. — May I meet you at half past ten to night. I have a capital excuse for your Mother. Do not say no but send word the earliest hour and I'll be with you.

One of Elisha's letters was printed in the book *The Love Life of Dr. Kane* as proof that he addressed Maggie as his wife.

"I have had a life of sorrow . . ."

Chapter 23 "SCIENCE WEEPS, HUMANITY WEEPS, THE WORLD WEEPS"

On his way home to Maggie, Elisha's weak heart caused a series of strokes which left him paralyzed and speechless. He died at thirty-seven in Havana, Cuba, February 17, 1857.

On hearing the news, Maggie fell in a dead faint. She was carried to bed, where she lay for weeks, delirious with grief. Mother and Kate cared for her. John Fox made a rare trip to New York City to comfort his distraught daughter, staying for months. Horace Greeley, Mrs. Walter, and many other friends visited. Even Leah wrote to her estranged sister. Maggie was inconsolable.

Dr. Kane's body made its way across the sea to the port of New Orleans the same week as President James Buchanan's inauguration, on March 4, 1857. The newspapers ran stories on Dr. Kane's last hours, the inaugural ceremonies, and continuing violence between pro- and

Proslavery congressman Preston Brooks beat abolitionist Senator Charles Sumner on the floor of the US Senate, almost killing him, May 22, 1856.

antislavery factions. Days later, on March 6, abolitionists railed against the Supreme Court's Dred Scott ruling which declared that slaves were not citizens and therefore not entitled to federal protection.

President Buchanan, utterly failing to understand his country's deep divisions, tried to subdue public opinion by labeling slavery's expansion "a matter of but little practical importance." Despite the President's words, the issues around slavery were so important that a few radical Southern (and some Northern) politicians threatened to break the United States apart: "I am for disunion." These politicians spoke of secession, starting a new country and ending the American experiment—the world's oldest democracy.

Still, for a few weeks, the fracturing country united in grief over the loss of Dr. Elisha Kent Kane, America's Arctic hero. As a series of steamboats and trains carried Elisha's body from Louisiana to Pennsylvania, thousands of Americans stood on riverbanks and alongside railroad tracks weeping, hats in hands, hands over hearts. This kind of nation-

Elisha Kent Kane's body lying in state at Philadelphia's Independence Hall

wide outpouring of love for a celebrity had never been seen before. Dr. Kane was making his way home for the last time. When Elisha's body reached Philadelphia a banner in the street proclaimed, "Science Weeps, Humanity Weeps, the World Weeps."

Elisha's corpse lay in state for three days at Philadelphia's Independence Hall. Crew members of the USS *Advance* draped the ship's tattered American flag over his coffin. Atop the flag lay his Navy sword with a mysterious floral wreath, "To the Memory of Dr. E. K. Kane, from Two Ladies." None of the Fox family, not even Maggie, attended his funeral; they weren't welcome. Elisha was buried on March 14, 1857, in the Kane family mausoleum, next to his little brother Willie.

Lost in grief, Maggie read and reread Elisha's last letter, "Dear Tutie, I am quite sick; and have gone to Havana; only one week from New

York. I have received no letters from you . . ."But Maggie *had* written him often, nearly every day. Newspapers had reported that Elisha was very sick. His mother and brother had kept a vigil at his bedside in Cuba. When Maggie had realized that the Kanes were keeping her letters away from Elisha, she had packed up and arranged passage to go to him. Now it was too late.

Maggie's weight plummeted. The long, shining hair that Elisha had loved was now dull and shorn. Scandalous rumors circulated about the couple's self-marriage. One Kane family letter suggested that Maggie had a child by Elisha. Whether or not this was true, whether the infant lived, and if so, who may have raised it, is entirely unknown. Maggie's deep depression lingered. Her friends and family worried about her future.

Mother Fox believed the Kane family should support Maggie as Elisha's widow. Elisha had promised that if anything happened to him, Maggie would be cared for. He had said he would leave money in his will for Maggie's support. Though Maggie's name wasn't mentioned, Elisha's will did list a separate, mysterious bequest of five thousand dollars (over $150,000 today) entrusted to his brother, Robert Kane. The will stated that instructions for this money would be found among Elisha's private papers. In April of 1857, Mrs. Fox wrote to Robert Kane asking about the bequest for Maggie; he didn't respond.

A little over nine months since she last saw Elisha, Maggie reached out to Robert Kane on her own behalf. She was not seeking money, but comfort, "I know the Dr. must have left some message for me." If Elisha *had* left Maggie a message before his death, Robert Kane had no intention of delivering it.

Neither Robert nor the Kane family believed that the couple's self-marriage was legal or believed it had even occurred. Under no circumstances was spirit rapper Maggie Fox to be treated as Dr. Elisha

Kane's widow. Especially now. Elisha turned out to be richer dead than he'd ever been while alive. The royalties from his second book flowed to his family—sixty thousand dollars in the first six months after his death (close to two million dollars today).

While Maggie wrote heartfelt words about her lost love, Robert sent Maggie short, polite notes. He visited her more than once to get Elisha's letters returned to the Kane family. Maggie refused: "the letters are mine to guard and cherish as long as I live . . . But do not think me so lost as to ever allow them to be published."

Maggie, considering herself a widow, dressed in mourning clothes and honored Elisha's memory in every way. She wrote politely and humbly, conducting herself as her husband would have expected. She kept away from mediumship; she tried to prove herself worthy of a place in the Kane family.

Robert Kane did not honor Elisha's will. Instead, he sent Maggie random sums—fifty dollars, ten dollars, fifteen dollars—to keep her quiet. The last thing Robert or his family wanted was the newspapers getting hold of Elisha's letters or asking Maggie for details about their so-called marriage.

Maggie was trapped between society's expectations for her gender, her profession, and her class. She didn't want to be a financial burden on her sister Kate, yet had to stay away from the séance table. She didn't trust the Kane family, yet needed their support. She didn't want to ruin Elisha's reputation, yet wanted to save her own. The correspondence between Maggie Fox and Robert Kane resulted in a standoff. He kept most of Elisha's money. She kept most of Elisha's letters.

"we were called upon by these old wretches to show our rapping . . ."

Chapter 24 WHEN FADS FADE

By mid-year of 1857, newspapers—even the *New-York Tribune*—now made "jibes at the Rochester rappers, of whom it used to be the champions," and warned against Spiritualism in any form. Reporters across the nation quoted experts on the connection between spirit belief and mental disturbance.

By one account, 573 people throughout the United States had been sent to asylums due to spirit-rapping obsessions and at least seventeen had committed suicide. The old fad of spirit circles was no joke. Spiritualism could be dangerous to vulnerable people.

John Fairbanks was an energetic, associate editor at *Scientific American*. But John had suffered two major losses in the past two years—the end of a long romance and his sister's death. Fellow lodgers at his New York City boardinghouse worried as the typically cheerful, young Fairbanks grew gloomy and distracted. John found great comfort in reading Spiritualist publications and started frequenting mediums.

Soon, Fairbanks was cornering office mates with wild talk about good and evil spirits. His fourth-floor neighbors were kept awake while John engaged in late-night spirit conversation "although he was quite alone." The young man said he'd contacted his dead sister and would see her one day in the heavenly Summerland.

On a rainy Saturday morning in early May 1857, John left his apartment and climbed up one flight. He let himself into an empty flat, opened a window, and walked out to meet his sister's spirit, falling five stories to his death.

Taking this and other tragic reports to heart, the editors of the *Boston Courier* intended to protect the American public by settling the "miserable delusion" of spirits once and for all (while hoping to increase readership, too). The *Courier* offered $500 (over $15,000 today) to any medium who could prove spirit communication to a committee of Harvard University science professors.

Three days of test séances were planned. A committee of Spiritualists negotiated and accepted all the conditions. At least seven famous mediums took on the *Courier*'s challenge, among them the Davenport brothers, teenage mediums whose impossible escapes from spirit cabinets were the latest in spiritual manifestations.

As Maggie no longer practiced mediumship, Leah and Kate were invited to appear before the *Courier* committee, all expenses paid. On June 25, 1857, Leah and Kate arrived as planned at apartment "No. 12" in Boston's Albion Building, where six Spiritualist believers greeted them. Four famous Harvard professors entered, trailed by assistants and an assortment of newspaper folks.

As the Spiritualists had requested, a large wooden board had been raised on wood strips, creating a low platform. A pine table about four feet square sat in the middle of that platform, surrounded by five or six chairs.

The Davenport Brothers, William (far left) and Ira (far right), in their spirit cabinet. Musical instruments were heard playing behind the cabinet doors even when the brothers were securely tied, allegedly proving spirit action.

Leah took her place at the table, Kate sat opposite, and three of the six believers joined them. The other believers, the professors, and the newsmen sat outside the circle to observe the actions of the mediums and participants. The séance began.

Rap . . . rap, rap . . . rap . . . rap.

The sounds were faint, irregular, not the confident sounds typically heard. Believers in the room worriedly asked the spirits if the room was the right temperature for manifestations.

Rap. Rap. Rap.

Yes. The spirits felt fine.

The Harvard men asked the believers to define the spirit manifestations. Leah said she felt the sounds throughout her body like "an electric shock." Another believer said the spirits were "a magnetic, electric force, going out from the person, and imponderable; this force comes in contact with . . . the mind."

These explanations left Harvard's science professors dumbfounded. Were the spirits making sounds, harnessing magnetism, or conducting electricity? Was this force physical or not physical? Did it affect the body or the mind? One sarcastic newsman in the room mused, "The spiritual force will appear to be a visible, imponderable, sound, which presents an idea mystical enough for the purposes only of those willing to see, hear and believe any thing and every thing."

The indefinable spirits grew louder.

Rap. Rap. Rap . . . Rap . . . Rap. Rap.

Yet, the raps were only heard when the investigators were talking among themselves; and not focused on the sisters. Most questions were answered inaccurately when they were answered at all.

Once the traditional table séance failed, other methods were suggested to bring forth the spirits. Leah and Kate stood—one on a chair, the other on a stool. A few faint raps were heard near them, so one of the investigators began.

Will you rap ten times? Silence. More silence.

The impatient scientists began talking and . . .

Rap. Rap. Rap. Rap. Rap. Rap. Rap. Rap. Rap. Rap.

Will you rap six times? Six hesitant raps sounded. No further answers were received.

Kate stood on a pine box and asked one of the men to listen closely. He put his ear to the box's corner but heard nothing at all. Kate stepped off, turned away, and then . . .

Rap. Rap.

One of the professor's assistants had rapped on the box with his knuckles while no one was looking. It sounded exactly like the Fox sisters' spirit sounds. The morning session ended.

As soon as they resumed for the afternoon session, raps sounded, and questioning began.

Are any spirits present?

Rap. Rap. Rap.

Yes.

One of the professors asked, *Are any of my friends here?*

Rap. Rap. Rap.

Yes.

Can you give your name? Silence.

The table was extended so that everyone in the room could sit together. Yet, two of the men insisted on observing from outside the circle. Questions were asked. Sometimes they heard raps, other times none; most seemed nearest Leah.

At this point, even a dedicated Spiritualist admitted, "The replies were confused." Another "thought they might be deceptive spirits, disposed to make sport of us." Leah declared that she felt "resisting influences" in the room.

The professors took Leah's opinion seriously and asked the spirits to identify any "resistors" by rapping. They called the name of each person present; the spirits didn't make a peep. Leah and Kate were invited to return another day. They refused.

The next two days of investigations went worse for the other mediums. The Harvard professors cooperated with all the mediums' requests, but carefully observed their actions at every moment and studied the room before and after the sessions. The Davenport brothers escaped from their spirit cabinet, but one of the professors discovered a piece of broken thread on the floor. The *Courier*'s Harvard professors dismissed them outright: "Good night, gentlemen."

Except for the Fox sisters' erratic rapping, none of the other mediums produced a single manifestation for the *Boston Courier* committee. No tables lifted. No instruments played. No messages were received. The newspaper kept its $500.

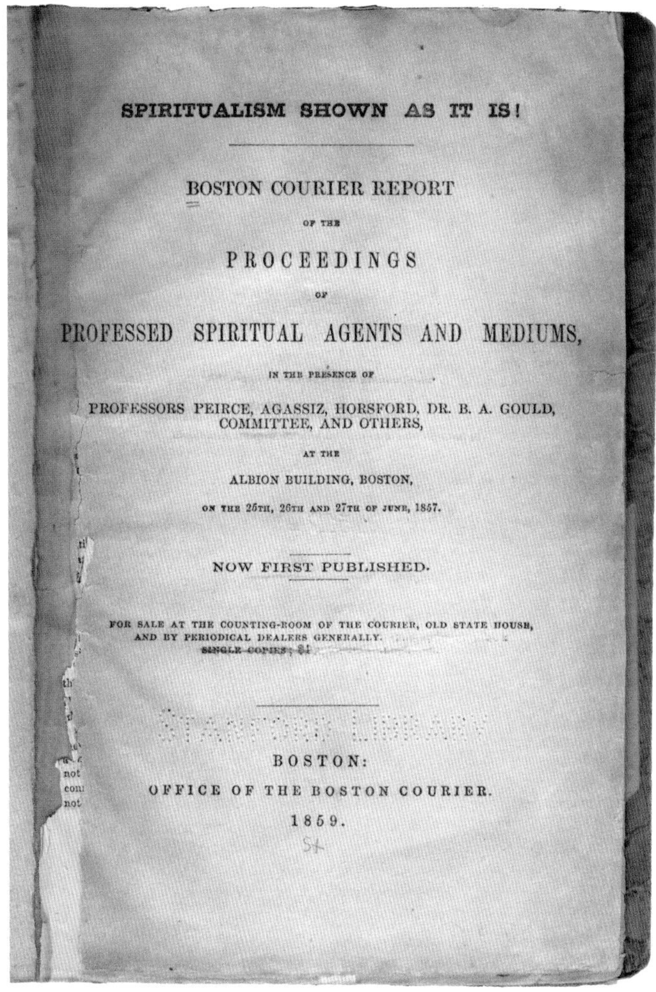

SPIRITUALISM SHOWN AS IT IS!

BOSTON COURIER REPORT

OF THE

PROCEEDINGS

OF

PROFESSED SPIRITUAL AGENTS AND MEDIUMS,

IN THE PRESENCE OF

PROFESSORS PEIRCE, AGASSIZ, HORSFORD, DR. B. A. GOULD, COMMITTEE, AND OTHERS,

AT THE

ALBION BUILDING, BOSTON,

ON THE 25TH, 26TH AND 27TH OF JUNE, 1857.

NOW FIRST PUBLISHED.

FOR SALE AT THE COUNTING-ROOM OF THE COURIER, OLD STATE HOUSE, AND BY PERIODICAL DEALERS GENERALLY.

SINGLE COPIES, $1

BOSTON:

OFFICE OF THE BOSTON COURIER.

1859.

The final report from the *Boston Courier*'s contest

The Harvard professors signed a statement: "Any connection with spiritualist circles, so called, corrupts the morals and degrades the intellect." The *Boston Courier*'s official report stated, "with every opportunity, means and motive to do their best, the spiritualists actually did nothing . . ." and proudly announced, "So ends this ridiculous and infamous imposture." The spirit trend didn't dissolve overnight, but skeptics had now exposed fraud often enough that belief among the general public was fading fast.

Leah and Kate returned to New York; but by the end of August, money was tight. An economic crisis, the Panic of 1857, had gripped the United States and the world. Large businesses began to fail and railroad stocks plummeted. People defaulted on loans, leaving banks shaken, and unemployment rising. People simply had no extra money to spend on spirit circles.

Horace Greeley came to the rescue. Because he traveled often to lecture, Greeley needed caretakers for his New York City townhouse. Mother, Kate, and Maggie began to live there rent-free.

Leah still earned enough to keep her own apartment where she led private séances mostly for long-term clients. When her old friend George Willets, one of their original Rochester supporters, moved to New Jersey, he wanted to introduce his new neighbors to the spirits that had given his family so much comfort over the years. Once a week, Leah began traveling to Jersey City to hold regular séances at various homes for Willets's circle.

Leah's followers wondered when she would produce new manifestations. The Spiritualist press ran stories about the more recent phenomenon of "apport" mediums, who channeled spirits that dropped gifts, like lilies or doves, into the laps of séance attendees. Leah's followers would have read about "direct voice" mediums too. These were typically female mediums who were entranced and spoke in the spirits' voices. Nineteenth-century séance attendees had the jaw-dropping experience of watching delicate lady mediums taken over by coarse sailor's spirits and cursing up a storm direct from Summerland.

Leah needed to stay current; rapping was not enough. For Willits's New Jersey friends, she finally agreed to attempt "mysteries hitherto unknown in the age of the world."

One rainy fall evening in 1857, a crowd of men and women sat shoulder to shoulder at her New Jersey hosts' parlor table. Leah's new friend, Mr. Daniel Underhill, had come with her by train from New York City. Mr. Underhill was a wealthy insurance executive who had first experimented with Spiritualism when he'd been widowed a few years back.

Leah asked for complete darkness as she began the ceremony. Though Daniel Underhill, George Willets, and others were dedicated believers, some of the guests were experiencing the spirits for the first time. When Leah rubbed her hands together, they sparkled, and the inexperienced company shouted their amazement.

Shouting was not allowed; every believer knew the spirits needed a calm atmosphere. When the company "could not or would not, for lack of common sense . . . follow all the directions," Leah brought her hosts, and a few more experienced believers, into an adjoining bathroom.

The door was closed. In the pitch-black room, Leah's hands now blazed with yellow spirit lights. Twinkling spirits bounced off the tiled surfaces. As the manifestations persisted, Leah felt faint. She rushed to the faucet to let cold water run over her burning hands.

Believing Leah was overcome by the spirits, her hostess took her out into the yard for some fresh air. Leah plunged her hands into the cool, wet earth, and quickly felt better. The hostess and the medium returned inside to receive congratulations on such a successful spirit evening. Leah returned to New York City accompanied by the spirit-believing, newly smitten Mr. Underhill.

The next evening, Leah's hostess took a walk in her yard. She saw white smoke rising from a patch in the ground! The earth that Leah had touched glowed faintly with yellow light. Her hostess found granules of a white substance in the dirt. It turned out to be the chemical phosphorus, known to light up when it hits the air.

As word spread of this discovery, many of the New Jersey guests cried fraud, claiming that Leah had coated her hands with phosphorous before the séance. Leah insisted she had no knowledge of the chemical; but long-time believer George Willets was embarrassed. Leah told Willets that perhaps spirits could materialize phosphorous, the way they apported flowers and doves. Her old friend Willets asked her to prove it.

Leah traveled to New Jersey again and again for test séances. Each time, her hands were examined, judged clean, plunged into sealed boxes of dirt; and found to produce solid phosphorous granules. To believers, this proved that spirits produced the chemical. But to skeptics, it only proved Leah was a very skilled trickster. Rumors that the oldest Fox sister had cheated would not die.

"I am a Catholic . . ."

Chapter 25 FOR WORSE FOR BETTER, FOR POORER FOR RICHER

There was talk about Maggie too. She could not accept Elisha's death. Before making any decision, no matter how small, people said that she asked, "Would dear Elisha like me to do this?" She was haunted by memories of her dead love, living in the past, still trying to please him.

Maggie remembered that Elisha had at one time suggested she convert to Roman Catholicism. The Catholic Church had strict rules against necromancy, communication with the dead. Elisha had thought that Catholic rituals might suit her interest in mystery, acting as a bridge away from Spiritualism. Maggie studied with a priest and joined the Catholic Church on August 15, 1858.

Since the days of the Puritans, America's Protestant majority frequently expressed prejudice against the Roman Catholic Church.

During the decade of Spiritualism's rise, immigration to the United States was growing. Well over a million new immigrants came from a single country, Ireland. The Irish immigrants were typically Catholic and very poor. Many native-born Americans "regarded the Irish as intruders and treated them as inferiors." News articles of the time criticized and stereotyped Catholics, the Pope, the Irish, and immigrants in general.

These same papers zealously covered Maggie's conversion to what was considered an alien religion: "Recantation of a Spiritualist," "Baptism of Miss (Spirit Rapper) Fox," "A Remarkable Conversion." Untruths filled these hastily written articles. One said that Maggie was the youngest Fox sister. Another claimed that Maggie converted to escape the devil. A few more implied that she had accused Kate and Leah of fraud.

The story of Maggie's baptism appeared in hundreds of papers, in big cities (Boston, Chicago, London, Belfast) and small towns (Maysville, California; Steubenville, Ohio; Shepton Mallet, England). The articles discussed who attended, what Maggie wore, and how the church looked. Some reports included the entire Catholic ritual, word for word; "it is so strange that what ever I may do finds its way to the newspapers . . . ," Maggie mused.

Her Catholic conversion did not provide Maggie the peace of mind she sought. She could not escape public interest in her life or the pain of missing Elisha. Maggie drank, often until she passed out, trying to escape her sadness.

Maggie also couldn't escape her lack of funds. Kate was not making enough to support herself, Mother, and Maggie also. An acquaintance named Elizabeth Ellet encouraged Maggie to fight for her legal rights as Elisha's widow. Ellet was that rare thing in the nineteenth century, not only a female author but one who had written about both women and scandals before. With Maggie's input, Ellet ghostwrote a book about

Maggie and Elisha's relationship. The famous Maggie Fox, who once earned more than most American men, now used her treasured love story to blackmail the Kanes for enough money to live on.

Robert Kane received notice that Ellet had prepared a book manuscript and that it contained transcripts of Elisha's letters to Maggie. Robert acted immediately, agreeing to a sum for Maggie's living expenses if she'd stop the book's publication. Maggie agreed and the book was not released. But Robert backtracked, he didn't pay Maggie; instead, he sent her Catholic priest a smaller portion of the money than he had promised.

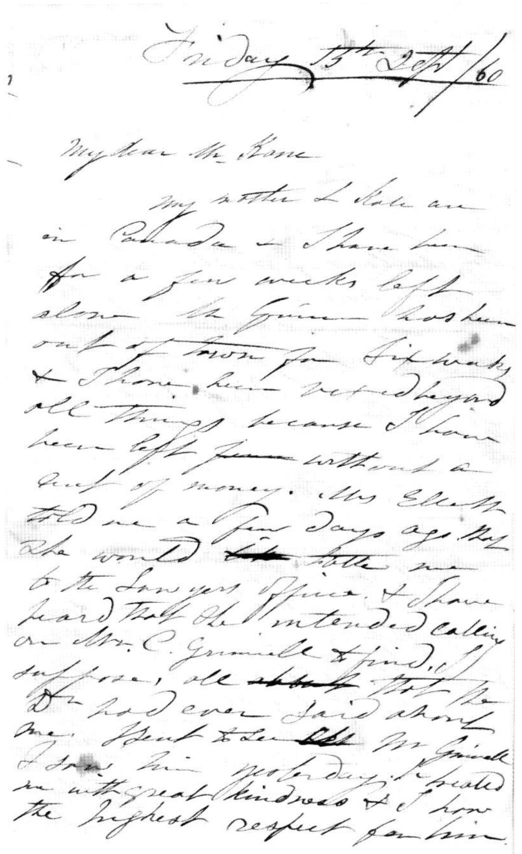

Friday 15th Sept /60

My dear Mr Kane

My mother & Kate are in Canada – I have been for a few weeks left alone the Grinnells have been out of town for six weeks & I have been vexed beyond all things because I have been left without a cent of money. Mrs Ellet told me a few days ago that she would take me to the Lawyers Office & I have heard that she intended calling on Mr C. Grinnell & find, I suppose, all that the Dr had ever said about me. I sent to see Mr Grinnell I saw him yesterday he treated me with great kindness & I have the highest respect for him

A scrawled letter from Maggie Fox to Elisha's brother, Robert Kane, September 15, 1860

Maggie's letters to Robert Kane swung wildly between resentment and melancholy: "The Margaret that Dr. Kane loved is dead. I am simply a Margaret without a heart, void of love or affection . . ." Lines scrawl across the page, as if written in a drunken state. The Kane family had not recognized the beautiful, famous Maggie Fox as Elisha's fiancée. They had less reason to recognize a drunk, unstable, former star as his widow.

From the surviving evidence, the Kanes could have afforded to support Maggie from Elisha's book royalties alone. Instead, they hardly paid and begrudged her every cent. Maggie publicly claimed the name, Margaret Fox Kane. But the name change didn't change reality—Elisha's family would not accept her. Her depression, her drinking, and her financial worries continued.

The rich and successful Leah (Fox, Fish, Brown) Underhill after her third marriage, around 1860

Leah never worried about money once she married again at the age of forty-five (while insisting she was in her late thirties). On November 2, 1858, her wedding to insurance executive Daniel Underhill took place in the Greeleys' town-home parlor. Though Daniel was a firm spirit believer, he insisted that Leah retire from public mediumship "to a quiet, well-ordered life . . ." Leah agreed (and after that humiliating experience in New Jersey, who wouldn't?).

Daniel bought Leah a four-story brownstone on New York's West Thirty-Seventh Street. She spent her days needlepointing cushions and playing the piano. She received guests in her front parlor with its cranberry glass chandeliers and blue velvet curtains.

The Underhill home filled with laughter as young nieces and nephews came for long visits. Some of them stayed so long, they called Leah "Ma." Daniel's daughter from his first marriage lived with them, too. Leah's daughter, Lizzie, must have lived nearby with her husband, as she saw these younger relatives off and on. But there is little evidence that Lizzie visited (or had much of a relationship at all) with her mother.

Daniel took care of Leah well. He surprised her with an aviary full of rare songbirds off their elegant dining room. When the birds sang, Leah sang along. Daniel said, "It was good for her to have the competition." His once driven, business-minded wife seemed totally content as a middle-class housewife. The spirits that Leah had called forth blessed her with abundance.

But the Spiritualist religion she had helped create was no longer growing. Despite the faith's promises of worldwide harmony, the year 1859 found the United States anything but peaceful. That October, militant abolitionist John Brown attempted to seize guns and start a revolt of enslaved people to destroy American slavery. He led fourteen white men and five black men on a raid of the government armory at Harpers Ferry, Virginia. Brown and his men were surrounded by US troops, shooting began, and ten of Brown's raiders were killed. A wounded John Brown was captured, tried, and hanged for treason. In the South, his execution was celebrated as the death of a dangerous terrorist. In the North, church bells tolled for Brown, a martyr to abolition. Little now held the country together; North and South no longer agreed on right and wrong.

Using language borrowed from those fighting the wrongs of slavery, Leah would champion Modern Spiritualists as "those [who] dared to stand before the world and battle for the right." Though officially retired, Leah's presence at séances was missed by her former clients; still her commitment to the cause continued.

By 1860, roughly two years after their marriage, Daniel allowed Leah to lead a few private séances once again. These social evenings at the Underhill home were run twice a month as a courtesy for believing admirers.

At one such gathering on October 13, 1860, Leah and Kate led a group that included Spiritualist Robert Dale Owen and his friend. The two men had come to investigate the strength of Kate and Leah's powers. At the Underhill's massive mahogany dining table, the alphabet was called.

Rap. Rap. Rap. Rap. Rap. Rap.

"Darken."

Rap. Rap. Rap. Rap. Rap. Rap. Rap. Rap. Rap.

"Join hands."

When the instructions were obeyed, participants were rewarded with dainty spirit lights near the floor. The lights grew larger, took shape in an outline of spirit hands, resting first behind Leah's head, then Kate's. The table rose, suspended for several seconds at a time.

The investigation-minded men had come prepared with a large steel scale. The table's weight was recorded at 120 pounds. The séance, and a test of the spirits' powers began—

Make the table lighter.

Slowly the scale moved, 100 . . . 80 . . . 60 pounds.

Make the table heavier.

Now the scale went in the other direction, 120 . . . 130 . . . 140 pounds.

This amazing demonstration set Robert Dale Owen on a path as a prominent investigator and spokesperson for the truth of Spiritualism. He would later explain his utter faith in the spirits as due to Kate's innocence, "She is one of the most simple-minded and strictly impulsive young persons I have ever met: as incapable of framing, or carrying on any deliberate scheme of imposition as a ten-year-old child is of administering a government."

On October 25, 1860, Owen arrived at the Greeley townhome where Kate, Mother, and Maggie resided. On being introduced to Maggie that night, he asked her to join his test séance. Mother and Kate knew Maggie hadn't called the spirits in years. Maggie surprised everyone. She agreed.

The doors to the parlor were locked. The company sat. The room was darkened. Spirit lights appeared.

BAM! BAM! BAM! BAM! BAM!

The center of the table shook as if a strong man was clubbing someone to death. Violent manifestations hadn't occurred since the early spirit days in Rochester. The frightened Mr. Owen wanted the lights turned up immediately. He examined the table. Neither the rough underside nor the polished top had a single scratch. It never occurred to him to question the sad, frustrated (perhaps drunk) woman who had joined them.

Maggie's Catholic faith required her to stay away from spirit contact. She was angry at herself for falling into old habits and agreeing to participate in Owen's séance. Soon afterward, Maggie moved out of the Greeleys' townhome to her own tiny apartment on New York's Barclay Street. She survived on the pittance the Kane family paid to keep her quiet, probably with extra support from family and old friends. Maggie hung black curtains in a closeted area, put up a portrait of Elisha, and surrounded it with flowers, letters, and candles like a saint's shrine. She spent hours in front of this memorial altar, drowning in sadness.

Maggie wrote Robert Kane obsessive, troubling letters,

> *Mr. Kane,*
>
> *I am afraid that I shall be insane. I have no longer slept neither day or night. I am fearfully frightened . . . Today I was better but it will not last . . .*
>
> *Margaret Fox*
>
> *[P.S.] Write at once.*

Two years after Elisha's death, she wrote her love a poem, "Oh, that I could die and be with thee!" Her wish was not granted. Maggie Fox lived on, alone and struggling.

By autumn of 1860, Americans struggled with the spread of armed conflicts over slavery, and American newspapers reflected the country's grim mood. Column space for joking articles about ghosts and gossip diminished as the idea of Southern secession grew more common. Two years prior, in 1858, a US Senate candidate from Illinois named Abraham Lincoln had predicted his troubled country's future, "A house divided against itself cannot stand. I believe this government cannot endure permanently half-slave and half-free. I do not expect the Union to be dissolved—but I do expect it will cease to be divided. It will become all one thing, or all the other."

Lincoln lost his senatorial race. Later running on a platform to prevent territorial slavery and preserve the Union, he was elected president on November 6, 1860. Threatened by Lincoln's stance against expanding slavery, South Carolina seceded in December. Before Lincoln's inauguration in March of 1861, Florida, Alabama, Georgia, Louisiana, and Texas had joined the secession movement and formed the Confederate States of America.

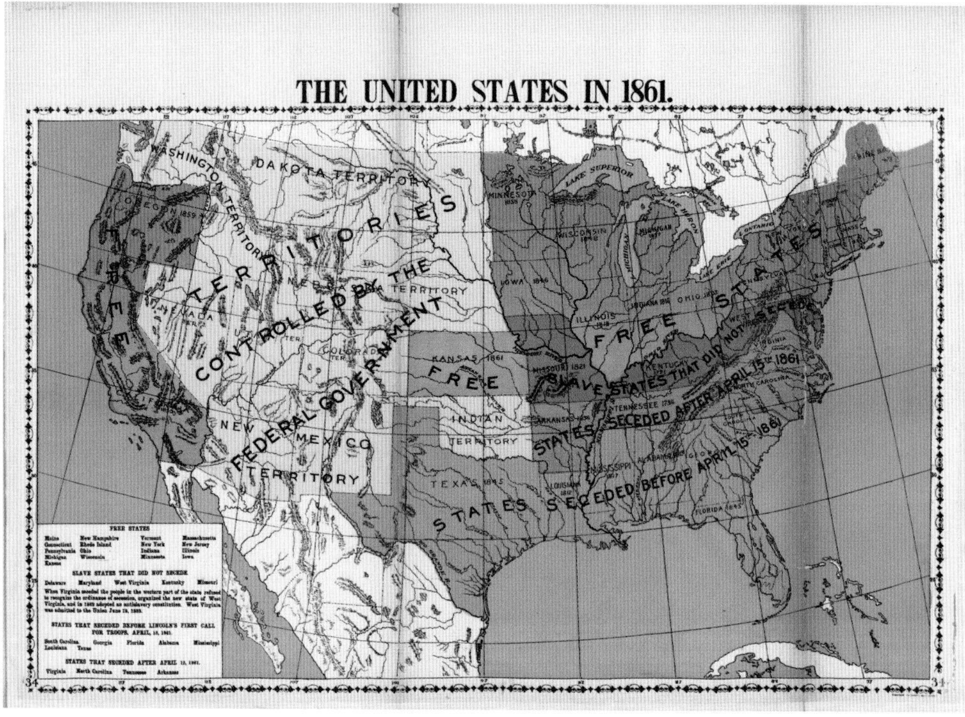

A map of the United States in 1861 shows the nation's divisions over slavery.

President Lincoln would not accept secession; he hoped to reunite the country without resorting to war. But Confederate forces began seizing United States property including military forts located in the south. Both the Union and Confederate governments stockpiled rifles and cannons in anticipation of conflict. The press and the public were on edge. No one knew when the war over slavery would start or what it could cost the country.

Even Horace Greeley, once so hopeful about the spirits, admitted that an evening spent "for two dreary, mortal hours in a darkened room . . . waiting for some one's disembodied grandfather or aunt to tip a table . . . ," seemed out of step with the seriousness of the times. When they wrote about spirits at all, most newspapers concentrated their efforts on exposing mediums as frivolous and fraudulent.

A parlor table with a rapping mechanism built inside that could be activated by means of a hidden lever

133. Spirit Table Lifting.

Same effect as above. Larger table used, and when started to move two or three persons cannot hold the table down. Requires operator and one assistant, suitable for gen-

tlemen only. Can be done anywhere with sleeves rolled up. Price................**$12.50**

134. Spirit Talking Glass Bell.

This is a fine clear cut glass bell, which can be examined minutely, and then placed on a wand, held in medium's hand when it commences to ring exactly as desired, tolling any number required, thus answering any question asked of it. Can be used anywhere at any time. Will also ring when placed on a skeleton stand. Complete, including bell, skeleton stand and wand.................~~**$15.00**~~ $18.00

135. New Spirit Glass Clock.

Polished plate glass clock dial, with handsome ornamental brass pointer. Gold num-

—17—

A page from *Gambols with the Ghosts*, a secretive catalog for mediums, listing tools of the trade, printed around 1900

News stories specified how mediums were caught mid-séance using tools to trick the public. Telescoping rods helped move objects in the dark. Tables were found to have rapping hammers inside. One such cabinetmaker boasted he'd make "two or twenty more if I can be paid for it." War loomed on the horizon; he may as well make a profit: "If people will give a dollar a piece to hear a little hammer strike inside a table bed, and run crazy about it, it is not my fault."

The alleged secrets of mediumship were divulged in booklets, often written by working magicians. Sealed envelopes could be expertly slit open; blank slates could be exchanged for those written in advance. There were rumors of "blue books" circulating among mediums. These books supposedly contained details on people who regularly attended séances—living and dead relatives, important dates, work histories, the questions asked, and answers given at prior sessions. Any medium who possessed this kind of information could seem like a miracle worker.

Some mediums straight-out confessed to fraud in newspapers, books, or magazines. Still, some long-term believers stayed true to the cause, unable or unwilling to accept facts. Believers developed conspiratorial theories to explain the mysterious relationship between mediums and spirits. They insisted that mischievous spirits could control mediums and force them to cheat. If a medium was caught cheating once, or even many times, followers insisted that didn't mean they cheated always. There were plenty who believed that the phenomena produced by the best mediums, Kate and Maggie Fox for example, were absolutely authentic.

Though they may have been suspected of fraud, at no time were the two youngest Fox sisters caught outright using chemicals, tools, or collaborators. Whatever the rapping peddler had first taught them, they learned well. The truth about Maggie and Kate's spirits remained hidden.

"She had many wealthy patrons here in New York—
Mr. Livermore, a wealthy banker . . ."

Chapter 26 THE WONDROUS MISS KATE

At twenty-three years of age, Kate Fox had spent more than half her life at the séance table. Still, the newspapers had always focused less on her than her two sisters. Leah had managed their careers and was often called upon as a spokesperson for Spiritualism. Maggie's dramatic romance and abandonment of mediumship made for great copy. Few news stories centered on the youngest Fox sister. Her opinions were rarely sought; she had no known romances to feed gossip. Kate Fox simply kept working—following where the spirits led.

They led her to Charles Livermore in January of 1861. Charles, a young, successful banker, had been passionately dedicated to his beautiful wife, Estelle. Estelle had died the year before, and Charles struggled to live without her. Spiritualist friends suggested a séance with Kate Fox might bring Livermore some much-needed peace.

Kate Fox in her early twenties, around 1860

Charles scheduled one session with Kate Fox, but was soon seeing her twice a week. They sometimes met at Kate's but most often in the parlor at Livermore's New York City home. On rare occasions one of Livermore's relatives or friends attended these sessions; but most evenings Charles and Kate sat alone, in the dark, holding hands.

Charles considered himself a skeptic. He kept a diary of séance specifics, noting weather conditions and the level of darkness in the room. Before the sessions began, the room was typically searched, the windows sealed, and the doors locked.

In their first séances, raps sounded, the tables lifted, and lights floated. While Kate called the alphabet, Charles received rapped messages from a spirit claiming to be his wife, that began, "**My dear** . . ."

After about a dozen sessions, Charles Livermore felt a spirit's touch. After more than two dozen, the spirit announced, "**I know that I can make myself visible to you** . . ."

In her years of séance work, Kate Fox had developed remarkable talents. She could transcribe spirit messages using either hand. Many of these communications were written backward, able to be read only in a mirror. Kate was able to mirror-write a message using her right hand, call the alphabet when raps sounded, and take down a separate rapped message with her left hand, at the same time. Whether or not they proved spirit intervention, Kate's skills were astounding.

On April 12, 1861, Confederate guns fired outside the Union Army's Fort Sumter. The long-feared Civil War began. That same week, inside Charles Livermore's parlor, Kate's spirit talents expanded to include the impossible.

It was Charles's forty-third spirit session. Though the weather was mild, the smell of a spring storm was in the air. At the mahogany parlor table, Charles and Kate sat, his left hand in her right, her left hand in his right. In this intimate circle they waited for any communication from Estelle's spirit. A silent half hour passed; Charles grew discouraged.

RAP!

The table rose and fell. The door rattled forcefully, the windows opened and shut; according to Charles, "everything movable in the room seemed in motion." A shape rose from the floor and loomed behind Kate in the darkness.

The hazy shape floated in the air and came to rest between Kate and Charles. Electricity crackled and popped like indoor lightning. The shape, "surrounded by a semi-circle of light about eighteen inches in diameter," formed itself into what looked like a human head. Some type of gauzy fabric wound beneath the chin; but Charles could not make out a face. The brilliantly lit head receded into the darkness, then returned to float in front of him once more. Raps instructed Charles to look closer.

Squinting into the bright light, an astonished Charles Livermore saw "a human eye" looking back at him.

The glowing head backed away, came forward once more. Charles made out a delicate hand holding an ethereal fabric veil across its face. The ghostly hand kept the lower half of the face covered but pulled back the fabric above the nose. Charles recognized, "*the upper half of the face of my wife*, the eyes, forehead and expression . . ." It was Estelle!

Kate Fox had brought his wife back from the dead.

As the figure moved, Charles heard silk rustling. He noticed Estelle's graceful arms and long, luxuriant hair, noting that "its shade of color, appeared like the natural tresses of my wife." Charles "asked her to kiss me if she could." Her arm wound round his neck, and he was kissed through a gauzy spirit substance. She wrapped her silky hair around his face and kissed him again. The electric crackling increased; the figure turned away. Charles gazed at his wife's brilliant spirit; five minutes turned to fifteen and still her figure remained.

This 1870s photograph shows famed medium Florence Cook slumped on a chair in an unconscious trance with a materialized spirit named Katie King standing behind her.

After half an hour, raps spelled out, "**Now see me rise.**" The spirit form sped toward the ceiling, then disappeared. *Where was she? There!* Estelle's face materialized in a mirror on the wall. The coming storm suddenly broke, rain crashed against the windows, "**The atmosphere has changed. I cannot remain in form.**" Estelle was gone.

The spirit of Estelle appeared to Charles Livermore throughout the summer of 1861, as the first battles of the Civil War were fought. Each time, she seemed more substantial—her hair pulled back with "a single, white rose," her perfume smelling of "freshly gathered violets." Estelle touched Charles's hands, head, shoulders; her passionate kisses were "audible in every part of the room." For a time, an enthralled Charles Livermore hired Kate Fox to work for him exclusively.

When the spirits wrote messages through Kate, Charles marked the stationery used in the séance, to verify that it hadn't been switched. One evening, he watched as a luminous hand took a sheet of paper he had previously marked and wrote while hovering "three or four inches from the carpet." The paper was returned with a loving note, his mark still intact. Charles recognized Estelle's handwriting and her perfect French, "not a word of which was understood by Miss Fox." One night, his papers and pencils were knocked to the parlor floor by Estelle's unearthly white gown which grew more solid, more real with each session.

As the months passed, the Civil War, imagined as potentially quick, became long-term reality for the American people. The battles continued; Union and Confederate troops traded small victories and bigger losses. In late July, the fighting intensified at the First Battle of Bull Run near Manassas, Virginia. Death marched alongside the roughly 18,000 barely trained soldiers from both North and South. It was an unsettling Confederate victory; in less than twelve hours, about a thousand men lay in a grassy field, never to rise again.

By February 1862, more than two thousand soldiers had been killed, and roughly a hundred thousand had been wounded in dozens of minor skirmishes and major battles. Soldiers died in combat, from wounds, and most often from epidemics of infectious diseases such as dysentery, typhoid fever, or measles. Eventually, so many casualties were racked up on both sides that no one knew how many soldiers had arrived in the land of the spirits. Interest in talking to the dead ticked up once more.

One of those newly fascinated by the possibility of spirit communication was First Lady Mary Todd Lincoln. Tragedy had struck the White House on February 20, 1862, when the Lincoln's son, eleven-year-old

The Lincoln family at the White House in 1865. Abraham and Mary are pictured with sons Robert, Willie, and Tad. Willie appears in the painting even though he died three years prior in 1862.

Willie, died of typhoid fever. Mary Lincoln took to her bed for weeks, grief-stricken.

The First Lady began attending séances at friends' homes in hopes of reaching young Willie. Mary Todd Lincoln was no stranger to tragedy. Another of the Lincoln's sons, a toddler named Eddie, had died years before, and when Mary was just six years old, her own mother had died in childbirth.

Mrs. Lincoln hosted as many as eight séances in the White House, using a local group of Washington, DC, mediums. The President attended a few sessions but treated these evenings more like entertainment than any kind of serious spiritual inquiry.

During the war years, the threat of skeptical public opinion kept the First Lady from a consistent practice of Spiritualism. However, she revealed the truth to her half-sister: "[Willie] lives . . . He comes to me every night and stands at the foot of the bed with the same sweet, adorable smile he has always had; he does not always come alone; little Eddie is sometimes with him . . . You cannot dream of the comfort this gives me."

Her husband may not have accepted the spirits, but Mary Todd Lincoln would forever believe.

Charles Livermore's belief strengthened as he sat through dozens more sessions with Kate Fox. He investigated Estelle's spirit in numerous ways. One night Charles aimed a lamp directly at Estelle's spirit. She flinched but allowed the bright light to play over her face, chest, and clothes. Another evening, Estelle's ghostly hand appeared on the table, covered in "something like a handkerchief of transparent gossamer" (which maybe *was* a handkerchief?). Charles couldn't help but reach out, and "we again grasped hands with all the fervour of long-parted friends, my wife in the spirit-land and myself here."

Thousands of grieving families wondered about the afterlife as war churned wives into widows and children into orphans. On September 12, 1862, Confederate forces met the Union army at Antietam, Maryland. It was the bloodiest one-day battle in US history. Of the twenty-three thousand injured, close to four thousand died that day, but many lingered, only to die weeks or months later. For the first time, photographs revealed war's result: young corpses piled one atop the other. Their faces haunted the American public.

As the brutal war persisted, Charles Livermore continued to see and feel Estelle's gentle spirit in his séances with Kate Fox. Were the spirit and the medium the same person? Charles thought the idea ridiculous.

The bodies of Confederate soldiers piled up in "Bloody Lane," a trench on the Antietam Battlefield. This photograph from September 1862 was taken by Alexander Gardner, who worked for Mathew Brady in documenting the Civil War.

He noted how he held Kate's hands in the sessions. The friends and relatives who attended these séances saw Estelle's spirit too. One friend, a retired doctor, was positive: "These manifestations could not have been produced by human means . . . I have no doubt, they are, in my opinion, conclusive evidence of spirit identity."

Often, a second figure materialized alongside Estelle, once so suddenly, that Kate reportedly "cried out in fear." It was a man "dressed in a white cravat, and a brown coat of the olden style." The people in the room that night recognized the familiar face of Benjamin Franklin, who had helped found the United States eighty years before.

A weary President Lincoln was doing his best to fight for the future of the country that Benjamin Franklin had so believed in. But was preserving the United States worth the deaths of so many, so young?

The pain of Lincoln's "republic of suffering" seemed never ending.

Soldiers fell far from home, their bodies often left on the battlefield. Neither the Union or Confederate armies had consistent procedures to remove or identify the dead. Family members wandered battlefields searching for the remains of fathers, sons, and brothers. About one in four Civil War soldiers never came home; and over 40 percent of the dead remained nameless. Never before had Americans, in the North or the South, experienced death on this scale.

In January of the new year 1863, the fighting further intensified as Lincoln issued the Emancipation Proclamation, freeing enslaved people in the Confederate states. One of Mary Lincoln's mediums would claim that spirits had influenced President Lincoln's decision. As Black men were freed, many joined the Union cause. Almost 180,000 Black men would fight with the Union Army, eventually making up 10 percent of its force. When the heroic Black officer André Cailloux died in combat, Spiritualists in the military led a séance to contact him. From his heavenly home in Summerland, Cailloux's spirit rallied his men, **"It will be I who receive you into our world if you die in the struggle, so fight!"**

In July of 1863, at the Battle of Gettysburg, over a hundred thousand Union and Confederate soldiers met in a savage battle. Union forces prevailed. In November, President Lincoln arrived to dedicate the battlefield as a national cemetery. Looking over the wooded slopes where seven thousand men had lost their lives, President Lincoln gave a 272-word speech that honored America's soldiers and echoed through the ages, "these dead shall not have died in vain—that this nation, under God, shall have a new birth of freedom—and that government of the people, by the people, for the people, shall not perish from the earth."

The butchery continued into 1864, as Abraham Lincoln was reelected after securing the helpful endorsement of abolitionist hero Frederick

A Harvest of Death, Gettsyburg, Pennsylvania. This famous photograph shows the bodies of Union soldiers in the aftermath of the Battle of Gettysburg.

Douglass. In July, Union General William Tecumseh Sherman, captured the city of Atlanta, Georgia. Sherman gave orders to "enforce a devastation more or less relentless" on Southern military targets and the civilian population as he marched his army from Atlanta to the Savannah coast. Union soldiers hacked pianos, tore apart featherbeds, rifled through drawers and diaries. Livestock, food, silver, and jewelry were stolen. Southern civilians were humiliated, attacked, and killed.

Misery and death touched every part of American life as the war raged through another year. The Confederacy would not surrender even in the face of an almost certain Union victory. The price was always paid in more corpses. Living through the carnage, Americans looked for ways to deal with so much loss.

Nearly every town had its mediums who were kept busy asking the Civil War dead: *Are you there? Are you happy? Will I ever see you again?*

"I received but little income from the book and have had few sources of revenue."

Chapter 27 ADDICTION AND REHAB

On a bitterly cold New York City night in December of 1864, Horace Greeley slipped on snow-covered cobblestones. He had failed to find a hansom cab out in the storm. As a gust tried to send his hat sailing down the emptied streets, Greeley turned up his collar against the thickly falling snow and made his way home on foot.

He was still several blocks away when a woman wearing a wide-brimmed bonnet and a fur cloak approached. She stumbled, struggling against the cutting wind. As she ran past him into the blinding snowfall, a concerned Greeley turned back, caught up, and grabbed her arm. The woman fought to free herself, staring at him wild-eyed. An alarmed Horace Greeley recognized Maggie Fox!

Too drunk to know her old friend, Maggie sobbed, "I always find him in the snow." She was looking for Elisha. The once vibrant Maggie

Fox had entirely disappeared into the broken addict that Horace Greeley walked home that night.

The year 1865 was one of sadness for the entire Fox family. At the start of the year Father John Fox died at the age of seventy-six and was buried on David's farm near Hydesville. Later that year, Mother Peggy Fox died of typhoid fever and was buried in the Underhill family plot in Brooklyn. Kate had never lived without Mother; she was lonely, and "found a way to quick forgetfulness," losing her private battle against alcoholism and most of her public following. Her name fell from mention even in the Spiritualist press.

In April of 1865, the most prominent of these Spiritualist papers, *Banner of Light*, announced the breaking news to its readers: "The End of the Rebellion!" With his hungry, ailing troops surrounded on the

The ruins of Charleston, South Carolina, after Union General William T. Sherman's March to the Sea

battlefield in Appomattox, Virginia, Confederate General Robert E. Lee had surrendered to Union General Ulysses S. Grant, ending the Civil War.

Only the spirits knew exactly how many Americans had died in four years of civil war. Roughly 2 percent of the population (equivalent to almost seven million people today) had been killed—an estimated 620,000 Union and Confederate soldiers, along with about 50,000 civilians. In some communities, up to 25 percent of the men under thirty were dead.

Mary Todd Lincoln sat for spirit photographer William Mumler, around 1872. The spirit of her husband, the assassinated president, appears with his hands resting on her shoulders. Mumler was later tried for fraud and acquitted.

And yet, the killing was not over. After Lincoln gave a speech supporting Black citizenship, Southern zealot John Wilkes Booth shot the President five days after the war ended. President Abraham Lincoln died on April 15, 1865.

Lincoln's memorial procession was "said to have been modeled" on the funeral of Dr. Elisha Kent Kane. A series of ferries and trains carried the President's body from Washington, DC, to Springfield, Illinois. In seven states, thousands of Americans stood weeping on riverbanks and train depots, hats in hands, hands over hearts. The heroic Abraham Lincoln was making his way home for the last time.

A crowd of ten thousand at the Baltimore depot on April 22, 1865 paid its respects to President Lincoln as his body traveled by train to his burial site in Springfield, Illinois.

The country was in tatters. Almost a billion and a half dollars in property had been damaged or destroyed (roughly 30 billion today). The war years had taken a serious toll on the country's trade, business, and financial markets. The Kane family of Philadelphia was among many who lost large sums due to ill-advised investments. As Congress ratified the Thirteenth Amendment forbidding slavery in the United States, sometime before the end of 1865, the Kanes cut off Maggie's meager support altogether.

In 1866, a New York publishing company released a book with a long title, *The Love Life of Dr. Kane, containing the correspondence, and a history of the acquaintance, engagement and secret marriage between Elisha K. Kane and Margaret Fox; with facsimiles of letters and her portrait.* By finally presenting 134 of Elisha's letters to the public, Maggie hoped to create outrage over her treatment by the Kane family. She expected the scandal to force the Kanes to acknowledge her marriage and support her permanently.

But Maggie was out of touch. Wrapped in her prolonged mourning for Elisha, she was unaware of how much the Civil War had changed the country. She hadn't worked as a medium for years and Elisha was no longer famous. The Arctic accomplishments of Dr. Kane paled next to the battlefield heroism of Civil War soldiers. Elisha had been dead eight years; Maggie had waited too long. No one cared about their old celebrity romance. The book sold few copies. Maggie was left with nothing, except a life-threatening dependence on alcohol.

She was not alone in her uncontrolled addiction. Kate was also regularly drunk between and probably during spirit sessions. Spiritualists, possibly also Leah and Daniel Underhill, offered to pay for both sisters to stay at a well-known residential rehab facility run by Dr. George Taylor and his wife, Sarah. Kate agreed to treatment. Maggie refused. Since Maggie wouldn't cooperate, she was asked by the Taylors and others to stay away from Kate during her recovery.

Maggie had already lost her relationship with Leah. According to *The Love Life of Dr. Kane*, "modest" Maggie had been forced into mediumship, "obliged . . . to sit in the spiritual circles . . . under the direction of another and older person," obviously Leah. Instead of using Leah's name, the book spurned her as, "The relative . . . in whose house Miss Fox was then living." The oldest Fox sister was also labeled "jealous" and Elisha's mocking nicknames for Leah, such as "the Tigress," were published for the first time.

Love Life's introduction admitted, "The profession of mediumship . . . was under the ban of public disfavor and suspicion." Yet, the book did not directly accuse any individual medium of fraud. It did not specify how Maggie, or her sisters, may have created spirit manifestations.

It portrayed Maggie and Kate's childhood powers as genuine, while blaming Leah and "the disciples of spiritualism" for any deceit.

Leah was mortified. *The Love Life of Dr. Kane* disparaged her, her friends, and the movement she believed in. Plus, Maggie had paraded what Leah considered a foolish relationship with a long-dead Elisha Kent Kane in front of the public. Leah could not forgive Maggie for her candor; Maggie would not forgive Leah for her deception.

Maggie continued to live alone, seeing few people and it's assumed, drinking. Kate lived with Dr. Taylor, his family, and other patients at the clinic. Receiving treatments like massage and hydrotherapy, Kate sobered, and remained sober for many months.

However, Kate was allowed to leave the Taylors' clinic to work. Charles Livermore still paid her to conjure Estelle's spirit. Through Kate's mediumship, "grief had departed from Charles Livermore" by early 1866. Charles had met a young woman (much younger than Kate) courted her, and planned to marry again. Expressing his great appreciation for the comfort (and the kisses?) Kate's mediumship had provided, he ended their sessions. The last occurred on April 2, 1866. Charles and Kate had been together for five years, three hundred and eighty-eight séances.

Soon after Livermore stopped seeing Kate, she left the Taylors, moved in with Maggie, and went on a bender. Spiritualist friends brought Kate back to the Taylors' clinic drunk. She sobered up again. She began repetitive cycles of sobering, running away, and drinking that went on for years. Kate made tearful promises not to see Maggie, then quickly broke them. Dr. Taylor found "there was no way to keep the two apart."

By 1869, Kate and Maggie's alcoholism seemed hopeless. It is not known exactly how Maggie supported herself; but she lived in poverty. Kate's Spiritualist friends stopped paying the Taylors' fee. She was desperate. In exchange for shelter, meals, and friendship, Kate provided Dr. George Taylor and Sarah Taylor the only collateral she had left—their dead children.

The Taylors had recently buried their three-year-old son, Frankie. Eighteen-month-old daughter, Leila, had died of scarlet fever a few years before. Kate led séances that brought the couple's children back home.

Photographing relatives after death was common in the nineteenth century. Postmortem photographs of children showed their bodies posed as if asleep or with toys as if still alive. Since photography was expensive, the only image parents often had was of their child's corpse.

In the darkness of her parlor, Sarah Taylor felt a tug at her skirt, a toddler's body pressed against her knees. As Sarah held hands in the circle, a child's legs struggled to climb up.

"Darling momma, let me get in your lap," the raps spelled as Kate translated.

Sarah had been told never to break the connection in a spirit circle. But she longed to feel her little daughter once more.

Leila's spirit repeated her request for help, spelling out, "**try to.**" But when Sarah reached forward to help her baby daughter up, the circle was broken, and Leila disappeared.

Spirit lights flashed. Raps echoed around the room so rapidly that Kate, mirror-writing as always, could barely keep up. With a pencil gripped in her left hand, she wrote in reverse on long lengths of rolled brown paper, taking down the spirit communications.

The Taylors' sessions were packed with spirits trying to come through. Benjamin Franklin was there, in charge of the energetic manifestations. Franklin made such frequent appearances at the Taylors that he soon quickly initialed his communications, "**B. F.**" Other spirit visitors included a deceased brother, grandparents, uncles, and cousins from George's and Sarah's families.

These spirits told jokes, gossiped, and argued like a mortal family. They told the Taylors all about the afterlife. In Summerland, spirits had bodies and clothes, lived in cottages or palaces, sat on sofas or under willow trees, sang and held tea parties, ate "**spiritual food**" for breakfast. The spirits also had many important postwar duties like "**preparing our homes for the poor wounded soldiers who are rapidly coming to our world.**" The Taylors' family spirits even met celebrities in Summerland; one saw "**John Brown walking arm and arm with Abraham Lincoln.**"

Every word of these busy, active spirit lives was told to the Taylors through the mediumship, mind, and body of Kate Fox. The family came to rely, sometimes daily, on Kate's skill to channel "all classes of spirits, high and low . . ." even when "dead drunk." Sarah Taylor wondered if "Drunkenness, like dying, releases evangelical power . . ."

Guests sometimes joined the Taylors' circles, including celebrities such as *Uncle Tom's Cabin* author, Harriet Beecher Stowe. The most frequent mortal attendees were Kate, George, Sarah, and their only remaining child, ten-year-old son Willie. The spirits Kate channeled provided superb advice, **"There is but one life to live on this earth. Enjoy it and be happy."**

Leila and Frankie, the Taylors' dead children, were the stars of these sessions. Sitting in the darkness, Dr. George and Sarah Taylor received proof that their children lived. According to the adult spirits who cared for them, Leila and Frankie were happily growing up in Summerland just as they would have at home: **"Your children live for you here and love you deeply."**

The family sat in sense-heightening darkness often for hours at a time. The Taylors and their guests were often given rapid instructions to help the spirits work—*hold hands, get a pencil, let go, converse, keep quiet, walk to the window, open the blinds, sit at the table, close your eyes, get light.* The family followed these directions to the letter; they couldn't risk missing Leila or Frankie, whose childhood pranks "would fill a book."

"The children played about us . . . Frankie pulled his Papa's long beard . . ." Sarah wrote. When the lights were turned up, George Taylor's beard lay twisted into three separate braids. *Silly Frankie!* In another spirit session, a house slipper was handed to Sarah as a joke. *Silly Leila!*

The mortals sang "The Lord's Prayer" as Leila's spirit strummed a heavenly harp, which, "resembled mostly those of a first-class music box (!), yet were different." They heard the repetitive squeak of Frankie rocking in his little chair. **"Papa, open your eyes and see my shadow,"** the boy's spirit spelled through Kate. The silhouette of a child appeared on the moonlit wall.

The family was asked to provide drawing paper and crayons. When they closed their eyes as instructed, the scratchy sounds of coloring were heard. They opened their eyes to gifts of spirit pictures—drawings of family members living in Summerland or a delicate sketch of rosebuds.

The immortals worried about Kate's drinking as much as Dr. George and Sarah Taylor did. The spirits fussed, **"We knew that if she went out . . . she would have drank . . . if Katie would only abstain . . ."** Messages *about* the medium from the spirits proved to Sarah Taylor that it was the spirits (not Kate) who were doing the communicating, "Imagine a normal person writing all that about herself." But Kate wasn't normal. Neither Sarah Taylor nor almost any person, except Maggie, could have possibly understood the kind of abnormality Kate Fox had lived with since she was eleven years old.

A spirit drawing said to be produced by the deceased Frankie Taylor in a session with Kate Fox. This image of a flower wreath and the name Frankie was given to his mother, Sarah Taylor, for Christmas around 1879.

One day, Sarah found a spirit message from Benjamin Franklin. It read, "**Private. We will meet at nine, but say nothing to Katie. B. F.**" Neither Dr. George nor Sarah Taylor seemed to question Kate's mental state. The Taylor family called her "the greatest medium, the one whose faculties for transmission were the purest . . ." and through Kate, stayed in touch with dead family members for more than twenty-two years.

When he grew up, Willie Taylor shared his family's story in a book that included spirit letters, spirit drawings, family photos, and diary entries—326 crowded pages of evidence that death had been conquered. Sixty years after his family's sessions with Kate Fox, Professor William (Willie) Taylor, graduate of Harvard and Columbia Law School, and a former chair in economics at the University of Nebraska, still believed.

"Many people . . . seemed to believe so firmly in it . . ."

Chapter 28 SPIRITS ACROSS THE SEA

As far back as 1868, one news article had claimed, "Mrs. Elisha Kent Kane Fox so-called, is again trying to 'call the spirits from the vasty deep.'" But, for the most part, despite years of financial need, Maggie had honored her commitment to Elisha and stayed away from the séance table.

In the early part of 1871, former war hero, now President Ulysses S. Grant, continued the process of Reconstruction. As America struggled to knit itself back together after the Civil War, Maggie had no choice but to make her own changes and return to mediumship. The Maggie Fox who had once turned away customers now ran ads in the back pages of Spiritual newspapers offering her services to anyone who paid a dollar.

Maggie's Catholic priest described her as a "humble, modest, and excellent soul." He gave his blessing for her to earn a living as long as she was honest with people. To that end, Maggie added a note to her business card, "Mrs. Kane does not claim any spirit power, but people must judge for themselves." This frank admission did not stop determined clients from using her services when Maggie was sober, and probably when she was not.

Kate also continued to seesaw between drunkenness and sobriety. No one mentioned the Taylors' conflicts of interest, but it was clear that their treatment of her alcoholism wasn't working.

Notice of Kate's work with Charles Livermore and the Taylors had made its way through the Spiritualist press to believers in England. Spiritualism was a "strange and fascinating American import." It had been brought to London by the American medium Mrs. Maria Hayden in 1852. Soon afterward, "An epidemic of table-turning had broken out . . ." and the number of England's Spiritualists and spirit publications grew. Estimates of English Spiritualists ranged widely from 10,000 to 100,000 believers by the end of the 1800s.

As part of a séance at the Taylors' in June 1871, Benjamin Franklin's spirit suggested Kate be allowed to travel to London. Despite Franklin's request, Sarah Taylor didn't want to lose contact with Leila and Frankie. In part, a mother-to-mother communication from the deceased Mrs. Fox helped Sarah let Kate go, **"I want to express my gratitude to you for your kindness to my child . . . you will be rewarded."**

In gratitude for his newfound happiness, Charles Livermore paid Kate's travel expenses, including a new wardrobe. The spirits suggested she take his help and **"not be prejudiced against her best friend, Mr. Livermore."** The Sunday before she left, Kate transcribed herself some additional advice from the spirits, **"Oh, never again touch the wine cup to your lips. We feel that the change has come. Go over the big waves, for the mighty change has come."** With one of Livermore's female relatives along as a chaperone, Kate sailed across the ocean for the first time at the age of thirty-four.

In London, Kate's drinking problems were not common knowledge; people only knew of her ability to produce the impossible. She shone, sober, at a reception given in her honor by Spiritualist friends. She met many believers that night; but a tall, fair-haired attorney named Henry Jencken stood out. Henry was in his late forties, once (unhappily) married, but now a widower. Toward the end of the elegant evening, the hosts poured champagne, "Drink with me to fair Kate Fox." Henry noticed Kate's panicked look, and gently removed the upraised glass from her hands.

From that evening on, it seemed as if every Spiritualist in London wanted a private séance with the famous Miss Fox. Kate was extraordinarily busy, far from home, and under great stress. Within weeks, her chaperone found Kate unconscious on a hotel room sofa, "an empty bottle flung upon the floor." Hotel servants fetched water, blankets, and towels, as her chaperone kept a desperately ill Kate alive that night.

In the morning, Kate and her chaperone left for Paris under the care of "a wise physician who had worked successfully with alcoholics." After hearing Kate's story, the doctor reportedly exclaimed, "I would drink too, if I lived in her world of spirit raps!" Under his care, Kate sobered up and stayed that way. But within weeks, Spiritualist supporters were begging to bring her back to London. The doctor warned against this move, "you must not look for any miracles." But providing miracles was the way Kate Fox had always made her living. She returned to her London public.

The attentive Henry Jencken was once again among the guests at an 1872 dinner and séance in London. When the courses were served, a servant came around with wine. With Henry by her side, Kate turned her wine glass over and refused alcohol. Her sober after-dinner séance was a great success. After the doors were locked, a glowing spirit arm appeared to write messages from beyond. The medium's hands had been tightly held, by her host on one side; and on the other by the handsome, charming Henry Jencken.

For the first time in her life, Kate was being seriously courted. As a believing Spiritualist, Henry was a trusting companion. As an older widower, he was an appropriate match. As a man, Kate thought him "good and kind." Though Henry and Kate kept details of their romance private, once they found each other, they spent little time apart.

In an Anglican ceremony in London on December 14, 1872, a joyful, clear-eyed Kate Fox married Henry Jencken. She wore a simple white lace dress with a half wreath of white flowers in her hair. Her chaperone stood beside her; her sisters did not attend. According to the press, one family member did make a surprise appearance. During the wedding breakfast, Mother Fox, dead more than seven years, showed up in spirit to speak to her new son-in-law, "expressing her approval of the marriage."

Kate's popularity in London increased her status back home. Articles about her wedding ran in newspapers from Rhode Island to Wisconsin, Vermont to Mississippi, and almost every state in-between. "Kate Fox at the Altar" described for the American public the wedding's dresses, décor, and celebrity sightings: a German prince and the Duke of Wellington's son.

Kate and Henry settled into family life. He worked in a London office, specializing in international law; she kept their home. Like Leah, Kate led intimate séances for friends but no longer for the paying public. On September 19, 1873, at the age of thirty-six, Kate gave birth to a baby boy named Ferdie, who seemed to have inherited his mother's talents.

Just before Christmas, London's leading spiritual periodical published an article, "Mediumship of a Baby." The paper had interviewed Henry and Kate's housemaid as well as little Ferdie's nurse. The household help repeatedly saw white veiled figures appearing and disappearing into two-month-old Ferdie's nursery. A gold ring floated in the darkness then knocked against Ferdie's crib; an unseen hand left a print on his little pillow. Henry Jencken told a reporter of holding bright-eyed Ferdie in early morning darkness. Raps in the room spelled "**We are looking at you through the eyes of the baby.**" Kate's role in these events went unquestioned.

By the time Ferdie was six months old, he had reportedly written his first spirit communication in pencil: "**I love this little boy, God bless his mama.**" It was reported Ferdie also wrote the biblical sentence, "**He who trusts in me shall live,**" in Greek, the original language of the New Testament. Ferdie Jencken's miraculous abilities were predictably covered in Spiritualist papers such as *Medium and Daybreak*, but also city newspapers in Chicago, Washington, DC, and New York. Even his Aunt Leah bragged of "this marvellous infant."

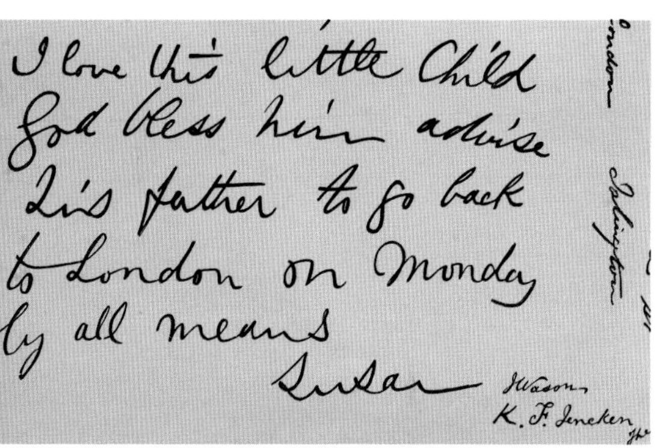

"Specimen of writing executed by Mrs. [Kate] Fox Jencken's Baby, aged nine days."

Soon Kate and Henry had a change of heart about the media's interest in their son. Before Ferdie was a year old, his parents decided to keep him "entirely aloof from mediumship" and out of the public eye, at least until he grew up. This resulted in the happily married Mrs. Kate Fox Jencken staying properly out of the spotlight also.

Maggie had taken a job in Philadelphia as medium-in-residence at the "Spiritual Mansion" of Henry Seybert, a trustee of the University of Pennsylvania. As the months passed, Seybert's frenetic requests for

Maggie included conjuring the spirits of biblical figures, like Elijah and Gabriel, as well as Saints Peter and Paul. Eventually objecting to Seybert's spirit "mania," Maggie resigned and returned to rented rooms in New York.

In the fall of 1874, when Kate and Ferdie visited New York, all three Fox sisters were in the same city once again. Kate was about six months pregnant with her second child. There were trips to visit relatives near Hydesville. Isaac Post and the Greeleys had passed on, but the sisters spent evenings with other old friends, such as Amy Post and Eliab Capron. Though Leah and Maggie remained estranged, both saw their youngest sister often, and doted on their one-year-old nephew.

Maggie's long-term alcohol abuse had caused permanent damage. A friend described her as in "feeble health," which may have indicated physical problems, emotional issues, or both. Yet, while Kate and Ferdie were in New York, Maggie made a heroic and successful effort to curb or stop her drinking.

It was in New York City, at Leah's home, that Kate's second son, Henry Jencken Jr. was born in the first months of 1875. His father, Henry Sr., came from London to see his new son and escort Kate and their two boys back to England. With few clients and no real ties keeping her in New York, Maggie soon followed Kate overseas.

Living among passionate Spiritualists in London, Maggie Fox once again developed a strong clientele. Though there were other famous mediums in England, Maggie's status as one of the originators allowed her to make a decent living. She lived in England for about five years, leading private séances. Kate stayed busy with her boys. And, as far as is known, they both stayed sober. Yet the happier the Fox sisters were, the less their names appeared in the papers. Every so often, tiny items ran only as fillers between bigger stories, reminding the American public "The three Fox Sisters . . . are alive."

In August of 1881, Maggie was hired to contact the spirits for attendees at a Massachusetts Spiritualist camp. For the next number of years, Maggie traveled between New York and London taking part in a variety of spirit investigations or other work as a medium.

Spiritualists gathered at summer camps beginning in the 1850s. Camp activities included séances, hymn singing, boating, archery, and picnics. This 1890s photograph shows the Maplewood Hotel at the Lilydale Assembly near Buffalo, New York. Other popular camps included Camp Etna in Maine, Camp Chesterfield in Indiana, and the Cassadaga Spiritualist Camp in Florida. These four communities still run Spiritualist programs today.

These happier times did not last. In November 1881, Henry Jencken suffered a stroke and died. Kate was left with little money as her husband's estate amounted to less than two hundred pounds. Kate hadn't performed publicly since Ferdie's birth. Now forty-four years old, she needed to support her children. When a Russian diplomat invited her to the court of Czar Alexander III, Kate packed her two boys, aged six and eight, and traveled to St. Petersburg. Kate and her sons lived in Russia for a few years. She claimed to have led séances for Russia's royal family.

Two years later, Maggie returned to Philadelphia in November of 1883 to call the spirits for her previous employer, the spirit-obsessed Henry Seybert, this time *after* his death. Seybert had left money in his will to fund a commission made up of ten University of Pennsylvania faculty tasked with proving the truth of Spiritualism. Yet, even in front of men chosen for their positive stance on spirit communication, Maggie's powers deserted her. She failed to produce accurate answers (and barely any raps either!). Before she was dismissed, she provided a reverse communication from Henry Seybert who resorted to scolding his own commission: **dah tey evah uoy sa emit a trohs os ni tbuod lla dnoyeb uoy yfsitas nac I taht tcepxe ton tsum uoY**

Seybert's spirit message ended with a jumble of words in Latin, a language Maggie did not know. Unfortunately for Maggie, the committee remembered that, unlike most educated men, Henry Seybert never knew Latin either. Even a committee set up specifically to prove the existence of spirits wound up concluding, "Spiritualism . . . presents the melancholy spectacle of gross fraud . . ." Maggie went back to her tiny New York apartment, barely eking out a living as a medium.

When they returned to New York in 1885, Kate, Ferdie, and Henry Jr. brought luxurious gifts from Russia. Kate and her boys first lived in a "handsomely furnished flat," but whatever money she had earned in Russia did not last long. She supported her sons with weekly public séances and private sessions for regular clients, including Dr. George and Sarah Taylor. Kate, Ferdie, and Henry Jr. lived with Leah and Daniel for a bit. Leah loved having her young nephews around so much that she encouraged them to stay permanently. But "Kate would not share her sons with anyone." She took Ferdie and Henry Jr. from Leah's, moved to the Taylors', then to her brother David's in Hydesville, and ended up with the boys in an apartment of their own in New York City by the late fall.

With her nephews gone, Leah put the finishing touches on her version of the Fox sisters' story. *The Missing Link in Modern Spiritualism*, "by A. Leah Underhill of the Fox Family" was published toward the end of 1885. Leah's book contained facts, fictions, and long sections that mixed both. Leah gave herself the starring role in the Spiritualist revolution: "nobody else possesses the means and the data necessary for the task of giving a correct account of the initiation of the movement known as Modern Spiritualism . . ." Only Leah's truth was to be trusted; Maggie and Kate were once again pushed out of their own story.

About six months later, in June of 1886, Kate Fox Jencken was found incoherent and drunk in a seedy New York City saloon. Leah had been embarrassed by her sisters' struggles with alcohol before. She believed that Ferdie and Henry Jr. might be better off in her care. It took a while to set a plan in motion.

An anonymous tip to child welfare resulted in a surprise visit to Kate's apartment the spring of 1888. The officers found her young teenage sons, Ferdie and Henry Jr., well dressed, clean, and fed. But they also found Kate noticeably intoxicated. She was arrested, charged with "drunkenness and flagrant neglect of her maternal duties," and spent the night in jail. Her boys were sent to a juvenile "asylum" to await the result of their mother's hearing, which gave relatives (like Aunt Leah) time to come forward and legally claim the boys.

New York's newspapers had a field day at Kate's expense: "One of the Fox Sisters Arrested," "Neglected Her Children," "Lamentable Downfall of Once Celebrated Spirit Rapper." The *Herald*'s editors made the shameful decision to run a play on words about alcohol addiction:

"The Spirits Too Much for Her." A typical story ended cruelly, "The once talented, vivacious and successful spirit rapper is now a total wreck."

On May 5, a *New York World* reporter showed up at Kate's apartment. "Age, worry, and dissipation have left deep lines on the medium's face—a face that at one time must have been handsome." The reporter got what he hoped for—a rambling, scandalous interview. The notorious Kate Fox admitted to being "a little fond of the bottle" and, more shockingly, called out Spiritualists as "fanatics."

Maggie was in England visiting friends when she read of Kate's arrest. Furious at Leah, Maggie schemed a way to get Kate's boys back. She wrote a false letter to the New York court, pretending to be Ferdie and Henry's British relative, "Uncle Edward." The ruse worked. The court believed Kate's sons would be safe with Uncle Edward, so her neglect case was dropped and the boys were released from the asylum. Kate, Ferdie, and Henry fled to London, as far away from Leah as they could manage.

Leah's attempt to take Kate's sons away drove a stake into the heart of the Fox sisters' already troubled relationships. The two youngest sisters were alcoholics who struggled to support themselves while their oldest sister had married a rich man and enjoyed the admiration of Spiritualists worldwide. In Maggie and Kate's view, they had followed Leah's rules, and she had left them with nothing. In Leah's view, her sisters were unsavable drunks who had disrespected the spirits and the followers who had made them famous.

Leah's interference with Kate's sons set a final confrontation in motion. After forty years of living with the public's praise and condemnation, Maggie and Kate knew how best to seek revenge against their oldest sister.

The newspapers.

"I think that it is about time that the truth . . . should be brought out."

Chapter 29 CONFESSIONS

It was close to midnight when a London hackney driver was hailed by a middle-aged woman wrapped against the nighttime chill. He learned she was American when she called out her destination, a London cemetery. The driver hesitated to take her at this hour, but the woman insisted. When the horses drew up to the graveyard's towering iron gates, she descended the carriage steps, and greeted the cemetery's watchman. Visitors weren't allowed on the burial grounds at this hour, yet this particular woman's request to enter was granted.

She set off down a shadowed path, wandering alone past obelisks, stone angels, and granite buildings in this city of the dead. Looking at the name on a random headstone, she concentrated her powers. *Are you there?* Silence. She turned toward another stone. *Are you happy?* Silence. She focused her thoughts on her lost lover. *Will I ever see you again?* “All was silent, and I found that the dead would not return.” The dead gave Maggie Fox the courage to move forward.

From England, Maggie shot off a letter to the *New York Herald*: “Spiritualism is a curse.” She sailed back to New York in September of 1888, trailed by rumors that she had more, much more, to say. As the spirit scandal brewed, the newspapers grew interested in the Fox sisters all over again.

Within a month, a *Herald* reporter stepped into Maggie’s tiny apartment on New York’s West Forty-Fourth Street. As she answered his questions, the “small, magnetic . . . negligently dressed” former celebrity paced the room, buried her face in her hands, and played “fitful floods of wild and incoherent melody” on a piano. Despite Maggie’s erratic behavior, the city reporter emphasized, “she knew what she was talking about.”

Maggie lashed out at Leah, “I hate her. My God! I’d poison her.” Their oldest sister “used us in her exhibitions and we made money for her . . . Oh, I am after her! You can kill sometimes without using weapons, you know.”

Maggie promised to tell the truth. She would give the public “one lecture, and no more,” which would expose spirit rapping. Maggie provided the *Herald* reporter with a brief demonstration.

Rap. Rap. Rap. The sound came from under his feet.

Rap. Rap. Now, under his chair and the table on which he leaned.

Rap. Rap. Rap. Rap. The sounds burst from a door and echoed inside a piano.

“How do you do it?” the astonished reporter asked.

“Well, I want to keep my explanation for the night of my lecture,” Maggie answered.

“Is it all a trick?”

“Absolutely.”

Leah did not respond to Maggie's newspaper accusations. Instead, Daniel Underhill gave an interview in Leah's defense: "My wife has done everything in the world for them." His two sisters-in-law could not "stay sober." He called Maggie "vicious as a devil." No one should pay attention to her: "I cannot think her in her right mind."

Maggie was giving a follow-up interview to the *New York Herald* when Kate, just in from London, burst into the room. The reporter described Maggie and Kate Fox embracing "upon each other's necks in an ecstasy of affection and delight at being together once again." Kate added to Maggie's interview, "I care nothing for spiritualism itself . . . The worst of them all is my eldest sister, Leah, the wife of Daniel Underhill . . . I think she is the one who caused my arrest . . . Spiritualism is a humbug from beginning to end. It is the biggest humbug of the century."

The story ran across the country, "Kate Fox Jencken . . . intends to co-operate with her sister—Margaretta Fox Kane—in her proposed exposé of the fraudulent methods of so-called spiritualism." Or, as the *Chicago Tribune* boasted, "KATY FOX WILL GIVE THE SNAP AWAY."

The *New York World* scooped other papers clamoring to run Maggie's confessional interview. Ads for the upcoming exposé ran within the *World* masthead:

> SPIRITUALISM EXPOSED. THE FOX SISTERS, ORIGINAL SPIRIT-RAPPERS, TELL THE STORY OF THEIR JUGGLERY. SEE THE SUNDAY WORLD. A CONFESSION WHICH WILL AMUSE AND ASTONISH THE COUNTRY.

On Sunday, October 21, 1888, the full-page story appeared. It was a history of the spirit rappings complete with illustrations of the Hydesville house, Maggie Fox, Kate Fox, Elisha Kane, and a séance in progress. The article's centerpiece was a written confession signed "Margaret Fox Kane."

SPIRITUALISM EXPOSED.

THE FOX SISTERS, ORIGINAL SPIRIT-RAPPERS, TELL THE STORY OF THEIR JUGGLERY.

SEE THE SUNDAY WORLD.

A CONFESSION WHICH WILL AMUSE AND ASTONISH THE COUNTRY.

Maggie revealed that she and Kate had been mischievous girls who "wanted to terrify our mother." So, "we used to tie an apple to a string and move the string up and down . . . making a strange noise every time it would rebound." The two youngest sisters progressed from bouncing apples to fooling the world under Leah's influence. New Yorkers who read the story in the Sunday morning paper flocked that evening to see Maggie's promised lecture.

The Academy of Music was once New York City's most elegant opera house. The theater had lost its luster and its high-society audience, reduced to booking vaudeville comedians, clog dancers, and trick dogs. The night of October 21, its red velvet seats filled once again. Two thousand souls, believers and skeptics in roughly equal numbers, anxiously waited to hear from Maggie Fox.

The show opened with a dentist turned magician. He produced spirit writing on a blank slate, then showed the audience how the magic trick worked. He read a message inside a sealed envelope, then did the trick again slowly, making obvious his substitution of one envelope, for another. After a time, the audience grew restless; "go and pull teeth!" someone yelled. The magician-dentist wrapped up and the main presentation began.

Maggie stepped from behind the heavy velvet curtain. The sounds of a deeply divided crowd washed over her. Believers hissed, certain that

New York's Academy of Music, site of Maggie's 1888 confession

the former celebrity medium was being paid to betray the spirits. Skeptics cheered, encouraged that one of the celebrated Fox sisters might finally tell the truth.

The major New York City papers had reporters stationed throughout the crowd to cover Maggie Fox's return to the stage. A wide, flowered bonnet covered her dark hair, streaked with gray. Her cheery hat contrasted with a black bombazine dress, suitable for mourning. Believers were correct; promotors had promised Maggie $1,500 for this public appearance (about $40,000 today). Skeptics were correct; Maggie Fox intended to tell her truth.

Maggie looked "nervous" as she crossed the stage to the wood lectern, noticeably trembling. Reporters described her as, "not in the best condition," "highly excited," and "ridiculous." She was not the lively Maggie Fox who had once enchanted the nation. Was she drunk? To those who knew her, she appeared unusually, but utterly, sober.

Kate sat near the stage in a chipped, gilded plaster box that once enshrined New York society's elite. Leah was nowhere to be found.

Maggie made an awkward curtsy to the audience. She put her reading glasses on, read a line of her prepared remarks to herself, took the glasses off, looked at the audience, and repeated the words. She halted and stumbled, line by line, making her way through only some of the speech. Many in the audience hooted as Maggie over-enunciated—raising her hands to heaven as if starring in some tragic play. Throughout Maggie's exaggerated performance, Kate applauded. With Kate nodding along, Maggie explained the source of the spirit sounds, "The rappings are simply the result of a perfect control of the muscles of the knee, which govern the tendons of the foot and allow action of the toe and ankles bones that are not commonly known."

When the audience did not understand, Maggie stopped speaking to demonstrate. Three doctors were invited on stage to hold Maggie's feet. A small, pine table was brought out. Maggie slipped off her shoes and stood on the table in her stockings. The rowdy audience shifted to absolute silence. The "black-robed, sharp-faced widow" in front of them appeared utterly motionless. But the sounds? They were everywhere.

Rap. Rap. Rap. Behind the heavy curtains.

Rap. Rap. Rap. In the ornate balconies.

Rap. Rap. Rap. Near the carved ceiling.

The doctors unanimously agreed that these rapping sounds came from Maggie's big toe.

"One moment it was ludicrous, the next it was weird," declared the *New York Herald*. Maggie sarcastically asked the "kind, dear spirits" to cooperate further, and "a hailstorm of responsive knocks" rained down as the audience roared, some in disbelief, others in approval. Maggie clapped her hands and hopped around the stage.

"It's a fraud," she cried. "Spiritualism is a fraud from beginning to end. It's all a trick! There's no truth to it!"

"this exposé will be a severe blow to her, and perhaps kill her"

Chapter 30 AS THE CURTAIN FALLS

The headlines screamed: "Spiritualism's Downfall," "The Fox Sisters Fraud," and "Mrs. Fox Kane's Big Toe." Capitalizing on the publicity, Maggie and Kate authorized their ghostwriter (in this case a literal term) to release their book titled, *The Deathblow to Spiritualism*. It told the story of a joke run wild, and two girls taken advantage of by a much older sister. The *New York Herald* assured its readers, "the confession of the two founders of Spiritualism and the complete exposure of the tricks of the mediums ends this form of swindling . . . it can never recover from this crushing blow."

The *Herald* turned out to be dead wrong.

The Fox sisters did make a return to the pages of the country's major newspapers, alongside stories of railroad strikes, and state visits by European royalty. But within a few days, the Fox story vanished. The sisters were no longer young or pretty, and the mystery that had always surrounded the spirits was left in ruins—the mainstream news lost all interest.

The Spiritualist press covered Maggie's exposure as a tragedy, not for the Spiritualist movement, but for the once great mediums Maggie and Kate Fox. "They are the slaves of strong drink, and are to be pittied: but there is one who needs pity more." That person was their saintly older sister Leah.

The Spiritualist newspapers mixed facts and fictions. Maggie and Kate were alcoholics, desperate, and therefore incapable of telling the truth. There were stories about a deep conspiracy against spirit believers. Enemies of Spiritualism (the Catholic Church, the mainstream news) had paid Maggie and/or Kate to make false confessions. Every true Spiritualist knew cracking joints could not explain the comfort they received from talking to the dead. Believers kept right on believing.

By confessing to fraud, Maggie and Kate didn't destroy the Spiritualist movement or their sister Leah. Instead, they destroyed their ability to earn a living. The truth didn't set them free; it kept them captive in poverty. Kate soon wrote a friend, "I think now I could make money in proving the raps were not made by the toes."

After a truth-telling lecture tour failed to attract much of an audience, Maggie retracted her confession: "I gave expression to utterances that had no foundation in fact." She met with a group of prominent Spiritualists to reiterate her retraction: "Those charges [against Spiritualism] were false in every respect." She suggested her willingness to once again lecture on behalf of the faith. Knowing Maggie's desperate finances, a Spiritualist scoffed, "for five dollars she would have denied her mother and would have sworn to anything." The damage was done. Maggie and Kate Fox were no longer wanted by either believers or skeptics.

Leah kept away from her sisters. The Spiritualist press referred to her as "honorable and estimable [respected]." About a year after

Maggie's confession, Leah's diligent work for the spirit cause was honored at an anniversary gathering of New York Spiritualists. She was described by a Spiritualist historian as, "The best test, rapping and physical medium I ever met, as well as one of the kindest and most noble-hearted of women."

Despite all the praise, the stress from her sisters' public revelations took its toll on Leah's health. On November 1, 1890, less than a year after Maggie's confession, Leah's heart failed due to "nervous excitability." She died in her New York City home with her loyal husband, Daniel Underhill, by her side.

Leah was buried at New York's elegant Green-Wood Cemetery, portrayed in this 1867 lithograph much like the heavenly Spiritualist Summerland.

Kate struggled on, living with her sons a few blocks from Central Park in a dingy apartment. Ferdie worked for New York's transit system, and helped support his mother and younger brother, Henry Jr. Suffering from kidney disease due to alcoholism, Kate passed away on

July 2, 1892, at the age of fifty-five. When reporters showed up to get the scoop, her bereaved sons insisted that Kate "died a firm believer" in the spirits. The corpse of the woman who "succeeded in mystifying the people of all classes" was put into temporary storage. There was no money for a permanent burial.

Upon learning of Kate's death, Maggie lost all interest in life. She spent her days drunk and sick, at some point moving to an almost-empty tenement on West Fifty-Seventh Street. On October 29, 1892, "An Earnest Appeal" was made in the Spiritualist press seeking donations of money to help "this very unfortunate sister."

The entrance to Cypress Hills cemetery in Brooklyn, New York, late 1800s. Kate's and Maggie's bodies were placed in a public vault due to lack of funds. Around 1894, an old friend offered to bury both sisters together in his plot at Cypress Hills. The headstone gave Maggie's birthdate as October 7, 1833, and Kate's birthdate as March 27, 1837. The original headstone became worn and was replaced by Spiritualists. Maggie's birthdate is now given as October 7, 1837, and Kate's as March 27, 1839, to conform with Spiritualist beliefs.

Either Maggie hadn't been forgiven, or she'd been forgotten; nationwide donations for her ongoing care amounted to less than ninety dollars. Maggie was moved to the Brooklyn home of a compassionate female Spiritualist where she died, just before sunrise, on March 8, 1893, at the age of fifty-nine.

That evening in Washington, DC, a group gathered in a darkened room. They joined hands as a male medium attempted communication with the spirits—*Are you there? Are you happy? Will I ever see you again?*

Before long, a female spirit materialized near a cabinet along the wall. She was not recognized by anyone in the room. The spirit wavered and made three separate attempts to move toward the circle's participants. It was clear that she was having great difficulty remaining in focus and disappeared before the séance ended.

The same participants and the same medium met again the following evening. Sure enough, the same woman's spirit joined them—repeatedly fading and materializing. This time, before she vanished into the darkness, a spirit message was transmitted, **"I am here to bid you greeting. The rappings shall still go on."** The communication was signed **"Maggie Fox Kane."**

How Maggie's spirit appeared at a séance in America's capital two days *before* her death was announced in the newspapers remains a mystery.

An exposé of Spiritualism appeared in the October 21, 1888, issue of the *New York World*. The article covered the history of spirit rapping and included a signed confession from Maggie. A portion of the text can be found below.

THE MEDIUM'S STATEMENT

Mrs. Margaret Fox Kane Tells the Story of Her Remarkable Life

I think that it is about time that the truth of this miserable subject "Spiritualism" should be brought out. It is now widespread all over the world, and unless it is put down soon it will do great evil. I was the first in the field and I have the right to expose it.

My sister Katie and myself were very young children when this horrible deception began. I was eight, and just a year and a half older than she.[1] We were very mischievous children and we wanted to terrify our dear mother, who was a very good woman and very easily frightened. At night, when we went to bed, we used to tie an apple to a string and move the string up and down, causing the apple to bump on the floor, or we would drop the apple on the floor making a strange noise every time it would rebound. Mother listened to this for a time. She could not understand it and did not suspect us of being capable of a trick because we were so young.

1. Maggie always maintained that she and Kate were much younger when they began rapping, as do most Spiritualists. But official records and the contemporaneous testimony of friends do not seem to support her version of their ages.

CHILDISH MISCHIEF AT FIRST

At last, she could stand it no longer and she called the neighbors in and told them about it. It was this that set us to discover the means of making the raps. I think, when I reflect about it, that it was a most wonderful discovery—a very wonderful thing that children so young should make such a discovery and all through our mischief. Children will always find means to accomplish mischief. As to the thought of spirits, this never entered our brains. We were too young to know anything about that.

Our eldest sister, Mrs. Underhill, was twenty-three years of age when I was home. She was in Rochester when these tricks first begun, but came to Hydesville, the little village in Central New York, where we lived and were born, shortly after. My father and mother were very good, honest people and great friends with the Hyde family for whom the village was named and who lived near. They took a great fancy to us and we were especial favorites of the Hydes, both before and after the notoriety that our rappings made became widespread. All the people around, as I have said, were called in to witness these manifestations. My sister, now Mrs. Daniel Underhill—she was Mrs. Fish then—began to form a society of spiritualists. There were so many people coming to the house that we were not able to make use of the apple trick except when we were in bed and the room was dark. Even then we could hardly do it so that the only way was to rap on the bedstead.

And that is the way we began. First as a mere trick to frighten our mother, and then, when so many people came to see us children, we were frightened ourselves and kept it up. We were then taken by Mrs. Underhill to Rochester. There it was that we discovered how to make the other raps. My sister Katie was the first one to discover that by swishing her fingers she could produce a certain noise with the knuckles and joints, and that the same effect could be made with the toes. Finding we could make raps with our feet—first one foot and then with both—we practiced until we could do this easily when the room was dark. No one suspected us of any trick because we were such young children. We were led on by my sister purposefully and by my mother unintentionally. We often heard her say, "Is this a disembodied spirit that has taken possession of my dear children?"

CONVINCED THAT MURDER HAD BEEN DONE

That encouraged our fun, and we went on. All the neighbors thought there was something, and they wanted to find out what it was. They were convinced some one had been murdered in the house. They asked us about it, and we would rap one for the spirit answer "Yes," not three, as we did afterwards. We did not know anything about Spiritualism then. The murder, they concluded, must have been committed in the house. They went over the whole surrounding country trying to get the names of people who had formerly lived in the house. They found finally a man by the name of Bell, and they said that this poor innocent man had committed a murder in the house, and that these noises came from the spirit of the murdered person. Poor Bell was shunned and looked upon by the whole community as a murderer. As far as spirits were concerned, neither my sister nor I thought about it.

I am the widow of Dr. Kane, the Arctic explorer, and I say to you now, as I hold his memory dear and would call him to me were it possible, I know that there is no such thing as the departed returning to this life. I have tried to do so in every form, and know that it cannot be done. Many people have said to me that such a thing was possible, and seemed to believe so firmly in it that I tried to see if it were possible. When in London, some years ago, I went to the sexton of a churchyard and asked him if I could go among the graves at 12 o'clock at night. He consented when I told him that I wanted to do this for a certain purpose. I left my servant at the gate outside. I went to each grave and stood over it, and called upon the dead, alone there in the dark, to come and give me some token of their presence. All was silent, and I found that the dead would not return. That is how I tested it. There is no test left that I have not thoroughly sifted. Mediums I do not visit. They are too low and too illiterate. Dr. H. Wadsworth, of 21 Queen Anne Street, London—a very dear friend of mine—sent me money for my expenses to go over to London. I said to him when I arrived; "I think too much of you to have you deceived, and there is nothing in Spiritualism. It is a fraud."

He answered me: "I thank you for telling me about it, Maggie. I know all the rest to be humbug. I thought I would have you to come in last." I said: "There are no dead or departed spirits that have ever returned." He said: "If you say so, Maggie, it must be true, because I have always believed in you." But still he seemed incredulous.

HOW THE SÉANCES WERE HELD

To return to the story of my childhood: I said I had gone with sister Katie and Mrs. Underhill, my oldest sister, to Rochester. It was here that Mrs. Underhill gave her exhibitions. She took us there and we were exhibited to a lot of Spiritualist fanatics. We had crowds coming to see us and Mrs. Underhill made as much as $100 to $150 a night. She pocketed this. Parties came in from all parts to see us. Many as soon as they heard a little rap were convinced. But as the world grew wiser and science began to investigate, my younger sister and myself began to adapt our experiments to our audiences. Our séances were held in a room. There was a centre-table in the middle, and we all stood around it. There were some who even believed that the spirits of living people could be materialized. There are many different forms of Spiritualism. To all questions we would answer by raps. When I look back upon that life, I almost say in defense of myself that I did not take any pleasure in it. I never believed in the spirits and I never professed to be a Spiritualist. My cards always say: "Mrs. Kane does not claim any spirit power, but people must judge for themselves." Nobody has ever suspected anything from the start, in 1848, until the present day as to any trickery in our methods. There has never been a detection.

HOW THE RAPPING IS DONE

Like most perplexing things when once made clear, it is astonishing how easily it is done. The rappings are simply the result of a perfect control of the muscles of the leg below the knee which govern the tendons of the foot and allow action of the toe and ankle bones that are not commonly known. Such perfect control is only possible when a child is taken at an early age and carefully and continually taught to practice the muscles which grow stiff in later years. A child at twelve is almost too old. With control of the muscles of the foot the toes may be brought down to the floor without any movement that is perceptible to the eye. The whole foot, in fact, can be made to give rappings by the use only of muscles below the knee. This, then, is the simple explanation of the whole method of knocks and raps.

Some very wealthy people, formerly of San Francisco, came to see me some years ago when I lived in Forty-second street, and I did some rapping for them. I made the spirit rap on the chair, and one of the ladies cried out, "I feel the spirit tapping me on the shoulder." Of course, that was pure imagination. A great many people, however, when they hear the rapping imagine at once that the spirits are touching them. It is a very common delusion. One fanatic gives Sunday services at the Adelphi Hall yet. He is called the "Old Patriarch." He said to someone the other day: "If Mrs. Kane says that she can make these rappings without the aid of the spirits, she lies." This person will be one of those who will see that I speak the truth.

THE MEETING WITH DR. KANE

As I have said before, my sister Katie and myself continued in this business until she was twelve years old and I thirteen and a half. After we left Rochester, we travelled all over the United States. I was thirteen years old when Dr. Kane took care of me and took me out of the miserable life. We began in 1848, and it was in 1853 that he took me away from this thing. It was at Philadelphia he met me. He sent me to a seminary and my vacations were spent with Mrs. Waters [Mrs. Walter] a sister of Senator Cockrell. She lives now at No. 7 East Sixty-second Street. She was a little inclined to believe in Spiritualism herself, although she never let Dr. Kane know it. I was taken away from all "spiritual" influences and for a long time did not see any of my old associates.

When Dr. Kane came into the room at Philadelphia, I told him that I hated this thing, that I had been pushed into it. I explained to him that it was a trick, that I had been forced into it and did not want to go on with it. I think not that if my brain had not been very round,[2] I should have been a maniac. Spiritualists say that I am mad now that if I attempt to expose these tricks that I am mad. I have had a life of sorrow, I have been poor and ill, but I consider it my duty, a sacred thing, a holy mission to expose it. I want to see the day that it is entirely done away with. After my sister Katie and I expose it, I hope Spiritualism will be given a death blow.

IN TERROR OF HER SISTER

Every morning of my life I have it before me. When I would wake up, I would brood over it, and Dr. Kane has said to me more than once, "Maggie, I see that the vampire is over you still." Dr. Kane was certainly not a believer in Spiritualism. He was often horrified at the blasphemy of these fanatics. One day he came into the room, at Philadelphia, and an old fanatic asked me to call up St. Paul. The doctor hurried in and took me out. He was shocked beyond measure. If those we love who have passed away before us can look down upon us from heaven—if we are ever to meet again—I know my dead husband is looking on me now and blessing me for my work.

I remember one time before my marriage the death of Mr. Brown the second husband of my sister Mrs. Fish, now Mrs. Underhill. Although Dr. Kane had no great devotion to Mr. Brown, he had respect for death. He sent his body servant Morton to sit up with the corpse. When he was laid out, he asked me to come and look at the dead and to see how dreadful it was to trifle with death. There were several champagne bottles in the room, I suppose for the refreshment of Morton—and as I entered the room a cork popped with a dreadful noise, and I made for the door terrified. My sister forced me to wear mourning for Mr. Brown and to go to the funeral in state. This is an example of how entirely under the influence of Mrs. Underhill I was during that dreadful time. Katie and I were led around like lambs. We went to New York from Rochester, then all over the United States. We drew

2. Maggie is probably referring to phrenology, the pseudoscience where head shape is thought to determine personality traits.

immense crowds. I remember particularly Cincinnati. We stopped at the Burnett House. The rooms were jammed from morning until night and we were called upon by these old wretches to show our rapping when we should have been out at play in the fresh air. We made the tour of the United States, and came back to New York where Mrs. Underhill left us. Mother went on to Philadelphia and took me and that is where Dr. Kane met me and brought me away from this life.

All during this dreadful life of deception I had been protesting. I have always rebelled against it. I have been going to expose it time and time again. After I married, Dr. Kane would not let me refer to my old life—he wanted me to forget it. He hated the publicity. When I was poor, after his death I was driven to it again. I have told my sister, Mrs. Underhill, time and time again: "Now that you are rich, why don't you save your soul?" But at my words she would fly into a passion. She wanted to establish a new religion and she told me that she received messages from spirits. She knew we were tricking people, but she tried to make us believe that spirits existed. She told us that before we were born spirits came into her room and told her that we were destined for great things. But we knew when to rap 'yes' or 'no' according to certain signs she made us during the séance. After my marriage my sister Katie still kept up the séances. She had many wealthy patrons here in New York—Mr. Livermore, a wealthy banker, and a Dr. Gray, a well-known homeopathic physician. They used to have regular meeting privately and Katie was the medium.

I have seen so much miserable deception that I am willing to assist in any way and to positively state that Spiritualism is a fraud of the worst description. I do so before my God, and my idea is to expose it. I despised it. I never want to lay eyes on any Spiritualists again, and I wish to say clearly that I owe all my misfortune to that woman, my sister, Mrs. Underhill. The last act of treachery she did—she has been persecuting me all along until recently—was to take my boys[3] from me. Her hand has been felt in all my sorrows and misfortunes.

Now I am, I hope, a Christian and a sincere one. I am a Catholic, baptized in the Roman Catholic Church by the Rev. Father Quinn in St. Peter's in Barclay Street. I want to do honor to my faith. Father Quinn said to me that as long as I was in this business and did not believe in it and had to support myself, to charge very high prices so that is would at least limit the number of my patrons; that I should not give any free exhibition, and never claim supernatural powers.

3. Maggie or whoever took down her statement was confused. The sons she speaks of were Kate's, not hers.

FRAUD, HYPOCRISY AND DELUSION

When Dr. Kane died, he left only $5,000 in trust for me. There was a suit over the possession of some of the doctor's letters which I wanted to publish. These letters have been in the care of a Catholic priest, and also of my lawyer. Afterwards some of these letters were published, although Dr. Kane's family strongly objected. The book was called 'The Love Life of Dr Kane.' I received but little income from the book and have had few sources of revenue. I now am very poor. I intend, however, to make the expose of Spiritualism because I think it is my sacred duty. If I cannot do it, who can?—I have been the beginning of it. I hope to reduce at least the ranks of the 8,000,000 Spiritualists now in this country. I go into it as a holy war. I do not want it understood that the Catholic Church has advised me to make these public disclosures and confessions. It is my own idea, my own mission. I would have done it long ago if I could have had the necessary money and courage to do it. I could not find any one to help me. I was too timid to ask.

My eldest sister, Mrs. Underhill, has gone to the country, and this expose will be a severe blow to her, and perhaps kill her. I am waiting anxiously and fearlessly for the moment when I can show the world, by personal demonstration, that all Spiritualism is a fraud and a deception. It is a branch of legerdemain, but it has to be closely studied to gain perfection. None but a child taken at an early age would have ever attained the proficiency and wrought such widespread evil as I have.

I trust that this statement, coming solemnly from me, the first and most successful in this deception, will break the force of the rapid growth of Spiritualism, and prove that it is all a fraud, a hypocrisy and a delusion.

—Margaret Fox Kane

BONES IN "OLD SPOOK HOUSE."

Apparent Confirmation of Story Told by Originators of Spiritualism.

NEWARK, N. Y., Nov. 22.—William H. Hyde, owner of what was known as the "Old Spook House," has discovered human bones under the cellar wall, which had fallen in as the result of being undermined by running water.

It was in the "Old Spook House" at Hydesville, Wayne County, N. Y., that the Fox sisters, daughters of Mr. and Mrs. John D. Fox, started the movement which has resulted in modern Spiritualism.

The Fox family occupied the house in the late forties. In 1848 the family were much disturbed by certain mylsterious "knocks" and "raps." It is alleged that at length Kate Fox, one of the two daughters, discovered that the cause of the sounds was intelligent, and that questions asked would be answered by the number of raps, one for "no" and three for "yes."

There is absolutely no doubt that the Fox girls declared that the rappings proceeded from the spirit of a certain peddler, whose throat had been cut by a previous tenant of the house, and whose body had been buried in the cellar.

An investigation of the matter seemed to show that none of the Fox family produced the rappings. Efforts were made to find the body of the peddler, but they were unsuccessful, probably because of the quantity of running water that was encountered when digging in the cellar was begun.

It was at Rochester, where the two Fox girls afterward went to live with a married sister, Mrs. Fish, that modern Spiritualism assumed its present form, and that communication was, it was asserted, established with the spirits of inquirers' relatives and with dead eminent men. Kate Fox and her sister were the first "mediums."

In 1904, the discovery of bones in the cellar wall at the original Fox family home in Hydesville was reported in states across the country including New York, California, Pennsylvania, Indiana, Alabama, Ohio, Kansas, Kentucky, Arizona, Montana, Arkansas, Utah, Vermont, and Wisconsin, as well as Washington, DC.

"It is a very common delusion . . . I know that there is no such thing as the departed returning to this life."

AUTHOR'S NOTE

In the five years I've spent researching the lives of the Fox sisters, I have moved from skepticism to belief, and back, hundreds of times. In large part, this is due to the quality of the available historical sources. The Fox sisters and the Spiritualist movement appear in hundreds of books, thousands of newspapers, journals, and magazines. Yet, most accounts are secondhand, and more problematically, written by either confirmed believers or confirmed skeptics. Objective primary sources about the sisters, and their spirits, are in such short supply as to be essentially nonexistent.

Leah's book, *The Missing Link in Modern Spiritualism,* is thorough, yet often unreliable, and obviously one-sided in support of the spirits. Though it once helped convince millions of the truth of spirit communication, her Victorian-era writing is so overdramatic, that today, most of the book reads as proof *against* spirit existence. Leah's book does extensively and for the most part accurately quote actual letters and newspaper clippings. From her correspondence with Amy Post and others, we see glimpses into what seems like the oldest Fox sister's real thoughts and feelings. However, due to her profession, Leah was both guarded and attempting to persuade the public with every word she wrote.

Books promoted as Maggie and/or Kate's memoirs were ghostwritten by others. Maggie's Crooksville journal, quoted by some old sources, is now lost. Only a handful of letters from Kate or Maggie exist. Early on, both sisters sound like typical young teens, sometimes teasing and full of fun, other times bored or frustrated. Later letters written by

Maggie, mostly to Robert Kane or Cornelius Grinnell, have to do with finances. After alcoholism set it, Maggie's letters swing wildly in subject and tone. From flirtation in French, "cher ami," to passive-aggressiveness, "I am sorry that you did not call again as promised," to insults, "The fact is you are all a set of cross kings . . . the only pleasant gentleman I have met is Mr. Grinnell, he was kind, he is a Christian, you are not." Considering its content, the signature on this derogatory letter is outrageous, "With love, truly your friend, Margaret Fox."

Neither Maggie nor Kate wrote much about séance specifics. One of Kate's letters to Amy Post from Cincinnati is typical of the level of detail, "the Spirits are doing wonderful things with us . . . the guitar was played. bells rang acordeon played. all while our feet were held." Overall, Kate comes across as a more solid believer in the spirits than Maggie.

Other than the 1888 *New York World* confession, news quotes are brief, a few sentences at most. Though we can learn much about the Fox sisters' actions from their believers and detractors, we have little direct evidence for what Maggie or Kate truly thought or felt about their lives. They are historical ghosts, glimpsed only in the mirror of others' opinions. All three Fox sisters lied repeatedly about their ages, excused their actions, and blamed each other. The historical evidence, even that written by the sisters, is never to be fully trusted.

So, I started out as a skeptic. I took a single primary source, Maggie's 1888 *New York World* confession, as the truth. I felt that Maggie Fox and her sister Kate got caught up in an April Fool's trick. They dropped an apple on a string, or rapped their toes on a headboard, and the resulting knocking sounds fooled their mother into thinking it was a spirit. The joke got out of hand once the neighbors arrived. Maggie and Kate were simply too scared of punishment or embarrassment, to admit the truth. They continued rapping by cracking their joints, which became how their older sister, Leah, made a living that supported them all.

The longer the original lie was kept secret, the harder it was to tell the truth. Plus, they enjoyed the attention, fun, and rich life their "spirits" provided.

Except, it is almost easier to believe in knocking spirits than the fact that the Fox sisters *taught themselves* to be world-class magicians and performers. Individually and together, they confounded relatives, friends, strangers, and some of the most prominent scientists, politicians, and writers of their time. The idea that two poorly educated teenagers (and their music teacher sister) could pull off such a long-standing hoax is truly miraculous.

So, for a time I thought there must have been at least some real supernatural power behind their mediumship. I moved toward the conclusion of a 1975 (!) University of Wisconsin history department dissertation, "the Fox sisters did possess extra-normal powers of extra-sensory perception, telepathy, and telekinesis." It is a reasonable conclusion given the manifestations the sisters produced and the number of sophisticated people they convinced.

However, I have learned that more than a century of scientific study has found no real proof of human extra-normal powers. As far back as 1882, Great Britain's Society for Psychical Research (SPR) studied mediumship and séance phenomena. In the US, the oldest such organization is the American Society for Psychical Research (ASPR), formed in New York City in 1884 and still housed there today.

By 1911, a professor at Stanford had performed some of the first university studies in extrasensory perception (ESP), which includes telepathy (communicating thoughts with the mind) and clairvoyance (ability to predict the future.) Other major US universities housed long-term paranormal studies or labs on parapsychology (the study of mental phenomenon not explained by traditional science). Among the most prominent were Duke, UCLA, Princeton, the University of Virginia, the

University of Arizona, and Cornell. For decades, these schools, and other institutions, studied subjects as varied as precognition, telepathy, psychokinesis, energy fields, reincarnation, and mediumship. Taken together, topics like these are known as psi, the scientific study of "processes of information or energy transfer that are currently unexplained in terms of known physical or biological mechanisms."

Though some psi studies continue today, most major universities have ended their programs due to inconsistent findings, lack of usefulness, or outright fraud. Interest in spirits and other parapsychology topics has usually increased in times of strife (during and after World War I in Great Britain, for example). But, as of this book's writing, no instance of spirit contact with mortals has been scientifically proven. Every medium so studied has been debunked, if not in the sessions, then by materials, photos, or interviews after the fact.

Scientific studies have found some proven psychological techniques used by many mediums and psychics, including the Fox sisters:

1. The Barnum (named for P. T. Barnum) effect: making statements so vague as to be true for most people, e.g., "You can be shy."
2. Observing and acting upon cues from body language, dress, and manner of speaking.
3. Framing the existing situation, e.g., if a medium or psychic says something is moving, people expect, and are more likely to experience, motion.
4. Confirmation bias. People believe what they desire, and they remember correct answers more than incorrect ones.
5. Sensory control. In séances, holding hands gives participants a feeling of safety, while ensuring they can't disrupt planned tricks, and darkness creates sensitivity to sound, motion, and feelings.

Skilled stage magicians can reproduce the phenomena of the Fox sisters and the mediums inspired by them. Same experience, no spirits needed. To scientists (and all magicians *are* scientists) the simplest explanation, deception, is the correct one.

However, Maggie's confession does not go nearly far enough. Spiritualist believers are correct in that it didn't explain all (or even most) of the manifestations that occurred. Cracking joints do not explain specific accurate answers like those given to James Fenimore Cooper. They do not explain how people like Reverend Hammond experienced sliding tables, unrolling window shades, and moving cabinet drawers. They do not explain the frantic, two-handed, mirror-writing that occurred with Dr. George and Sarah Taylor. And they certainly don't explain physical manifestations of spirits like that of Estelle Livermore or the ever-present Benjamin Franklin.

Yet, other mediums, operating much like the Fox sisters, were exposed outright while producing very similar manifestations. All were found to be fraudulent—tricks of costuming, light, accomplices, secret tools, background research, and lots of practice.

Except, I was once greatly comforted by a psychic medium, a total stranger, who told me what I took to be specific details about my much loved, deceased grandfather. She started our session, "his name begins with an S"; and in fact, my grandfather's name was Stanley, which she couldn't have known. She told me how he was laughing (he had a terrific sense of humor), that there might be something unusual about his face (he had vitiligo, a condition in which the skin loses pigment), and how he watched over me and my family. Even if magician's tricks can produce similar results, people (like me) have still received great comfort in messages from deceased loved ones. Not all truth is scientific.

Yet, taking Maggie's confession as fact, it's obvious that the Fox sisters preyed on vulnerable people. How many grieving mothers did

Maggie lie to? How many desperate husbands did Kate trick? How many trusting friends did Leah manipulate to make herself rich? The presumed deception, including within their own family, is so deep as to be unfathomable.

Plus, there's the fact that Maggie did not tell the whole truth, not even in 1888. In the *World* story, Maggie said she was eight years old and Kate, six, when they began dropping apples and snapping toes in Hydesville, where she also falsely claims they were born. Maggie threw the blame on Leah for taking two innocent children and forcing them into a life of lies. In reality, Maggie and Kate Fox were fourteen and eleven when the rappings began, certainly old enough to know the difference between right and wrong. It seems true that as a manager, Leah controlled her sisters, then later rejected them—a familiar celebrity story even today. But it's hard to believe that a childhood fear of exposure was enough to explain forty years of deception.

Instead, it's possible that Maggie and Kate believed in their own powers much of the time. Growing up in an era of ecstatic religious feeling, brought up by a fervent father and superstitious mother, the youngest Fox sisters may have been susceptible to the notion of spirits.

When the girls were brought to Leah's house, *the spirits were declared real*. Leah was the only sister who never denied their existence. She was the only sister who expressed a lifelong belief in Spiritualism. Whether Leah truly believed or whether she kept up a false story to propel herself into the comfortable middle class cannot be known.

At Leah's, Maggie and Kate were fed a relentless narrative that they had been chosen to speak to the dead. Maggie said that Leah "told us that before we were born spirits came into her room and told her that we were destined for great things." The fame, adult praise, new clothes, and excitement of their celebrity were benefits that almost any teenager would love. If Kate or Maggie's self-belief ever faltered, they had only to listen to their supporters or read the media, constantly feeding the world the story of the Fox sisters' marvelous powers.

So, wasn't society responsible also? These were intelligent women, born into a working-class life; one already had a daughter to support. In a boom town like Rochester, they watched as men of their class turned into financial and social success stories. Perhaps they longed for similar opportunities.

In the mid-1800s, the Fox sisters, like almost all women, were not allowed to support themselves in business, law, education, medicine, or the trades. Being female meant they could not legally own property or vote; even their children belonged to their husbands. Instead, society told them if they were obedient, polite, and followed the rules, they would be taken care of by men. Society lied. Their father stayed poor. Mr. Fish left. Calvin Brown died. Elisha Kane died. Henry Jencken died. Perhaps, communicating with spirits was the way they made their livings, built lives, and saved themselves.

But, if Maggie's confession is true, then the Fox sisters' long hoax also took advantage of grief and is therefore despicable and unforgivable.

And still, for me, there is a troubled admiration for the Fox sisters' advance within a society that insisted they stay powerless. By developing their skills, socializing with influencers, and pursuing risks that encouraged sensational press promotion, Leah, Maggie, and Kate claimed power for themselves in a particularly individual, American way.

I was struck over and over by similarities between their times and ours, including: countrywide divisions, political name-calling, competing media outlets, new technologies, conspiracy theories, an addiction crisis, a pandemic, and the emphasis on fame. Like many celebrities today, the Fox sisters broke social norms. The séance format that they developed allowed three working-class, barely educated women to advise higher-class, well-educated men, who never would have listened otherwise.

The Fox sisters' early success led other women into public careers as spiritual speakers and writers. Many of them, like Sojourner Truth and Victoria Woodhull, became important spokeswomen for other social justice movements. Modern Spiritualism helped normalize female leadership—advancing the public power and wisdom of women's voices.

Leah cultivated that power and social standing, enjoying riches and respect for the rest of her life. For a time, her sisters, Kate and Maggie Fox, held greater power and a larger place in the public consciousness as the original spirit mediums. Then addiction, fueled perhaps by genetics, stress, or guilt, took that power away. Once again, a familiar celebrity story today. For the famous, it's always been hard to hang on to the truth and easy to lose one's real self.

So, let's imagine sitting at a table, in the dark, holding hands. For, in the end, maybe only the spirits can answer the many questions left by the lives of the Fox sisters.

Were they fakers? Were they faithful? Were they villains? Were they victims?

Rap. Rap. Rap.

ACKNOWLEDGMENTS

The opinions and conclusions expressed in this book about both spirits and mortals are my own. However, I owe a great debt to the following people, believers and skeptics both, who were kind enough to share their thoughts and provide resources about the Fox sisters, historical locations, performance, and women's history including: Chris Davis, Executive Director, Newark-Arcadia Historical Society Museum; William Keeler, Librarian Archivist, Rochester Historical Society; Autumn Haag, Assistant Director, Rare Books, Special Collections and Preservation, University of Rochester River Campus Libraries; Cynthia Howk, The Landmark Society of Western New York; Jane Milem, Wayne County Historian Office (NY); Tracy Murphy, Historian and Caretaker, Fox Sisters and Hydesville Property; Keith Mages, Curator, R. L. Brown History of Medicine Collection, University at Buffalo Libraries; Jonathan Pritchard, Mentalist; Neil Tobin, Mentalist; Brandon Hodge, Occult Historian; Ron Nagy, Historian, Lilydale Assembly. I also appreciate the work of librarians Sonia Schoenfield and Amy Heatherman, Cook Memorial Library, as well as the dedicated staff of: The Rochester Public Library; The Rochester History and Science Center, City of Buffalo Library; and Chicago's Newberry Library. Additional thanks to James Lundberg, Associate Professor of History, The University of Notre Dame.

SOURCE NOTES

CHAPTER 1—FOOL'S EVE

"My sister Katie . . .": "The Medium's Statement." *New York World*, Oct. 21, 1888.

"almost sick": Lewis, 6.

"the simplest things . . .": Jackson, Jr., 2.

"As fast as . . ." and "Now do this . . ." and "Count ten": Lewis, 6.

"Only look . . .": Cadwallader, 8.

"Is it a spirit?": Jackson, Jr., 3.

"not a believer . . .": Lewis, 9.

"Will this noise . . .": Lewis, 7.

"smart girls, bright . . .": Jackson, Jr., 20.

"much frightened" and "Now count . . ." and "Count fifteen" and "If you are . . ." and "we are innocent . . .": Lewis, 30.

CHAPTER 2—LOCAL CELEBRITIES

"All the people . . .": "The Medium's Statement," *New York World*, Oct. 21, 1888.

"It has caused . . .": Lewis, 10.

"A, . . ." and "B, . . ." and "C": "Singular Revelations," *New-York Tribune*, Nov. 29, 1849.

"Charles B. Rosna": National Spiritualist Association of Churches, nsac.org/who-we-are/history/.

"Rosema": Sieber, et al., 306.

"Rasme": "Singular Revelations," *New-York Tribune*, Nov. 29, 1849.

"Rosma": Doyle, *History*, vol. 1, 61.

"I cannot . . .": Lewis, 21.

"examined the premises . . .": Lewis, 25.

"I have no. . . .": Lewis, 20.

"The good people . . .": "Great 'Ghost' Excitement," *Western Argus*, Apr. 12, 1848.

"APRIL FOOL": *Newark Herald*, May 4, 1848, from Jackson, 16.

"I couldn't tell . . .": Hoeltzel, 81.
"They all seemed . . .": Lewis, 22.
"supernatural" and "haunt": Lewis, 3.
"murder": Lewis, 4.
"if the excitement . . .": *Newark Herald*, May 4, 1848, from Jackson, Jr., 17.
"Now do this . . .": Lewis, 6.
"Here, Mr. Splitfoot . . .": Peck, 510.

CHAPTER 3—THE DEVIL KNOCKS, A SISTER ANSWERS

"Our eldest sister . . .": "The Medium's Statement," *New York World*, Oct. 21, 1888.
"If my father . . .": Underhill, 31.
"information superhighway": "Canal in Song," nyheritage.org/exhibits/two-hundred-years-erie-canal/canal-song.
"Mr. Fish . . ." and "on business" and "delighted to find . . .": Underhill, 31.
"just at this . . . got Saved.": Jorgensen, 182.
"My Much Loved . . ." and "you Cant think . . .": Maggie Fox to Amy Post, Aug. 21, 1849, ID: 751 (RBSCP-Post).
"the haunted house": Underhill, 23.
"put a stop . . .": Underhill, 32.

CHAPTER 4—SPIRITS ABOUT THE HOUSE

"We were then . . .": "The Medium's Statement," *New York World*, Oct. 21, 1888.
"one end of . . ." and "a dreadful sound . . ." and "Why, what is . . .": Underhill, 33.
"the instant we . . .": Underhill, 34.
"we were awakened . . ." and "haunted": Underhill, 35.
"entirely from the . . ." and "We cannot much . . .": Underhill, 37.
"evil spirits" and "conquer or die . . .": Underhill, 38.
"the head-board in . . .": Underhill, 39.
"Is the Spirit . . . opposite side?": Webb, 236–238.

CHAPTER 5—THE INFLUENCERS

"I owe all . . .": "The Medium's Statement," *New York World*, Oct. 21, 1888.

"circles": Underhill, 87.

"Your family was . . .": Frederick Douglass to Amy Post, Apr. 28, 1846, from Powalski, 5.

"paid no more heed . . ." and "we do not . . ." and "very anxious" and "enjoy what they . . ." and "our little Dutch . . ." and "love very much . . ." and "they always speak . . ." and "it has been . . .": Isaac Post to Joseph & Mary Post, Nov. 23, 1848, SC-176 (SFHL-PFP).

"atrocious" and "refused to answer": Douglass from Powalski, 10.

"crazy" and "Drag out . . .": Underhill, 25.

"Great God! here . . .": Underhill, 24.

"Dear faithful friends . . .": Jackson, Jr., 38.

"How we all . . .": Underhill, 25.

"God will reward . . .": Jackson, Jr., 38.

"Several bones were . . ." and "In the name . . .": Underhill, 24.

"sunk in the . . .": Jackson, Jr., 39.

"You are welcome . . .": Underhill, 27.

"Is the Spirit . . . require her to bow": Webb, 240–242.

"Ma, how can . . .": Davenport, 128.

CHAPTER 6—SPIRIT INVESTIGATORS

"we were frightened . . .": "The Medium's Statement" *New York World*, Oct. 21, 1888.

"rap my age" and "rap four times" and "rap seven" and "I resolved to test . . .": Capron, *Modern Spiritualism*, 75.

"the change which takes . . .": Capron, *Modern Spiritualism*, 32.

"Will the Spirit come tonight?": Webb, 240.

"put her asleep": Braude, 15.

"magnetized": Isaac Post from Powalski, 9.

"put in the clairvoyant state": Willets from Capron, *Modern Spiritualism*, 70.

"black cholera": Daly, 143.

"bad air": "150th Anniversary of John Snow and the Pump Handle," Centers for Disease Control and Prevention, cdc.gov/mmwr/preview/mmwrhtml/mm5334a1.htm.

"wilds of the West": Underhill, 104.

"Make ready for the work": Underhill, 58.
"We want you . . .": Underhill, 60.
"One morning, on . . ." and "Each coffin . . ." and "If you do not . . .": Underhill, 59.
"several weeks": Capron, *Modern Spiritualism*, 101.
"nothing could please . . .": Capron, *Modern Spiritualism*, 88.
"We will now . . .": Capron, *Modern Spiritualism*, 89.
"The spirits have . . ." and "The spirits have . . .": Jones, 143.
"Perhaps they will . . ." and "And so they . . .": Underhill, 60.
"Hire Corinthian . . .": Underhill, 62.
"enough to pay . . .": Capron, *Modern Spiritualism*, 91.
"Wonderful Phenomena" and "COME AND INVESTIGATE . . . ladies": *Rochester Daily Advertiser* quoted in Jackson, Jr., 48.

CHAPTER 7—ALTOGETHER RIGHT, ALTOGETHER WRONG

"that I should . . .": "The Medium's Statement," *New York World*, Oct. 21, 1888.
"gaping ears": "A Chapter on Ghosts," *Rochester Republican*, Nov. 29, 1849.
"the more the . . .": *Rochester Daily Democrat*, Nov. 16, 1849, from Stuart, 52.
"humbug": "A Chapter on Ghosts," *Rochester Republican*, Nov. 29, 1849.
"not altogether right . . ." and "entirely failed . . .": "Singular Revelations," *New-York Tribune*, Nov. 29, 1849.
"If I cannot . . .": Pond, 42.
"howling mob": Underhill, 71.
"Life, Liberty and . . .": National Archives, Declaration of Independence, archives.gov/founding-docs/declaration.
"slavery question": "Fifteen 'fixed facts,' or facts which cannot be successfully controverted," *Daily Nashville Union*, Nov. 10, 1851.
"Northern and Southern . . . & etc.": "Correspondence of the *Baltimore Sun*" from *Plain Dealer*, Jan. 18, 1850.
"A Chapter on . . .": "A Chapter on Ghosts," *Rochester Republican*, Nov. 29, 1849.

CHAPTER 8—THE SPIRITUAL TELEGRAPH

"we were destined . . .": "The Medium's Statement," *New York World*, Oct. 21, 1888.

"That Rochester Ghost . . .": "That Rochester Ghost is still knocking at . . . ," *Detroit Free Press*, Nov. 23, 1849.

"SINGULAR REVELATIONS . . .": "Singular Revelations," *New-York Tribune*, Nov. 29, 1849.

"Go West, young . . .": "The *New York World* Says," *Democrat and Chronicle*, Apr. 24, 1873.

"smart": "A PUNNING LETTER," *The Daily Crescent*, June 18, 1850.

"portly": A Searcher After Truth, 19.

"gentle": Dewey, 1st ed., 58.

"sparkling and irrepressible": Kane and Fox, 35.

"dreamy": Susannah Moodie quoted in Weisberg, 142.

"sensitive": Harriet Beecher Stowe quoted in Weisberg, 215.

"ladies": various, see "Stop Dat Knocking," *Louisville Daily Courier*, Dec. 5, 1849.

"The matter is . . .": *Rochester Daily Magnet*, Feb. 26, 1850, from Capron, *Modern Spiritualism*, 82.

"Persons of such . . .": "The people of *Rochester*. . . ," *Hartford Courant*, Dec. 3, 1849.

"similar to the . . .": Dewey, 1st ed., 60.

"Now I am . . . FRANKLIN.": Dewey, 1st ed., 61–62.

"shut up until . . .": "From the *New-York Tribune*. Those Rochester 'Rappings,'" *Plain Dealer*, Mar. 11, 1850.

"music teacher": *Rochester City Directory*, 1849, 113.

"mysterious knocker": *Rochester City Directory*, 1851, 125.

"forced to charge . . .": Taylor, W. G., 147.

"The sum thus . . .": "News of the Day," *Alexandria* (VA) *Gazette*, Mar. 27, 1850.

"every part of . . .": Hammond quoted in Dewey, 1st ed., 29.

"passed out of . . ." and "Will the spirit . . ." and "spirit's song" and "a transparent hand . . ." and "played back and . . ." and "That any of . . .": Hammond quoted in Dewey, 1st ed., 31–32.

"the Foxy abode . . . at my school.": Strong, 5–6.

CHAPTER 9—MAKING MEDIUMS

"I have tried . . .": "The Medium's Statement," *New York World*, Oct. 21, 1888.

"let us prepare . . .": Isaacs, 70.

"fools are not . . .": "It is really wonderful that in Western *New York* . . . ," *Hartford Courant*, Apr. 22, 1850.

"A reformation is . . .": Parker, 268–269.

"without any action . . .": Capron, *Modern Spiritualism*, 99.

"twelve years of . . ." and "apparently 17 or 18 . . .": *NY Merchant's Day Book* from Dewey, 1st ed., 58.

"world of spirits": "Spiritual World (Afterlife)," Swedenborg Foundation, swedenborg.com/emanuel-swedenborg/explore/spiritual-world/.

"Poughkeepsie Seer": Butler, "The Poughkeepsie Seer—Andrew Jackson Davis," poklib.org/the-poughkeepsie-seer-andrew-jackson-davis/.

"another link in . . .": Capron, *Modern Spiritualism*, 7.

"perfectly willing" and "say for themselves . . .": Capron and Barron, *Singular Revelations*, 80.

"pro or con . . .": Dewey, Preface, 1st ed., i.

"Additional Facts": Dewey, 2nd ed., 77.

"a turnip covered . . .": Dewey, 2nd ed., 78.

"I this morning . . .": Eliab Capron to Margaret Smith Fox, Feb. 2, 1850 (RBSCP-Post).

"we were directed . . .": Underhill, 115.

"The people in . . .": "Stop That Knocking!," *Weekly Argus*, Feb. 16, 1850.

"blasphemy against . . .": Underhill, 118.

"quiet, gracious . . .": Pond, 53.

"rests on extremely . . ." and "worthy of . . .": "Communion with Spirits," *Brooklyn Daily Eagle*, Jan. 17, 1850.

"We incline to . . ." and "a great many . . .": "From the New-York Tribune. Those Rochester 'Rappings'" from *Plain Dealer*, Mar. 11, 1850.

"The Rochester 'Spirits' . . .": "The Knockings," *Troy Daily Whig*, May 1, 1850.

CHAPTER 10—BIG-CITY SPIRITS

"They took a . . .": "The Medium's Statement," *New York World*, Oct. 21, 1888.

"half-intoxicated": Davenport, 130.

"The daughters of . . .": "Who's That Knocking," *Baltimore Sun*, June 4, 1850.

"they do not mean . . ." and "private investigations . . .": "The Mysterious Rappings," *Evening Post*, June 1, 1850.

"ATTENTION is specially . . . One Dollar": "Miss Fox's Seances Twenty Years Ago," *Medium and Daybreak*, Dec. 6, 1872.

"seemed to be. . . ." and "Are you a friend?" and "Are you a relative?" and "double thump . . ." and "How many years . . ." and "whole deportment . . ." and "We are not willing . . ." and "hoped to have some . . .": "An Hour with 'The Spirits,'" *New-York Tribune*, June 5, 1850.

"considerably prettier . . .": "Post Mortuum Soiree," *Home Journal*, June 15, 1850.

"a very pretty . . .": "A Visit to the Knocking Family," *New York Herald*, June 17, 1850.

"Will the Spirits converse . . . prepossession in their favor.": "An Evening with the 'Spirits,'" *New-York Tribune*, June 8, 1850.

"the 'demonstration' . . .": "Post Mortuum Soiree," *Home Journal*, June 15, 1850.

"correcting an erroneous . . .": "The Rochester Knockings," *Evening Post*, June 15, 1850.

"penny papers": University of Illinois, library.illinois.edu/hpnl/tutorials/antebellum-newspapers-city/.

CHAPTER 11—STARDOM!

"wanted to establish . . .": "The Medium's Statement," *New York World*, Oct. 21, 1888.

"Firm, united let us be, / Rallying round our liberty": lyrics, "Hail Columbia," songofamerica.net/song/hail-columbia/.

"Summerland": Davis, 126.

"All is rejoicing . . .": Isaacs, 221.

"Rochester Knockings": Underhill, 128.

"a new farce . . .": advertisement for "Mysterious Knockings," *Sunday Dispatch*, May 19, 1850.

"Ladies, you are . . ." and "keep the rabble . . .": Underhill, 128.

"first in the . . .": "The Medium's Statement," *New York World*, Oct. 21, 1888.

"One would think . . .": "Here's a Knocking, Indeed—," *Indiana State Sentinel*, July 11, 1850.

"the women who . . .": "Grimes on Knockings, & etc.," *New York Daily Tribune*, July 9, 1850.

"There are many . . .": "The Disembodied Spirits at Rochester," *New York Herald*, Jan. 23, 1850.

"ludicrous": "To all our Readers and Correspondents," *Holden's Dollar Magazine*, Sept. 1850, 574.

"trifling and nonsensical": "More of the Knockings," *Cleveland Herald*, July 3, 1850.

"a farce": "Mysterious Knockings," *Southern Press*, June 24, 1850.

"dunderheads": "Another Humbug Exploded," *Hinds County Gazette* (MS), July 12, 1850.

"fools": "We have devoted . . ." *Wayne County Herald*, PA, May 29, 1851.

"lunatic asylums": Isaacs, 110.

"socialistic": "The Socialistic Humbugs of the Day," *New York Herald*, June 16, 1850.

"extreme imbecility": *Northern Christian Advocate* from Jackson, 71.

"Modern Spiritualism": various, see "Putnam's Monthly," *Boston Evening Transcript*, Dec. 27, 1852.

CHAPTER 12—SEPARATIONS

"Katie and I . . .": "The Medium's Statement," *New York World*, Oct. 21, 1888.

"Castle Doleful": Lundberg, 48.

"a mere fraud . . .": Horace Greeley quoted in Stuart, 78.

"these singular sounds . . .": H. G. (Greeley) "The Mysterious Rappings," *New-York Tribune*, Aug. 10, 1850.

"O how I . . .": Kate Fox to "My Dear Friend," Oct. 26, 1850 (RBSCP-Post).

"murderous" and "Five villanous-looking . . ." and "A deep plot . . .": Underhill, 123.

"Send your mother . . .": Underhill, 124.

"You must be . . .": Underhill, 125.

"sick and nearly . . .": Underhill, 127.

CHAPTER 13—THE "BUFFALO GHOSTBUSTERS"

"the world grew . . .": "The Medium's Statement," *New York World*, Oct. 21, 1888.

"Buffalo Ghostbusters": Henning and Mages, 59.

"the muscles inserted . . .": *Buffalo Commercial Advertiser* from Underhill, 170.

"*spiritual rappings* may . . .": "To the Editor of the Commercial Advertiser," *Buffalo Commercial Advertiser*, Feb. 17, 1851.

"Buffalo Doctors": "More About the 'Rappings'—S. B. Britten," *New-York Tribune*, Feb. 27, 1851.

"a waste of time . . .": "To the Editor of the Commercial Advertiser," *Buffalo Commercial Advertiser*, Feb. 17, 1851.

"Gents" and "we do not . . .": Jackson, 94.

"The Rochester knockings . . .": Henning and Mages, 59.

"harsh": Underhill, 189.

"cruel": Underhill, 190.

"conceited": Underhill, 258.

"bigotry of modern . . .": Underhill, 173.

"a large Dinner Bell . . .": Charles White Kellogg quoted in Weisberg, 126.

"he had other . . .": Henning and Mages, 60.

"a more striking . . ." and "if they were to . . . their followers.": Lee, Charles, "Dr. Lee on Spiritualism," *New-York Tribune*, July 22, 1859.

CHAPTER 14—TRUTHTELLERS OR TRAITORS?

"Unless it is . . .": "The Medium's Statement," *New York World*, Oct. 21, 1888.

"Money flowed to . . .": Pond, 104.

"had brought them . . .": Pond, 126.

"from all parts . . .": Underhill, 250.

"warm" and "contempt" and "abuse" and "revilement": "The Compromise a Finality," *New York Times*, Dec. 9, 1851.

"Wonders of the . . .": "Wonders of the Nineteenth Century," *National Era*, Aug. 8, 1850.

"I did not write . . . his dictation.": Fields, 377.

"admirable": "Uncle Tom's Cabin," *Eastern Argus,* Mar. 26, 1852.

"too truthful": "Frederick Douglass' Paper," University of Virginia, Apr. 29, 1853, utc.iath.virginia.edu/africam/afar03pt.html.

"founded on imaginary . . ." and "historic amount . . .": Petschauer, "Fear and Resentment: The Southern Reaction to Uncle Tom's Cabin Before and After the War," ycphistpolisci.com/fear-and-resentment-the-southern-reaction-to-uncle-toms-cabin-before-and-after-the-civil-war/.
"delusion": Burr, 5.
"the self appointed . . .": Burr, 46.
"Spiritual Knockings Exposed": Chapin, 94.
"Rochester girls": Burr, 55.
"toe-o-logy": various, see "The Burrs are still giving . . . ," *Pittsburg Daily Post*, May 23, 1851.
"more than fifty": Burr, 5.
"Rochester Rappings": Burr, 26.
"I can now . . .": Burr, 6.
"nineteen": Burr, 30.
"about sixteen . . .": Burr, 34.
"aged about . . .": Burr, 42.
"A little girl . . ." and "feeble": Burr, 35.
"poorly educated": Burr, 46.
"a swarm of . . .": Burr, 63.
"fraud": Burr, 5.
"The Fox girls . . ." and "suspect that they . . ." and "consult the spirits . . ." and "satisfy . . ." and "assist her in . . ." and "should probably be . . ." and "sit next to . . ." and "After I had . . .": Carpenter, 150.
"was the first . . .": Carpenter, 151.
"too conscientious . . .": Carpenter, 151–152.
"At first it . . .": Carpenter, 150.
"I have sometimes . . ." and "told me how . . ." and "the countenance . . ." and "when I wished . . ." and "Dutch servant-girl . . .": Carpenter, 151.
"was very much . . ." and "I meant to . . ." and "they would never . . .": Carpenter, 152.

CHAPTER 15—SURPRISES ON TOUR

"It is astonishing . . .": "The Medium's Statement," *New York World*, Oct. 21, 1888.
"come immediately . . ." and "Burr is here . . .": Underhill, 221.
"it is not . . .": Burr, 15.

“a woman of . . .”: “New Way of Determining the Philosophy of Spirit Rappings,” *Plain Dealer*, May 15, 1851.

“It is not very manly . . .”: *Pittsburg Post* from Underhill, 239.

“Notwithstanding the burlesques . . .”: “A Change is Going On,” *Plain Dealer*, May 20, 1851.

“There are to . . .”: “Spirits Coming,” *Plain Dealer,* May 5, 1851.

“the strength . . .”: “Spiritual Accession,” *Plain Dealer,* May 31, 1851.

“the most perfect . . .”: “Spiritual Accession,” *Buffalo Daily Republic*, June 4, 1851.

“Make a Little Speculation . . .” and “Much of my trouble . . .”: Underhill letter to Amy Kirby Post, July 22, 1851 (RBSCP-Post).

“life was despaired . . .” and “all business . . .” and “for several days”: Underhill, 223.

“a bad manager”: Underhill letter to Amy Kirby Post, July 22, 1851 (RBSCP-Post).

“arrested him”: Underhill, 221.

“I pity her” and “very distant relatives” and “shamefully slandering”: “‘Mysterious Rappings’—The Fox Family—Mrs. Culver’s Statement,” *New-York Tribune*, Oct. 18, 1851,

“itinerant, catch-penny . . .”: *Pittsburg Post* from Underhill, 239.

“dunces”: “A Change is Going On,” *Plain Dealer*, May 20, 1851.

“accomplished mountebanks”: *Pittsburg Post* from Underhill, 238.

“bricks, broken eggs . . .” and “Welcome to . . .”: Underhill, 228.

“The Burrs . . . breeze”: *Cincinnati Nonpareil* from Underhill, 239.

“It has become . . .”: *Cincinnati Nonpareil* from Underhill, 241.

“Our progress . . .”: Underhill, 225.

“Ohio Campaign”: Underhill, ix.

“Oh so homesick . . .”: Catherine Fox letter to Amy Post, Nov. 185[?] (RBSCP-Post).

“We are still . . .”: Margaret Fox Kane letter to Amy Kirby Post, 185[?] (RBSCP-Post).

“dear sister”: Underhill, 229.

“what was supposed . . .”: Underhill, 230.

CHAPTER 16—A SCIENTIFIC FAITH

"It was a most . . .": "The Medium's Statement," *New York World*, Oct. 21, 1888.

"Rochester Rappers": various see, "The mysterious Rochester . . . ," *Brattleboro Eagle* (VT), June 6, 1850.

"handsome": Underhill, 252.

"the piano . . .": Catherine Fox to Amy Kirby Post, June 19, 1850[?] (RBSCP-Post).

"the spiritual telegraph": various see "Remarks," *New-York Tribune,* April 2, 1851.

"Ki-e-lou-cou-ze-ta": "Letters from Dr. Bristol," *Spiritual Telegraph*, Dec. 25, 1852.

"very eccentric": Hardinge, *Modern*, 110.

"fine, clairvoyant . . .": Hardinge, *Modern*, 166.

"the whole mass . . .": "A plain talk about Spiritualism and its Tendencies," *St. Albans Weekly Messenger* (VT), Sept. 8, 1853.

"an illustration . . .": "'Progress of Imposture,'" *Weekly National Intelligencer*, March 6, 1852.

"a singular . . .": "Spiritualists Convention," *New York Herald*, Aug. 8, 1852.

"a Rat-revelation . . .": Wilson, 248.

"I would exchange . . ." and "idiots, inspired . . .": Wilson, 249.

"luminous clouds" and "winding its way . . .": Partridge, "Spiritual Manifestations," *The Spirit Messenger and Harmonial Guide*, Nov. 8, 1851.

"Don't, I don't . . .": Elliott, 167.

"played upon . . .": Partridge, "Spiritual Manifestations," *The Spirit Messenger and Harmonial Guide*, Nov. 8, 1851.

"I'm touched . . .": Elliott, 167.

"always *under*. . ." and "most peculiar . . .": Elliot, 165.

"after various theatrical . . .": Elliott, 166.

"entirely disgusted . . ." and "listened for about . . .": Elliott, 167.

"the most absurd . . ." and "a chorus of . . ." and "I left them . . .": Elliott, 168.

"Does James miss . . . Wafer.": Britten, *Nineteenth Century Miracles*, 133.

"Spirits . . . are compelled . . .": Underhill, 182.

"You know I . . .": Ballou, 140.

CHAPTER 17—THE DOCTOR AND THE TEENAGE MEDIUM

"and that is where . . .": "The Medium's Statement," *New York World*, Oct. 21, 1888.
"It is at all . . ." and "quiet city": Kane and Fox, 22.
"I beg your . . .": Kane and Fox, 23.
"This is the . . ." and "I am . . .": Pond, 108.
"read in a penny . . .": Kane and Fox, 237.
"by Jove, I saw . . .": Kane and Fox, 238.
"open polar sea": various, see "Naval Defenses of the United States: Explorations and Surveys," *New York Herald*, Dec. 8, 1852.
"This is no life . . .": Kane and Fox, 26.
"Were you . . .": Kane and Fox, 27.
"Ask the . . .": Jackson, Jr., 124.
"Dr. Kane will . . .": Kane and Fox, 27.
"the richest . . .": Kane and Fox, 42.
"Dr. Kane leaves . . .": Kane and Fox, 27.
"Although I am . . .": Kane and Fox, 31.
"My Dear Miss . . .": Kane and Fox, 27–28.
"a very pleasant . . .": Pond, 116.
"practice in anything . . .": Kane and Fox, 72.
"I could not resist . . .": Kane and Fox, 28.
"Tell Miss Maggie . . ." and "favorite cousin": Kane and Fox, 29.
"a winning grace" and "reserve" and "self-control" and "a soul far . . .": Kane and Fox, 24.
"joyous": Kane and Fox, 36.
"repartee and mimicry": Jackson, Jr., 20.
"Leading her . . . marches to the grave": Kane and Fox, 36–37.
"Here, Margaret . . ." and "had suffered . . ." and "Maggie, you . . ." and "Elisha loves you . . .": Kane and Fox, 37.
"simpering behind . . .": E. K. Kane letter to Eliza Lieper, May 1853, from Stuart, 106.
"if I had my . . .": Kane and Fox, 66.
"an obscure . . .": Kane and Fox, 105.
"weary" and "dreary" and "deceit": Kane and Fox, 30.
"preacher": Kane and Fox, 37.
"a high position . . .": Kane and Fox, 42.

"very gentle . . .": Kane and Fox, 63.
"Wear your undersleeves . . .": Kane and Fox, 64.
"thinking too much" and "My dear . . .": Kane and Fox, 45.
"warmth and affection . . .": Kane and Fox, 53.
"darling": Kane and Fox, 51.
"sweet pet" and "sugar plum": Kane and Fox, 88.
"loveable": Kane and Fox, 48.
"You have more . . .": Kane and Fox, 46.
"I had no idea . . .": Kane and Fox, 47–48.
"Now, Doctor—": Kane and Fox, 46.
"It haunts me . . .": Kane and Fox, 49.
"I was unwilling . . .": Kane and Fox, 43.
"How disgusting . . .": Kane and Fox, 60.
"you should know . . .": Kate Fox to E. K. Kane, n.d. (APS-EKK Papers).
"I believe . . .": Kane and Fox, 106.
"Remember then . . .": Kane and Fox, 49.

CHAPTER 18—SHOULD I STAY OR SHOULD I GO?

"There were several . . .": "The Medium's Statement," *New York World*, Oct. 21, 1888.
"Tell Katie . . .": Kane and Fox, 253.
"examining recruits . . .": Elder, 175.
"Maggie darling—Why . . .": Kane and Fox, 51.
"How can I . . ." Kane and Fox, 52.
"a vain, pompous . . .": Pond, 125.
"How awful 'tis . . .": John Taylor letter to Elisha Kent Kane, January 4, 1846, from Sawin, 35.
"I miss you . . .": Kane and Fox, 54.
"walk past . . .": Kane and Fox, 55.
"The idea seems . . .": Kane and Fox, 56.
"Devil of . . .": Chapin, 127.
"Ly": Kane and Fox, 111.
"Cousin Peter": Kane and Fox, 63.
"F. Webster": Kane and Fox, 84.
"dark horse": "Franklin Pierce," The White House, whitehouse.gov/about-the-white-house/presidents/franklin-pierce/.

“We have been carried . . .”: “Franklin Pierce Inaugural Address,” University of California, Santa Barbara, presidency.ucsb.edu/documents/ inaugural-address-32.
“a time of . . .”: “Franklin Pierce,” The White House, whitehouse.gov/ about-the-white-house/presidents/franklin-pierce/.
“a curse . . .”: *Congressional Globe*, 33rd Congress, 1024.
“Am I obliged . . .”: *Congressional Globe*, 33rd Congress, 339.
“Only imagine Maggie . . .” and “low remarks” and “I am tired . . .”: Underhill, 270.
“tiresome life . . .”: Maggie Fox to Elisha Kent Kane, 1853 (APS-EKK Papers).
“visited daily . . .”: Sawin, 171.
“How does Washington . . .”: Kane and Fox, 64.
“*know* I have loved . . .”: Kane and Fox, 74.
“Is it any wonder . . .”: Kane and Fox, 65.
“a very fine . . .” and “This is all . . .”: Underhill, 270.
“if my sister . . .”: Underhill, 270–71.
“old country inns”: Kane and Fox, 88.
“her warm kisses . . .”: Kane and Fox, 77.
“first gave me . . .” Kane and Fox, 91.
“Come out . . .”: Kane and Fox, 81.
“refined, educated . . .”: Kane and Fox, 94.
“for my Maggie . . .”: Kane and Fox, 117.
“What have I . . .”: Maggie Fox to Elisha Kent Kane, 1853 (APS-EKK Papers).
“the old wretch”: Chapin, 127.
“sent her $75 . . .”: envelope, Leah Brown to Elisha Kent Kane, April 12, n.d. (APS-EKK Papers).
“purported to come . . .” and “a husband . . .”: Underhill, 253.
“Shall I go . . .”: Kane and Fox, 132.
“solemnly never . . .”: Kane and Fox, 133.
“Don’t rap . . .”: Kane and Fox, 114.
“Tell me how . . .”: Kane and Fox, 117.
“One final wish . . .”: Kane and Fox, 161.
“My own dear . . . Farewell, E.K. Kane”: Kane and Fox, 150-1.

CHAPTER 19—POOR GIRLS WITH PRETTY FACES

"Dr. Kane . . . brought . . .": "The Medium's Statement," *New York World*, Oct. 21, 1888.

"On the morning . . .": Kane and Fox, 149.

"intrepid" and "the indefatigable . . ." and "nothing . . .": "The Arctic Expedition," *New York Herald*, June 1, 1853.

"Just standing out . . .": Kane and Fox, 157.

"Don't mope . . .": Kane and Fox, 160.

"Dr. Kane's . . .": various, see "Dr. Kane's Arctic Expedition," *Baltimore Sun*, Feb. 24, 1853.

"treasured all . . .": Kane and Fox, 154.

"Slave Power": various, see "Snow Camp, Alamance co . . . ," *National Era*, Jan. 6, 1853.

"thieves" and "serving the devil": "The Union with Slaveholders," *Liberator*, Aug. 26, 1853.

"crazy men" and "Atheists": "Decline of Abolitionism," *Charleston Daily Courier*, Oct. 28, 1853.

"nothing could . . .": Kane and Fox, 162.

"poor patient . . .": Britten, *Autobiography*, 40.

"I am very lonely . . .": Margaret Fox to Cornelius Grinnell, undated (APS-EKK Papers).

"necessary expenses": Margaret Fox to Cornelius Grinnell, folder 2, 1855, undated (APS-EKK Papers).

"Will you also . . .": Margaret Fox to Cornelius Grinnell, Wednesday evening, Aug. 9 (APS-EKK Papers).

"I should prefer . . .": Margaret Fox to Cornelius Grinnell, Aug. 15, 1854 (APS-EKK Papers).

"Will you please send . . .": Margaret Fox to Cornelius Grinnell, folder 1, 1853–1855 (APS-EKK Papers).

"a poor girl . . .": Robert Patterson Kane to Cornelius Grinnell, February 13, 1854, from Chapin, 146.

"with the intention . . .": Cornelius Grinnell to E. K. Kane, June 2, 1855, from Chapin, 147.

"hopeful and . . .": "Kane's Arctic Expedition," *Baltimore Sun*, Jan. 18, 1854.

"Miss F . . .": Robert Patterson Kane to Cornelius Grinnell, Feb. 13, 1854, from Chapin, 146.

"it has occurred . . .": Cornelius Grinnell to Robert Patterson Kane, Feb. 4, 1854, from Sawin, 173.
"the bodies . . .": various, see "The Body of Sir John Franklin Found by Dr. Kane," *Baltimore Sun*, Dec. 2, 1854.
"P.S. I saw . . .": Kane and Fox, 180.
"gloom rested . . .": Kane and Fox, 178.
"sweet and touching" and "What is more . . .": Kane and Fox, 170.
"my own angel": Kane and Fox, 157.

CHAPTER 20—ARCTIC DREAMS, ARCTIC NIGHTMARES

"Dr. Kane, the Arctic . . .": "The Medium's Statement," *New York World*, Oct. 21, 1888.
"Dear, Dear Maggie . . .": Kane and Fox, 175–176.
"amputating knives": Kane, *Arctic Explorations in the Years 1853, 54, 55*, v. 2, 251.
"Experience has taught . . .": Kane, *Arctic Explorations in the Years 1853, 54, 55*, v. 2, 24.
"Bad! Bad! . . .": Kane, *Arctic Explorations*, 1859, 204.
"an anomalous . . .": Kane, *Arctic Explorations in the Years 1853, 54, 55*, v. 2, 180.
"There broke upon us . . .": Kane, *Arctic Explorations in the Years 1853, 54, 55*, v. 2, 399–401.
"I saw that . . .": Kane, *Arctic Explorations in the Years 1853, 54, 55*, v. 2, 399.
"strapped on . . .": Kane and Fox, 145.

CHAPTER 21—GOSSIP AND GLORY

"He wanted me . . .": "The Medium's Statement," *New York World*, Oct. 21, 1888.
"Dr. Kane to . . .": "Dr. Kane to Marry One of the Fox Girls," *Daily American Organ*, Oct. 31, 1855.
"Dr. Kane's . . .": "Dr. Kane's Prospects," *New-York Tribune*, Nov. 6, 1855.
"Dr. Kane on . . .": "Dr. Kane on a Fox Hunt," *Plain Dealer*, Nov. 7, 1855.
"Every tongue did . . .": "The Kane Expedition," *Boston Evening Star*, Oct. 13, 1855.
"DR. KANE . . .": "DR. KANE HOME AGAIN," *New York Times*, Oct. 12, 1855.

"The newsboys ran . . ." and "An army . . .": "The Kane Expedition," *Boston Evening Star*, Oct. 13, 1855.
"Remember your newspaper . . . ourselves.": Thomas Kane to E. K. Kane, May 31, 1855 (APS-EKK Papers).
"If Dr. Kane . . .": Pond, 161.
"the same as . . ." and "sister and brother": Kane and Fox, 195.
"a daring that . . .": *Family Mirror*, Dec. 6, 1856, from Sawin, 257.
"Maggie, is . . ." and "No—no—. . .": Kane and Fox, 196.

CHAPTER 22—NOBODY'S BUSINESS

"if we are . . .": "The Medium's Statement," *New York World*, Oct. 21, 1888.
"I can't bear . . .": Kane and Fox, 202.
"bright": "Dr. Kane," *Buffalo Courier*, Nov. 22, 1855.
"beautiful": "Dr. Kane's Prospects," *Plain Dealer*, Nov. 7, 1855.
"foolish": "Dr. Kane," *Buffalo Courier*, Nov. 22, 1855.
"all this talk . . .": Kane and Fox, 222.
"If this were . . ." and "Whether they have . . .": "Dr. Kane's Prospects," *New-York Tribune*, Nov. 6, 1855.
"I from this . . .": Mrs. Fox to Elisha Kent Kane, June 24, 1856 (APS-EKK Papers).
"I have seen . . ." and "I must either . . ." and "you have my love": Kane and Fox, 210.
"friend": Kane and Fox, 224.
"the betrothed . . .": Kane and Fox, 228.
"the Royal Family": Kane and Fox, 245.
"cared no longer . . .": Kane and Fox, 228.
"I really can not . . .": Kane and Fox, 233.
"It is now . . .": Kane and Fox, 243.
"to be shut . . .": Kane and Fox, 245.
"ten thousand kisses": Kane and Fox, 259.
"You must not . . .": A Searcher After Truth, 139.
"a sort of sanctuary . . .": Kane and Fox, 236.
"The book . . .": Elder, 218.
"I . . . twice dreamt . . .": Kane and Fox, 260.
"the simple pleasure . . .": Kane and Fox, 246.

"magnificent": "Specimen Pages of Dr. Kane's Arctic Expedition," *Knickerbocker*, Oct. 1856, 417.

"stirring": Chapin, 186.

"be in the hands . . .": "Dr. Kane's Second Expedition," *United States Magazine*, Dec. 1856, 538.

"They will all . . .": Kane and Fox, 263.

"If I send . . ." and "Certainly . . ." and "I fear you . . .": Kane and Fox, 269.

"Maggie is my . . .": Kane and Fox, 271.

"Tell me . . .": Kane and Fox, 275.

CHAPTER 23—"SCIENCE WEEPS, HUMANITY WEEPS, THE WORLD WEEPS"

"I have had . . .": "The Medium's Statement," *New York World*, Oct. 21, 1888.

"Science Weeps . . .": various, see "Eulogy on Dr. Kane," *Pittsburg Post*, Mar. 6, 1857.

"a matter of . . .": "James Buchanan's Troubled Legacy as President," National Constitution Center, constitutioncenter.org/blog/james-buchanan-why-is-he-considered-americas-worst-president.

"I am for . . .": "The Crisis of 1850," Digital History-The University of Houston, digitalhistory.uh.edu/disp_textbook.cfm?smtid=2&psid=3273.

"To the Memory . . .": Elder, 364.

"Dear Tutie, I . . .": Kane and Fox, 277.

"I know . . .": Margaret Fox to R. P. Kane, June 1, 1857 (APS-EKK Papers).

"the letters . . .": Maggie Fox to R. P. Kane, May 27, 1858 (APS-EKK Papers).

CHAPTER 24—WHEN FADS FADE

"we were called . . .": "The Medium's Statement," *New York World*, Oct. 21, 1888.

"jibes at the Rochester . . .": "Ghost Walking," *The New York World*, Aug. 20, 1863.

"although he . . .": "Suicide of a Spiritualist," *New-York Tribune*, Dec. 1, 1856.

"miserable delusion": Lunt, 2.

"No. 12": Lunt, 4.

"an electric shock" and "a magnetic, electric . . .": Lunt, 6.

"The spiritual force . . .": Lunt, 7.

"The replies . . ." and "thought they might . . ." and "resisting influences": Lunt, 9.

"Good night . . .": Underhill, 317.

"Any connection . . .": Hardinge, *Modern*, 187.

"with every opportunity . . .": Lunt, 20.

"So ends . . .": Lunt, 19.

"apport": Doyle, vol. 2, 212.

"direct voice": various, see "My Talks with the Dead," The Arthur Conan Doyle Encyclopedia, arthur-conan-doyle.com/index.php/My_Talks_with_the_Dead.

"mysteries which hitherto . . ." and "could not or would . . .": Underhill, 286.

CHAPTER 25—FOR WORSE FOR BETTER, FOR POORER FOR RICHER

"I am a Catholic . . .": "The Medium's Statement," *New York World*, Oct. 21, 1888.

"Would dear Elisha . . .": Kane and Fox, 284.

"regarded the Irish . . .": Potter, 243.

"Recantation of . . .": "Recantation of a Spirit Rapper," *New York Herald* from *St. Mary's Beacon*, Aug. 26, 1858.

"Baptism of . . .": "Baptism of Miss (Spirit Rapper) Fox," *Courier Journal*, Aug. 19, 1858.

"A Remarkable . . .": "A Remarkable Conversion," *Vicksburg Daily Whig*, Sept. 3, 1858.

"it is so strange . . .": Margaret Fox to R. P. Kane, Friday, 13th (Aug. ?), 1858 (APS-EKK Papers).

"The Margaret . . .": Margaret Fox to R. P. Kane, Sept. 2, 1858 (APS-EKK Papers).

"to a quiet . . .": Pond, 190.

"Ma": Underhill, 252.

"It was good . . .": Pond, 192.

"those [who] dared . . .": Underhill, 24.

"Darken." and "Join hands.": Owen, *Debatable Land*, p. 468.

"She is one . . .": Taylor, W. G., 97.

"Mr. Kane, I . . .": Maggie Fox to R. P. Kane, Sept. 1, 1860 (APS-EKK Papers).
"Oh, that I . . .": Kane and Fox, 281.
"A house divided . . .": Lincoln, "House Divided Speech," June 16, 1858. nps.gov/common/uploads/teachers/lessonplans/Primary_Sources.pdf.
"for two dreary . . .": Greeley, 239.
"two or twenty . . ." and "If people will . . .": Mattison, 174.

CHAPTER 26—THE WONDROUS MISS KATE

"She had many . . .": "The Medium's Statement," *New York World*, Oct. 21, 1888.
"My dear . . .": Sargent, *Communications*, 17.
"I know that . . .": Owen, *Debatable*, 484.
"everything movable . . .": Sargent, *Communications*, 18.
"surrounded by . . .": Sargent, *Communications*, 17.
"a human eye" and "*the upper half* . . ." and "its shade of . . .": Sargent, *Communications*, 18.
"asked her . . .": Sargent, *Proof Palpable*, 17.
"Now see . . ." and "The atmosphere . . .": Owen, *Debatable*, 486.
"a single . . .": Sargent, *Communications*, 19.
"freshly gathered . . ." and "audible in . . .": Sargent, *Proof Palpable*, 17.
"three or four . . .": Sargent, *Communications*, 21.
"not a word . . .": Owen, *Debatable*, 488.
"[Willie] lives . . .": Helm, 227.
"something like . . ." and "we again grasped . . .": Sargent, *Proof*, 18.
"These manifestations . . .": Sargent, *Communications*, 19.
"cried out . . .": Pond, 211.
"dressed in . . .": Sargent, *Communications*, 23.
"republic of suffering": Frederick Law Olmstead from Faust, xiii.
"It will be I . . .": Faust, 182.
"these dead shall . . .": Lincoln, Gettysburg Address, Nov. 19, 1863, Library of Congress, loc.gov/resource/rbpe.24404500/?st=text.
"enforce a devastation . . .": "The March to the Sea Begins," The Civil War Monitor, civilwarmonitor.com/blog/the-march-to-the-sea-begins.

CHAPTER 27—ADDICTION AND REHAB

"I received but . . .": "The Medium's Statement," *New York World*, Oct. 21, 1888.

"I always find . . .": Pond, 221.

"found a way . . .": Pond, 243.

"The End . . .": "The End of the Rebellion," *Banner of Light*, Apr. 15, 1865.

"said to have . . .": Weisberg, 208–209.

"modest": Kane and Fox, 24.

"obliged . . . to sit . . .": Kane and Fox, 51.

"The relative . . ." and "jealous": Kane and Fox, 99.

"the Tigress": Kane and Fox, 106.

"The profession . . .": Kane and Fox, 17.

"the disciples . . .": Kane and Fox, 18.

"grief had departed . . .": Pond, 210.

"there was no . . .": Pond, 233.

"Darling momma . . .": Taylor, W. G., 173.

"try to.": Taylor, W. G., 173.

"B. F.": Taylor, W. G., 92.

"spiritual food": Taylor, W. G., 201.

"preparing our homes . . .": Taylor, W. G., 247.

"John Brown walking . . .": Taylor, W. G., 221.

"all classes . . .": Taylor, W. G., 273.

"dead drunk" and "Drunkenness, like dying . . .": Taylor, W. G., 164.

"There is but . . .": Taylor, W. G., 283.

"Your children live . . .": Taylor, W. G., 149.

"would fill . . .": Taylor, W. G., 175.

"The children played . . .": Taylor, Susan, 111.

"resembled mostly . . .": Taylor, W. G., 176.

"Papa, open . . .": Taylor, W. G., 174.

"We knew that . . ." and "Imagine a normal . . . ": Taylor, W. G., 151.

"Private. We will . . .": Taylor, W. G., 152.

"the greatest . . .": Taylor, W. G., 204–205.

CHAPTER 28—SPIRITS ACROSS THE SEA

"Many people . . .": "The Medium's Statement," *New York World*, Oct. 21, 1888.

"Mrs. Elisha Kent . . .": *Pittsburgh Weekly Gazette*, Sept. 21, 1868.

"humble, modest . . .": Father Quinn to R. P. Kane, Oct. 18, 1858 (APS-EKK Papers).

"Mrs. Kane does . . .": "The Medium's Statement," *New York World*, Oct. 21, 1888.

"strange and fascinating . . .": Diniejko, "Victorian Spiritualism," The Victorian Web. victorianweb.org/victorian/religion/spirit.html.

"An epidemic . . .": Podmore, 7.

"I want to . . .": Taylor, W. G., 157.

"not be prejudiced . . .": Taylor, W. G., 156.

"Oh, never again . . .": Taylor, W. G., 318.

"Drink with me . . .": Pond, 254.

"an empty bottle . . .": Pond, 255.

"a wise physician . . ." and "I would drink . . .": Pond, 256.

"you must not . . .": Pond, 257.

"good and kind": Weisberg, 222.

"expressing her approval . . ." and "Kate Fox . . .": "Kate Fox at the Altar," *Sun*, Jan. 30, 1873.

"Mediumship of . . .": "Mediumship of a Baby," *The Spiritualist*, Dec. 13, 1873.

"We are looking . . .": Underhill, 93.

"I love this . . ." and "He who trusts . . .": Taylor, W. G., 101.

"this marvellous . . .": Underhill, 94.

"Specimen of writing . . .": Britten, *Nineteenth Century*, plate after 550.

"entirely aloof . . .": Underhill, 95.

"Spiritual Mansion": Davenport, 164.

"mania": Davenport, 166.

"feeble health": Elizabeth Ellet to R. P. Kane, Dec. 1, 1858 (APS-EKK Papers).

"The three Fox . . .": "About People," *Plain Dealer*, Sept. 16, 1878.

"dah tey evah . . .": Seybert Commission, 45.

"Spiritualism . . .": Seybert Commission, Appendix, 26.

"handsomely . . .": "Spirits Led Her to Drink," *Rochester Democrat and Chronicle*, May 7, 1888.

"Kate would not . . .": Pond, 287.
"by A. Leah . . .": Underhill, interior title page.
"nobody else . . .": Underhill, 1.
"drunkenness and flagrant . . .": *New York Herald*, May 5, 1888, from Midorikawa, 242.
"asylum": "Neglected Her Children," *Auburn Morning Dispatch*, May 5, 1888.
"One of the . . .": "One of the Fox Sisters Arrested," *New York Times*, May 5, 1888.
"Neglected Her . . .": "Neglected Her Children," *Auburn Morning Dispatch*, May 5, 1888.
"Lamentable Downfall . . .": "Lamentable Downfall of Once Celebrated Spirit Rapper," *Rochester Democrat and Chronicle,* May 5, 1888.
"The Spirits Too . . .": "The Spirits Too Much for Her," *New York Herald,* May 5, 1888, from Midorikawa, 242.
"The once talented . . .": "Wreck of a Talented Woman," *Chicago Tribune*, May 5, 1888.
"Age, worry . . ." and "a little fond . . ." and "fanatics": "Spirits Led her to Drink," *Rochester Democrat and Chronicle*, May 7, 1888.

CHAPTER 29—CONFESSIONS

"I think that it . . ." and "All was silent . . .": "The Medium's Statement," *New York World*, Oct. 21, 1888.
"Spiritualism is . . .": "To the Editor of the [*New York*] *Herald*," from Davenport, 30.
"small, magnetic . . ." and "fitful floods . . ." and "she knew what . . ." and "I hate her . . ." and "used us in . . ." and "one lecture . . ." and "How do you . . ." and "Well, I want . . ." and "Is it all . . . Absolutely.": "God Has Not Ordered It," *New York Herald*, Sept. 24, 1888.
"My wife has done . . ." and "stay sober" and "vicious as . . ." and "I cannot think . . .": "Gotham Gossip," *Times-Picayune*, Oct. 7, 1888.
"upon each other's . . ." and "I care nothing . . . century.": "And Katy Fox Now," *Spokane Falls Review,* Oct. 19, 1888.
"Kate Fox Jencken . . .": "Against Spiritism," *Buffalo Morning Express,* Oct. 12, 1888.

"KATY FOX WILL . . .": "KATY FOX WILL GIVE THE SNAP AWAY," *Chicago Tribune*, Oct. 12, 1888.

"SPIRITUALISM EXPOSED . . . Astonish the Country": "SPIRITUALISM EXPOSED The Fox Sisters . . .", see advertisement in masthead of *New York World*, Oct. 20, 1888.

"Margaret Fox Kane" and "wanted to terrify . . ." and "we used to tie . . .": "The Medium's Statement," *New York World*, Oct. 21, 1888.

"go and pull teeth!": "Those Toe 'Spirit' Raps," *New York World*, Oct. 22, 1888.

"nervous": "Done with the Big Toe," *New York Times*, Oct. 22, 1888.

"not in . . .": "Those Toe 'Spirit' Raps," *New York World*, Oct. 22, 1888.

"highly excited": "Spirit Mediums Outdone," *New-York Tribune*, Oct. 22, 1888.

"ridiculous": "Pranks the Spirits Play," *New York Sun*, Oct. 22, 1888.

"The rappings . . .": "The Medium's Statement," *New York World*, Oct. 21, 1888.

"black-robed . . ." and "One moment . . .": "Spiritualism's Downfall," *New York Herald*, Oct. 22, 1888.

"kind, dear spirits" and "a hailstorm . . .": "Spirit Mediums Outdone," *New-York Tribune*, Oct. 22, 1888.

"It's a fraud. Spiritualism . . .": "Spiritualism's Downfall," *New York Herald*, Oct. 22, 1888.

CHAPTER 30—AS THE CURTAIN FALLS

"this exposé will . . .": "The Medium's Statement," *New York World*, Oct. 21, 1888.

"Spiritualism's . . .": "Spiritualism's Downfall," *New York Herald*, Oct. 22, 1888.

"The Fox Sisters . . .": "The Fox Sisters Fraud," *Boston Evening Transcript*, Oct. 25, 1888.

"Mrs. Fox Kane's . . .": "Mrs. Fox Kane's Big Toe," *Chicago Tribune*, Oct. 22, 1888.

"the confession . . .": "Spiritualism's Downfall," *New York Herald*, Oct. 22, 1888.

"They are the slaves . . .": "Mrs. Underhill and Spiritualism," *Better Way*, Jan. 12, 1889.

"I think now . . .": Pond, 314.
"I gave expression . . .": "Spirits Called Her," *Weekly Press*, Nov. 20, 1889.
"Those charges . . .": "Mrs. Kane's Recantation," *Banner of Light*, Mar. 25, 1893.
"for five dollars . . .": Funk, 241.
"honorable and estimable": "Mrs. Underhill and Spiritualism," *The Better Way*, Jan. 12, 1890.
"The best test . . .": Britten, *Autobiography*, 106.
"nervous excitability": Weisberg, 257.
"died a firm . . .": "Medium Kate Fox Dies Suddenly," *New York Herald*, July 3, 1892.
"succeeded in mystifying . . .": "Mother of Spiritualism," *Rochester Democrat and Chronicle*, July 4, 1892.
"An Earnest Appeal" and "this very . . .": "An Earnest Appeal," *Progressive Thinker*, Oct. 29, 1892.
"I am here . . ." and "Maggie Fox Kane": "Exposures of Mediums," *Globe Democrat*, Mar. 26, 1893.

AUTHOR'S NOTE

"It is a very common . . .": "The Medium's Statement," *New York World*, Oct. 21, 1888.
"cher ami": Margaret Fox to R. P. Kane, July, 1858 (APS-EKK Papers).
"I am sorry . . .": Margaret Fox to R. P. Kane, May 16, 1860 (APS-EKK Papers).
"The fact is . . ." and "With love . . .": Margaret Fox to R. P. Kane, "Sunday Night" (APS-EKK Papers).
"the Spirits . . .": Catherine Fox to Amy Kirby Post, 185(?) (RBSCP-Post).
"the Fox sisters did possess . . .": Isaacs, 57.
"processes of information . . .": Bern, 407.
"told us . . .": "The Medium's Statement," *New York World*, Oct. 21, 1888.

BIBLIOGRAPHY

BOOKS

A Searcher After Truth. *The Rappers: the mysteries, fallacies, and absurdities of spirit-rapping, table-tipping, and entrancement.* New York: H. Long & Brother, 1854.

Ballou, Adin. *An Exposition of Views Respecting the principal facts, causes and peculiarities involved in Spirit Manifestations.* Boston: Bella Marsh, 1852.

Braude, Ann. *Radical Spirits.* Boston: Beacon Press, 1989.

Britten, Emma H. *Nineteenth Century Miracles.* New York: William Britten, 1884.

Britten, Emma Hardinge. *Autobiography.* London: Mrs. Margaret Wilkinson, 1900.

Burr, Heman. *Knocks for the Knockings.* New York: Burr Brothers, 1851.

Cadwallader, M. E. *Hydesville In History.* Chicago: Progressive Thinker Publishing House, 1917.

Capron, Eliab W., and Henry D. Barron. *Singular Revelations, Explanation and History of the Mysterious Communion with Spirits, comprehending the rise and progress of the Mysterious Noises Generally Received as Spiritual Communications.* Auburn, NY: Finn & Rockwell, 1850.

Capron, Eliab W. *Modern Spiritualism.* Boston: Bella Marsh, 1855.

Carpenter, William B. *Mesmerism, Spiritualism, &c.* New York: D. Appleton & Co., 1895.

Chapin, David. *Exploring Other Worlds.* Amherst: University of Massachusetts Press, 2004.

Cronise, Adelbert. *The Beginning of Modern Spiritualism in and around Rochester.* Rochester: Historical Society Publication Fund Series, V, 1926.

Davenport, Reuben Briggs. *The Death Blow to Spiritualism.* New York: G. W. Dillingham, 1888.

Davis, Andrew Jackson. *Morning Lectures.* New York: Plumb & Co., 1865.

Dewey, D. M. *History of the Strange Sounds or Rappings.* Rochester, NY: D. M. Dewey, 1850, 1st ed. (March) and 2nd ed. with appendix (June).

Doyle, Arthur Conan. *The History of Spiritualism*, vols. 1 and 2. London: Cassell & Company, 1920.

Elder, William. *Biography of Elisha Kent Kane*. Philadelphia: Childs & Peterson, 1858.

Elliott, Charles Wyllys. *Mysteries: or, Glimpses of the Supernatural*. New York: Harper & Brothers, 1852.

Faust, Drew Gilpin. *This Republic of Suffering*. New York: Knopf, 2008.

Fields, Annie, ed. *Life and Letters of Harriett Beecher Stowe*. Boston and New York: Houghton, Mifflin and Company, 1898.

Funk, Isaac K. *The Widow's Mite and Other Psychic Phenomena*. New York: Funk and Wagnalls, 1904.

Greeley, Horace. *The Autobiography of Horace Greeley*. New York: E. B. Treat, 1872.

Hardinge, Emma. *Modern American Spiritualism*. New York: published by the author, 1870.

Helm, Katherine. *Mary, Wife of Lincoln*. New York: Harper Brothers, 1928.

Hesketh, Kristy. "Spiritualism and the Resurgence of Fake News." In *Navigating Fake News, Alternative Facts, and Misinformation in a Post-Truth World*, edited by Kimiz Dalkir and Rebecca Katz. Hartsford, PA: IGI Global, 2020.

Hoeltzel, Bob. *Hometown History: Village of Newark Town of Arcadia*. Newark, NY: Arcadia Historical Society, 2000.

Jackson, Jr., Herbert G. *The Spirit Rappers*. New York: Doubleday, 1972.

Kane, Elisha Kent. *Arctic Explorations in the Years 1853, 54, 55*, vols. 1 and 2. Philadelphia: Childs & Peterson, 1856.

———. *Arctic Explorations*. London: T. Nelson & Sons, 1859.

Kane, Elisha Kent, and Margaretta Fox. *The Love Life of Dr. Kane*. New York: Carleton, 1865.

Lewis, E. E. *A Report of the Mysterious Noises Heard in the House of Mr. John D. Fox*. Canandaigua, NY: Lewis, 1848.

Lundberg, James M. *Horace Greeley: Print, Politics, and the Failure of American Nationhood*. Baltimore: Johns Hopkins University Press, 2019.

Lunt, George. *Spiritualism Shown as It Is*. Boston: Boston Courier Press, 1859.

Mattison, Hiram. *Spirit Rapping Unveiled*. New York: J. C. Derby, 1855.

Midorikawa, Emily. *Out of the Shadows, Six Visionary Victorian Women*. Berkeley: Counterpoint, 2021.

Moore, R. Laurence. *In Search of White Crows, Spiritualism, Parapsychology and American Culture*. New York: Oxford University Press, 1977.

Oppenheim, Janet. *The Other World, Spiritualism and Psychical Research in England, 1850–1944*. Cambridge: Cambridge University Press, 1988.

Owen, Robert Dale. *The Debatable Land Between This World and the Next*. New York: G. W. Carleton & Co., 1872.

Parker, Jenny. *Rochester: A Story Historical*. Rochester: Scranton, Wetmore, and Co., 1884.

Peck, William. "The Rochester Rappings." In *Semicentennial History of the City of Rochester*. Syracuse, NY: D. Mason & Co., 1884.

Podmore, Frank. *Modern Spiritualism*, vols. 1 and 2. London: Methuen, 1902.

Pond, Mariam Buckner. *Time is Kind*. Clinton, CT: Centennial Press, 1947.

Potter, David Morris. *The Impending Crisis, 1848–1861*. New York: Harper & Row, 1976.

Sargent, Epes. *Communications from Another World*. Melbourne: G. Robinson, 1869.

———. *The Proof Palpable of Immortality*. Boston: Colby & Rich, 1881.

Sawin, Mark. *Raising Kane: Elisha Kent Kane & the Culture of Fame in Antebellum America*. Philadelphia: American Philosophical Society, 2008.

Seybert Commission, University of Pennsylvania. *Preliminary report of the Commission appointed by the University of Pennsylvania to investigate modern spiritualism, in accordance with the request of the late Henry Seybert*. Philadelphia: J. B. Lippincott, 1887.

Strong, Augustus Hopkins. *Reminiscences of Early Rochester*. Rochester: Rochester Historical Society, 1916.

Stuart, Nancy Rubin. *The Reluctant Spiritualist: The Life of Maggie Fox*. New York: Harcourt, 2005.

Taylor, Susan. *Fox Taylor Automatic Writing 1869–1892*, unabridged. Minneapolis: Tribune Great West Printing, 1932.

Taylor, W. G. Langworthy. *Katie Fox and the Fox-Taylor Record*. Boston: Bruce Humphries, Inc., 1936.

Thompson, Susan. *The Penny Press: The Origins of the Modern News Media, 1833–1861*. Northport, AL: Vision Press, 2004.

Underhill, A. Leah. *The Missing Link in Modern Spiritualism*. New York: Thomas R. Knox, 1885.

Weisberg, Barbara. *Talking to the Dead: Kate and Maggie Fox and the Rise of Spiritualism*. New York: Harper One, 2004.

WEBSITES*

American Antiquarian Society, "The News and the Making of America," americanantiquarian.org/earlyamericannewsmedia/exhibits/show/news-in-antebellum-america.

The Arthur Conan Doyle Encyclopedia, "My Talks with the Dead," arthur-conan-doyle.com/index.php/My_Talks_with_the_Dead.

Centers for Disease Control and Prevention, "150th Anniversary of John Snow and the Pump Handle," *Morbidity and Mortality Weekly Report*, Sept. 3, 2004, cdc.gov/mmwr/preview/mmwrhtml/mm5334a1.htm.

The Civil War Monitor, "The March to the Sea Begins," civilwarmonitor.com/blog/the-march-to-the-sea-begins.

Library of Congress, *Congressional Globe*, "American Memory," memory.loc.gov/ammem/amlaw/lwcg.html.

Library of Congress, Gettysburg Address, loc.gov/resource/rbpe.24404500/?st=text.

National Park Service, "Lincoln Home," "House Divided Speech," nps.gov/liho/learn/historyculture/housedivided.htm.

National Spiritualist Association of Churches (NSAC), "History," "Who We Are," nsac.org/who-we-are/history/.

New York Heritage Digital Collections, "Canal in Song," "Two Hundred Years on the Erie Canal," nyheritage.org/exhibits/two-hundred-years-erie-canal/canal-song.

Poughkeepsie Public Library, "The Poughkeepsie Seer-Andrew Jackson Davis," by Shannon Butler, poklib.org/the-poughkeepsie-seer-andrew-jackson-davis./

Rochester Public Library, *Rochester City Directories*, 1849 at libraryweb.org/rochcitydir/images/1849/1849complete.pdf and 1851 at libraryweb.org/rochcitydir/images/1851/1851d-h.pdf.

Swedenborg Foundation, "Spiritual World (Afterlife), The World of Spirits," swedenborg.com/emanuel-swedenborg/explore/spiritual-world/.

University of California Santa Barbara, "The American Presidency Project: Franklin Pierce," presidency.ucsb.edu/documents/inaugural-address-32.

University of Houston, "Digital History," "The Crisis of 1850," digitalhistory.uh.edu/disp_textbook.cfm?smtid=2&psid=3273.

* Websites active at time of pulication

University of Illinois Library, "American Newspapers, 1800–1860," "City Newspapers," library.illinois.edu/hpnl/tutorials/antebellum-newspapers-city/.
University of Virginia, "Uncle Tom's Cabin and American Culture," by Daniel Petschauer, excerpts from Frederick Douglass' Paper, unsigned, Rochester, April 29, 1853. utc.iath.virginia.edu/africam/afar03pt.html.
U. S. Government, Declaration of Independence, US, 1776, archives.gov/founding-docs/declaration.
The Victorian Web, victorianweb.org.
The White House, whitehouse.gov.
York College of Pennsylvania, "Fear and Resentment: The Southern Reaction to Uncle Tom's Cabin Before and After the War," by Daniel Petschauer, ycphistpolisci.com/fear-and-resentment-the-southern-reaction-to-uncle-toms-cabin-before-and-after-the-civil-war/.

LIBRARY COLLECTIONS

American Philosophical Society, Elisha Kent Kane Papers (APS-EKK Papers).
University of Rochester, River Campus Libraries, Rare Books, Special Collections and Preservation, Isaac and Amy Post Family Papers (RBSCP-P).
Swarthmore College, Friends Historical Library, Post Family Papers (SFHL-PFP).

JOURNALS AND DISSERTATIONS

Bern, Daryl. "Feeling the Future: Experimental Evidence for Anomalous Retroactive Influences on Cognition and Affect." *Journal of Personality and Social Psychology*, Mar. 2011: 407–425.
Daly, Walter. "The Black Cholera Comes to the Central Valley of America in the 19th Century—1832, 1849, and Later." *Transactions of the American Clinical and Climatological Association*, 119 (2008): 143–153.
Flint, A., C. A. Lee and C. B. Coventry. "Discovery of the Source of the Rochester Knockings." *Buffalo Medical Journal*, Mar. 1851: 628–642.
Gaunt, Paul J., ed. "Hydesville—Fox Special." *Psypioneer*, Jan. 2012: 1–41.
Henning, Jan and Keith C. Mages. "Buffalo Ghostbusters: Doctors, Mediums and an Examination of the Spirit World." *Western New York Heritage*, Spring 2016: 54–63.

Isaacs, Ernest. "A History of Nineteenth Century Spiritualism as a Religious and Social Movement." PhD diss., University of Wisconsin, 1975.

Jones, R. D. "Modern Spiritualism." *Spiritual Offering*, Nov. 1878: 31–145.

Jorgensen, Loreen. "The Diary of Michael Prindle, Methodist Minister, 1840–1885." Unpublished, from transcription at Wayne County Historian's Office, Lyons, New York.

Moore, R. Laurence. "Spiritualism and Science: Reflections on the First Decade of the Spirit Rappings." *American Quarterly*, Oct. 1972: 474–500.

———. "The Spiritualist Medium: A Study of Female Professionalism in Victorian America." *American Quarterly*, May 1975: 200–221.

Natale, Simone. "Spiritual stars: religion and celebrity in the careers of spiritualist mediums." *Celebrity Studies*, Mar. 2013: 94–96.

———. "Spreading the Spirit Word: Print Media, Storytelling and Popular Culture in Nineteenth-Century Spiritualism." *communications+1* 4, no. 1 (2015).

———. "The medium on the stage: Trance and performance in nineteenth-century spiritualism." *Early Popular Visual Culture* 9, no. 3 (2011): 239–255.

Nickell, Joe. "A Skeleton's Tale: The Origins of Modern Spiritualism." *Skeptical Inquirer*, July/Aug. 2008: 17–20.

Powalski, Caitlin. "Radical Transmissions: Isaac and Amy Post, Spiritualism, and Progressive Reform in Nineteenth Century Rochester." *Rochester History*, Fall 2009: 1–25.

Sieber, Robert, Kathy Peterson, Marjorie Seal, and Lemuel Clark. "The Fox Sisters in Action: A Clergyman's Account." *New York History*, July 1974: 301–318.

Warwood, Lis J. "The Fox Sisters: Riddle of the Records." *Psypioneer*, Sept. 2008: 186–196.

Webb, Wheaton Phillips, A. H. Clark, and Lemuel Clark. "Peddler's Protest." *New York History,* Apr. 1943: 228–50.

Wilson, John B. "Memoranda and Documents: Emerson and the 'Rochester Rappings.'" *New England Quarterly*, June 1968: 248–258.

NEWSPAPERS

Alexandria Gazette (VA)
Auburn Morning Dispatch (NY)
Baltimore Sun
Banner of Light (Boston)
Better Way (Cincinnati)
Boston Evening Star
Boston Evening Transcript
Brattleboro Eagle (VT)
Brooklyn Daily Eagle
Buffalo Commercial Advertiser
Buffalo Courier
Buffalo Daily Republic
Buffalo Morning Express
Charleston Daily Courier
Chicago Tribune
Cleveland Herald
Courier-Journal (Louisville, KY)
Daily American Organ (Washington, DC)
Daily Crescent (New Orleans)
Daily Nashville Union
Detroit Free Press
Eastern Argus (Portland, ME)
Evening Post (New York, NY)
Globe Democrat (St. Louis)
Hartford Courant (CT)
Hinds County Gazette (Raymond, MS)
Holden's Dollar Magazine (New York, NY)
Home Journal
Indiana State Sentinel (Indianapolis)
Knickerbocker (NY)
Liberator (Boston)
Louisville Daily Courier
National Era (Washington, DC)
Newark Herald (Newark, NY)
New York Daily Tribune
New York Herald
New York Sun
New York Times
New-York Tribune
New York World
Northern Christian Advocate (Auburn, NY)
Pittsburg Post
Pittsburg Weekly Gazette
Plain Dealer (Cleveland)
Progressive Thinker (Chicago)
Rochester Daily Advertiser
Rochester Daily Democrat
Rochester Democrat and Chronicle
Rochester Republican
Southern Press (Washington, DC)
Spirit Messenger and Harmonial Guide (New York, NY)
Spiritual Telegraph (New York, NY)
Spokane Falls Review (WA)
St. Albans Weekly Messenger (Vermont)
St. Mary's Beacon (Leonard Town, MD)
Sunday Dispatch (New York, NY)
Times-Picayune (New Orleans)
Troy Daily Whig (Troy, NY)
United States Magazine (New York, NY)
Vicksburg Daily Whig (VA)
Wayne County Herald (Honesdale, PA)
Weekly Argus (Albany, NY)
Weekly National Intelligencer (Washington, DC)
Weekly Press (New York, NY)
Western Argus (Lyons, NY)

PICTURE CREDITS

Albany Institute of History and Art: *Before the Days of Rapid Transit* by Edward Lamson Henry (1841–1919) c. 1900, pencil and watercolor on paper, Albany Institute of History & Art purchase, 1976.7.2: 28–29.

Brandon Hodge, MysteriousPlanchette.com: *The Missing Link in Modern Spiritualism* by Leah Underhill: 26; 66; *Leslie's Illus. Magazine*: 103; *Ballou's Pictorial Drawing Room Companion*, June 14, 1856: 176; *Gambols with Ghosts: Mind Reading, Spiritualistic Effects, Mental and Psychical Phenomena and Horoscopy* by Ralph E. Sylvestre, Chicago, 1901: 204.

Cleveland Museum of Art, Dudley P. Allen Fund, *Rapping Spirits* by Honoré Daumier, 1851: 84.

Cypress Hills Cemetery: 246.

Green-Wood Historic Fund Collections, *Greenwood Cemetery, New York* by John Bachmann: 245.

Indiana University–Purdue University Indianapolis, University Library, Camp Chesterfield Collection/Hett Museum of Art: 119, 124, 198, 207, 225.

iStock, klyaksun: 6–7.

Johns Hopkins University, the Sheridan Libraries, the Lester Levy Sheet Music Collection: 90.

Kane, Elisha K., and Margaret Fox, *The Love Life of Dr. Kane,* 1865: 151, 180.

Laurel Hill Cemetery: 138.

The Library Company of Philadelphia, *The Death Watch* by DeWitt Clinton Baxter: 183.

Library of Congress: 2004664278: 20, 2003674027: 25, 10034181: 58, 2004663966: 81, 2003674674: 97, 2017660885: 145, 2004669987: 155, 96519333: 188, 2009581130: 202, 2014646926: 213, 2006685384: 215, 2018666922: 217, 2015645306: 219.

Library of the American Philosophical Society: 132, 197.

Lilydale Museum, Ron Nagy: 233.

Lincoln Financial Foundation Collection: 218.

Lunt, George, *Spiritualism Shown as It Is!: Boston Courier Report*, Second Edition, 1859: 191.

Metropolitan Museum of Art: Rubel Collection, Gift of William Rubel, 2001:

42; Costume Institute, Gift of Lee Simonson, *Children 1860–1864, Plate 049*: 75 (top); Costume Institute, Gift of Woodman Thompson, *Women, 1855–1856, Plate 010*: 75 (bottom); Gift of Mary Knight Arnold, 1974: 169.

Missouri Historical Society: 117.

National Portrait Gallery, Smithsonian Institution: 161.

Newark-Arcadia Historical Society: 12.

Newcastle Historical Society/Horace Greeley House: 99.

Newsbank.com, *The Plain Dealer*, Cleveland, Ohio, October 26, 1855: 168.

Newspapers.com, *New York Times*, November 23, 1904: 255.

New-York Historical Society: "Notice. Preventives of Cholera!" by New York Board of Health; Broadside SY1849, no. 64: 92; "The Greatest Book of the Age," lithograph. PR031, Bella C. Landauer Collection of Business and Advertising Ephemera, 38219: 110; The Lincoln Family by Francis Bicknell Carpenter, ca. 1865, oil on canvas, 27 x 36 3/3 in., Gift of Warren C. Crane, 1909.6: 211.

New York Public Library, Miriam and Ira D. Wallach Division of Art, Prints and Photographs: 424521: 79; b16513338: 182; G91F216_039: 241.

The New York World, October 20, 1888, p. 1: 240.

Olive Tree Genealogy Collection: 52.

Peary-MacMillan Arctic Museum, Bowdoin College: 165.

Philadelphia Museum of Art, Gift of Mr. and Mrs. Wharton Sinkler, 1958: 64.

Pierce Brigade at the Franklin Pierce Manse, Concord, NH: 150.

Research Gate, *The Illustrated London News*, July 16, 1853: 112.

Rochester Historical Society: 203.

Rochester Public Library, Local History & Genealogy Division: 32, 56.

Smithsonian American Art Museum: 15.

SuperStock: 209.

Thanatos Archive: 89, 222.

University at Buffalo Libraries, R.L. Brown History of Medicine Collection, *Les mystères de la science* by Louis Figuier, Paris, 1880: 106, 125.

University of Rochester, River Campus Libraries, Department of Rare Books, Special Collections and Preservation: 38, 40, 70.

Wellcome Collection, *A practitioner of Mesmerism using Animal Magnetism*: 34; *A dead victim of cholera at Sunderland in 1832*, coloured lithograph attributed to J.W. Gear: 50.

Wikimedia Commons: *Arctic Explorations: The Second Grinnell Expedition in Search of Sir John Franklin, 1853, '54, '55* by Elisha Kent Kane, 1856: 162; *Nineteenth Century Miracles*, by Emma Hardinge Britten, 1884: 231.

INDEX

Page numbers in bold refer to images or captions.